Double Zero
and Soviet Military Strategy

Double Zero and Soviet Military Strategy

Implications for Western Security

Dennis M. Gormley

Revised and updated
Paperback Edition

TRI-SERVICE

PRESS

© Dennis M. Gormley, 1988, 1990

First published by
Jane's Publishing Company Limited 1988

This revised, updated edition published 1990 by
Tri-Service Press Limited
42–43 Lower Marsh
London SE1 7RQ

British Library Cataloguing in Publication Data
Gormley, Dennis M., *1943–*
    Double zero and Soviet Military strategy. – Rev. ed
    1. Soviet Union. Military Policies. Implications of
    arms control treaties
    I. Title
    355′.0335′47

ISBN 1–85488–025–X

Printed in Great Britain by
Antony Rowe Ltd, Chippenham, Wiltshire

*To my wife JJ
and my children Douglas and Jennifer*

Contents

List of Tables

List of Figures

Acknowledgements

For having originally encouraged me to pursue research in the area of this book, I am grateful to Robert Nurick of the Rand Corporation. Books cannot be written without time for research, contemplation, and writing. Many individuals helped me in this regard. Bob Nurick provided the encouragement, and Frank Thomas and the late Gary Lang of Pacific-Sierra Research Corporation furnished the wherewithal for me to spend six months as a Research Associate at the International Institute for Strategic Studies during 1984. I am especially grateful to the many kind and superbly talented members of the Institute's staff. I could not have finished the book without the enduring patience, understanding, and support of my wife JJ. For her insight, sensitivity, and care in guiding me through the publication process, I am indebted to Anne-Lucie Norton. Many of my colleagues at Pacific-Sierra Research were generous in sharing their considerable wisdom and expertise with me as I pursued my efforts. Particular thanks go to Charles Appleby, John Barker, Bonnie Driggers, Doug Hart, Kerry Hines, Bill Koenig, Steve McKay, John Tritak, and Notra Trulock. Last, but by no means least, I thank Sheri Barnes for imposing organisation and discipline on an otherwise chaotic final production phase.

List of abbreviations

AAFCE   Allied Air Forces Central Europe
AFCENT   Allied Forces Central Europe
ALCM   air-launched cruise missile
ALRS   alternate launch and recovery strip
ARM   anti-radiation missile
ATACMS   army tactical missile system
ATAF   Allied Tactical Air Force
AWACS   airborne warning and control system
C^2 command and control
C^3 command, control and communications
CEP   circular error probability
COB   collocated operating base
CPSU   Communist Party of the Soviet Union
CRC   control and reporting centre
CRP   control and reporting post
CSBM   confidence and security building measure
CSCE   Conference on Security and Co-operation in Europe
CST   Conventional Stability Talks
FAE   fuel air explosive
GLCM   ground-launched cruise missile
GSFG   Soviet group of forces, Germany
INF   intermediate-range nuclear forces
IRBM   intermediate-range ballistic missiles
JSTARS   joint surveillance and target acquisition radar system
KT   kiloton (1000 tons TNT equivalent)
LRA   Long-Range Aviation

MIRV   multiple independently targetable re-entry vehicle
NADGE   NATO Air Defence Ground Environment
OMG   operational manoeuver group
POMCUS   pre-positioned overseas materiel configured to unit sets
R^3 rapid runway repairs
RTA   Rocket Troops and Artillery (Soviet)
RVGK   Reserves of the Supreme High Command (Soviet)
SACEUR   Supreme Allied Commander, Europe
SALT   Strategic Arms Limitations
(I + II)   Treaty
SAM   surface-to-air-missile
SDI   Strategic Defence Initiative
SEP   selective employment planning
SHAPE   Supreme Headquarters Allied Powers Europe
SLBM   submarine-launched ballistic missile
SLCM   sea-launched cruise missile
SOC   sector operations centre
SP   self propelled
SRF   Strategic Rocket Forces
SRINF   short-range INF
SSBN   ballistic-missile nuclear submarine
START   Strategic Arms Reduction Talks
TVD   theatre of military operations
USAF   United States Air Force
VGK   Supreme High Command (Soviet)

Introduction

This book is largely meant for those with a specialist bent in the national security field. Military strategy, operational art, and the related instruments of war in the European theatre play a featured role. As the title suggests, its quest is twofold: it first assays the consequences for Soviet military strategy of eliminating all ground-based ballistic and cruise missiles with ranges between 500 and 5500 km – the so-called "double zero" intermediate-range nuclear forces (INF) agreement; it then turns to considering the implications of these consequences for Western security planning.

The book's novel feature is its perspective. There has been no shortage of expert judgement of the INF treaty's impact on Western security interests, but the same cannot be said regarding the treaty's meaning for Soviet national security. To inject more balance into evaluating the treaty's overall strengths and shortfalls, the book assesses the impact of the INF treaty on Western security interests but only after first focusing on how the Soviet military might view the treaty's effect on their responsibilities as they have traditionally come to see them.

Even though the book's focus is on the mechanics of military strategy and forces in the European theatre, one is inescapably compelled to view the complexities of military science through a political prism. Until recently, the interaction of politics and military planning was far more decidedly a Western phenomenon than a Soviet one. But now there is persuasive evidence that the Soviet military no longer has exclusive control – as it once did under a more pliant Brezhnev leadership – over the military-technical dimension of Soviet national security planning. Some view this development as offering new hope for substantive agreement in, say, conventional arms control. But there are also possible dangers ahead if the INF negotiating record is any gauge of how politics can either serve or harm basic national security needs. One important conclusion of the book in regard to the INF treaty is that Mikhail Gorbachev not only achieved important political results but also generally served the basic interests of the Soviet military establishment. By contrast, the Reagan Administration's achievements were largely political.

There is a certain irony in the fact that Mikhail Gorbachev can now reap the benefits of Leonid Brezhnev's enormous accumulation of military power between 1965 and his death in 1982. If there is anything certain about the Soviet accumulation of military power over that time, it is that its purpose has been to challenge both the operational utility of Western military strategy and the political consensus needed to sustain its credibility.During this period of virtually unfettered national defence growth, the Soviet military developed a wide array of new military capabilities to meet broadened contingency needs below the strategic nuclear level. The fruits of these development programmes can now be effectively exploited to expose the tension in the West between the political desire for arms control and the military need for a coherent strategy of credible deterrence.

Developing a broad popular consensus on the nature of the Warsaw Pact threat has become increasingly difficult with the advent of a shrewd political leadership in Moscow. To a growing number of Europeans, the Soviet Union is now perceived as a partner rather than a potential aggressor. Under such circumstances, the new Kremlin leadership has begun a skilful program of exaggerating tensions within NATO over what to do about yet another of the asymmetric military advantages the Soviets have accumulated over the years. The latest nuclear deployment issue testing Alliance cohesion is over battlefield nuclear weapons, or those delivery means (with the primary focus being on missiles) with ranges under the INF treaty's 500-km lower limit.

Albeit belatedly, Western publics have now begun to recognise that the shorter-range dimension of Soviet theatre nuclear forces has undergone a significant transformation over the last decade. While the Alliance was preoccupied with Soviet SS-20 missile deployments, the Soviet military began a modernisation programme that includes major quantitative and qualitative improvements in dual-capable artillery, strike aircraft, and short-range ballistic missiles. Because these weapons are dual-purpose (they can deliver either nuclear or non-nuclear munitions), they have provoked concern in two ways. On the one hand, coming in the context of NATO's decision at Montebello, Canada in late 1983 to begin a downward trend in its nuclear stockpile (primarily in shorter-range weapons), Soviet developments have drawn attention to a destabilising asymmetry that is of special concern to West Germans, who understandably feel singularly threatened by weapons that would land, for the most part, on German soil. On the other hand, improvements in the conventional delivery capability of Soviet short-range missiles and strike aircraft have also provoked concern about the growing potential of these weapons to exploit NATO vulnerabilities below the nuclear threshold. Because Soviet military planners show a strong preference for conventional-warfare contingencies, many are beginning to conclude that new Soviet dual-capable systems should be viewed primarily in a conventional military context.

However one chooses to view the predominant role of new Soviet dual-capable delivery means, they will increasingly dominate NATO's future defence and arms control agendas. Never before has there been such a pressing need for NATO to develop a coherent framework that rationalises military strategy, force modernisation, and arms control. Understanding the enduring features of Soviet military strategy and the forces that underpin it – especially in the aftermath of the INF treaty – is an essential component of forging NATO's much-needed security framework. This book is intended to assist in that endeavour.

Chapter 1 sets the historical context surrounding the Soviet pursuit of new military capabilities below the strategic force level. The general similarities between Soviet military doctrine and strategy under Khrushchev and contemporary expressions of doctrine and strategy mask a rich evolutionary history of changing Soviet views on escalation, methods of war, military contingencies, and the types and forms of combat action required to support favoured contingencies. Chapter 1 finds that contemporary Soviet contingency preferences have a marked conventional orientation, but not without a full appreciation of the dilemmas of substituting conventional for nuclear mass at the very outset of war. How new dual-capable missiles and aircraft have come to play an increasingly prominent role in escalating and conventional contingencies is an issue that receives close scrutiny. The chapter ends on a note of uncertainty. The contingencies and related military forces covered in the chapter were amassed during the Soviet military's unprecedented position of autonomy under the Brezhnev regime. While these military instruments certainly provide Mikhail Gorbachev with useful bargaining leverage, there are signs that the Soviet military no longer retains the powerful bureaucratic position it once held under Brezhnev, even in regard to such matters as the military-technical content of doctrine. Here a note of caution seems in order, for the chapter concludes with the judgement that there is no inherent contradiction between discussions of a so-called "defensive" military doctrine and the traditional Soviet emphasis on the offensive. In fact, Soviet military planners view the introduction of highly accurate long-range conventional firepower – where they currently hold a noticeable advantage over the West – as compelling a closer interaction between offence and defence. Relating this operational interaction to notions of "non-provocative defence," which have been popular amongst the European left, has largely been an initiative led by Soviet civilian defence intellectuals. It must be viewed as part of a carefully orchestrated program of Soviet public diplomacy in the aftermath of INF.

Public diplomacy aside, the Soviet military possesses a vast array of dual-capable forces, the INF treaty notwithstanding.

Chapter 2 turns to a description and analysis of the current transitional state of Soviet dual-capable theatre forces (artillery, strike aircraft, and short-range ballistic missiles), including their delivery means, current and projected deployment numbers, and payload options (nuclear, chemical, and conventional). Chapter 2 also considers how Soviet planners might legally compensate for the elimination of shorter-range missiles under the INF treaty.

Moscow's efforts to redress the military impact of the INF treaty inevitably call for making compromises that can be understood only in the context of the Soviet approach to force employment in the theatre – the subject of Chapter 3. Attempts to compensate for INF reductions mean that Soviet planners must evaluate complementary relationships between affected and unaffected classes of weapons. Clearly, the latter classes represent a means by which to reconstitute lost target coverage that results from the elimination of entire categories of weapons. To assist in evaluating Soviet circumvention alternatives, Chapter 3 describes the Soviet force employment process for theatre targeting, with special attention given to NATO targets (priorities, numbers, vulnerabilities) against which INF weapons have been aimed, and unaffected weapons could be, in the future.

With forces described and a force employment framework in hand, Chapter 4 assesses the role of particular Soviet weapon systems in each of the three dominant planning contingencies that Soviet planners worry about today. Because the book seeks to understand the impact of the INF treaty on Soviet military strategy, Chapter 4 focuses on a pre-INF setting; in other words, the role of forces eliminated under the treaty is examined to establish a baseline for assessing the damage caused by the INF treaty. That damage assessment is one of the subjects of Chapter 5 in which the analysis generally suggests that the elimination of intermediate-range missiles (especially the SS-20 force) will impose unwanted constraints on several aspects of Soviet planning for nuclear contingencies in both Europe and Asia. The only reliable way of compensating for the SS-20's elimination is to draw upon ICBMs and per-

haps some SLBMs, but these forces may be dramatically reduced as part of a future START treaty.

In contrast to the loss of intermediate-range forces, the
elimination of shorter-range missiles (500 to 1000 km) will
cost the Soviets little, particularly with respect to preferred
conventional contingencies. The "second zero" has such marginal effect because over 80% of the targets of interest to a Soviet
planner are located within 300 to 350 km of the inter-German
border. Below the 500–km INF threshold, the Warsaw Pact
holds an enormous advantage over NATO in short-range ballistic missiles, and the treaty does nothing to control qualitative or quantitative improvements in this catetgory. Finally,
removing INF missiles as targets permits Soviet planners to
focus even more heavily in the preferred conventional contingency on exploiting NATO's vulnerable airpower infrastructure.

Consideration of military factors alone probably would
have made total elimination of the SS-20 force unacceptable
to the more narrowly focused Brezhnev leadership. The
Gorbachev leadership, by contrast, seems far more willing to
put aside clinical military detail – especially when the constraints only affect the least preferred nuclear contingencies
and furnish such important political benefits as well. Foremost in the latter regard is a fostering of the erroneous notion
that Pershing II and cruise missiles were deployed simply to
counter the SS-20 force. Instead, the Alliance rationale for
INF deployments had just as much, if not more, to do with
bolstering US extended deterrence *vis-a-vis* improving Soviet
conventional warfare capabilities – ironically, the very
capabilities which likely sustain Moscow's confidence that the
SS-20 can be safely traded for Pershing and cruise missiles.

The second subject taken up in Chapter 5 is the story behind the "second zero," which clearly was not in the West's
national security interests. Whereas the "second zero" cost the
Soviets very little, the same cannot be said for NATO. Soviet
planners depend on short-range ballistic missiles primarily
for conventional fire missions, while their NATO counterparts rely on a significantly smaller arsenal (about one-six-
teenth the size of the Warsaw Pact's) of shorter-range missiles

exclusively for nuclear missions. NATO simply counts on nuclear options for deterrence far more than does the Warsaw Pact. If the relative impact of shorter-range reductions so favoured the Soviets, why did the USA raise the issue of shorter-range constraints in the first place? Upon closer analysis, the reasons behind the US position – largely having to do with the fear that the Soviets could circumvent SS-20 limits by depending more on shorter-range missiles – reflect a dangerously myopic view of the role of these weapons in Soviet strategy. The better Soviet shorter-range missiles perform in their primary mission of conventional fire support to the air operation, the less chance they could in any way replace lost SS-20 coverage. Certainly, this apparent failure to understand the effect of US positions on the Soviet military is a poor basis upon which to fashion on arms control negotiating strategy. As a consequence, the USA clumsily ventured into a negotiating area where the Soviets held most of the cards. That the USA kept the shorter-range issue alive as an obstacle to an INF treaty till the very end, thereby permitting Mikhail Gorbachev to appear as if he were making a selfless gesture in acceding to a "double zero" agreement, does not augur well for the future of arms control as it affects basic Western security interests.

Given the conclusions of Chapter 5, it is only appropriate that the final chapter weigh the implications of the preceding ones for the future of Western security and arms control policy. Coherent defence and arms control planning rests on a sound understanding of the Soviet military's weaknesses as well as its strengths. The INF negotiating record suggests that serious improvements must be made in this regard if the West is to achieve a closer linkage between arms control and national security planning. Chapter 6 identifies several important areas of uncertainty with respect to the Soviet approach of coping with Western military strategy. Exaggerating these uncertainties should be a major focus of Western defence planning in the future.

In the aftermath of the INF accord, the Western Alliance should concentrate on two comparatively modest goals. The first entails recognising the continuing importance of survivably based and credibly planned nuclear options. Chapter 6 evaluates several alternative compensatory measures that should be considered in the light of the elimination of Pershing II and cruise missiles. At the same time, the INF treaty and Soviet expansion of short-range nuclear forces compel a re-examination of NATO's nuclear modernisation decisions made at Montebello in late 1983. Special attention is given to assesssing the utility and vulnerability of dual-capable artillery. The analysis concludes that while a significant drawdown of nuclear artillery (compensated for by an increase in air-to-ground nuclear missiles) could be tolerated over the next decade, a continuing requirement exists for a modernised stockpile of these weapons. Finally, considerable attention is devoted to the matter of nuclear weapon survivability. The fundamentally political nature of NATO has predetermined the outcome of virtually all of the Alliance's nuclear weapon survivability programmes: the Alliance does not lack technical solutions, only the political will to execute them. Because the mere existence of nuclear weapons is viewed as sufficient to deter any rational adversary, weapon vulnerability receives low priority in peacetime. But it is during deep crises when deterrence is put to its most stressful test. The way NATO postures its nuclear stockpile ought to be a stable feature of flexible response. Instead, it currently stands as one of NATO's top instabilities: it could provoke the very action it seeks to deter.

The second goal is a corollary of the first. To bolster the credibility of nuclear and conventional deterrence, the Alliance must show an improved capacity to survive the weight of the Warsaw Pact's initial conventional blow. Given Warsaw Pact improvements in conventionally armed missiles and aircraft, this appears especially crucial in the area of air-base survivability. Soviet planners have great respect for the airpower component of NATO's nuclear and conventional forces. Without success in the air, Soviet planners believe the Warsaw Pact cannot win on the ground, tank asymmetries notwithstanding. Therefore, NATO security planners must focus attention on determining the most cost-effective counters to

Soviet short-range ballistic missiles below the INF treaty's 500-km threshold.

Chapter 6 argues that NATO should place top priority on finding ways to cope with conventionally (and perhaps chemically) armed ballistic missiles, not nuclear-armed ones. Although the dramatically improved accuracy of these missiles means that the Soviet Union could, if it chose, deliver very low yield nuclear warheads with great effectiveness and reduced collateral damage, there would still be immense escalatory risks associated with such attacks. NATO has somehow managed to deter nuclear missile attacks over several decades. A far more serious and plausible threat lies in the Warsaw Pact's emerging capacity to use conventionally armed missiles and aircraft to exploit longstanding NATO vulnerabilities below the nuclear threshold. Despite the seriousness of this threat, the advent of the SDI programme has had a profound adverse effect on Western analysis of counters to short-range ballistic missiles. As a consequence, the threat of conventionally armed ballistic missiles has been both exaggerated and understated. SDI proponents have a tendency to see these missiles as capable of independently destroying complex targets like airfields, which today are assigned to either nuclear weapons or several conventionally armed fighter-bombers. Such robust capabilities justify ATBM defences of the more exotic type. Conversely, SDI's opponents, who have difficulty separating ATBM from SDI (the former is seen as a "stalking horse" for the latter), downgrade the threat by simply taking the proponents' exaggerated argument and disproving it.

Building on Chapter 4's analysis of combined-arms warfare, Chapter 6 evaluates the role missiles play in the air operation and the utility of various passive and active counters in blunting their effectiveness. Their role is basically one of leveraging the effectiveness of aircraft strikes by temporarily tying up critical operations (launch and/or recovery of aircraft) until aircraft can follow up with a more telling blow. In view of the importance NATO attaches to its aircraft for both conventional and nuclear deterrence, NATO should pursue a modest programme of active and passive counters against conventionally armed missiles. For reasons of cost-effectiveness and potentially adverse impact on the Soviet operational style of warfare, furnishing the Patriot air defence system with a self-protection capability against missiles has substantial merit. This measure should be combined with such passive measures as additional runways at airfields where space is already available, and more and better rapid runway repair capability as well. The only effective way to counter this package of modest measures – at much greater economic and political cost to the Pact countries than to NATO – is for the Soviets to greatly proliferate missile launchers in Eastern Europe. In a sense, this modest programme of counters could create strong incentives for Soviet political decision-makers to accept a missiles-only "triple zero" agreement, which would substantially reduce fears of surprise attack in Central Europe. Barring the attainment of such an admittedly optimistic agreement, the analysis in Chapters 4 and 6 should still serve well as a useful framework for assessing the relative contribution of various arms control (missile launcher ceilings, say), active, and passive measures in coping with the weight of the Warsaw Pact's initial blow.

Introduction to the paperback edition

Sparked by the unexpected political liberalisation of Eastern Europe, Western perceptions of the Warsaw Pact military threat have changed dramatically in the year and a half since I completed the hardback edition of this book. Albeit more ambiguous, change is also evident in the character of Soviet military doctrine and capabilities. Yet, it seems fair to say that the book's account of the logic underlying Mikhail Gorbachev's willingness to accede to a "double zero" Intermediate-Range Nuclear Forces (INF) agreement anticipated the direction, if not the scope and pace, of Soviet initiatives in conventional arms control. After nearly fifteen years of false starts in Mutual and Balanced Force Reduction Talks, there is strong reason to believe that current negotiations on Conventional Armed Forces in Europe (CFE) will soon produce an agreement that could eliminate the threat of a Soviet blitzkrieg attack in Europe. But more than just the prospect of CFE success has influenced Western perceptions. Gorbachev's skilled diplomacy has displaced rhetoric with action, as demonstrated by the Soviet Union's willingness to unilaterally reduce its forces in Central Europe before any CFE agreement is signed.

Notwithstanding the dizzying pace and positive direction of Soviet policy, opinion differs over the long-term consequences of these developments for Western security. Although many view Gorbachev's unilateral force reductions as a legitimate stimulus to a mutually acceptable CFE outcome, others fear that the initiative is meant more as a screen for restructuring Soviet military forces outside the formal scrutiny of CFE verification. Moreover, some argue that the military rationale for restructuring predates Gorbachev by several years and rests on a solid appreciation of how new technology will shape future warfare. Thus, rather than producing a Soviet military structurally incapable of offensive operations, force restructuring could ultimately yield a more effective Soviet military, especially if events in Eastern Europe induce a deep malaise in Western defence planning while the Soviet economy is primed for an inevitable renewal of military-technical competition with the West.[1]

Any prediction of the long-term Soviet future is fraught with great uncertainty. From today's vantage point prospects for a successful economic restructuring look dim. That the Soviet economy is in such a woeful state helps explain the Soviet military's willingness to accept a substantial narrowing of its traditional planning framework. The West's continued widening of the high-technology gap is so inimical to the Soviet military's view of future war that it has prompted a convenient alliance of interests. A conservative Soviet military has much to gain from the success of Gorbachev's reform-oriented *perestroika*. But it is shortsighted to suggest a convergence between Gorbachev's arms control agenda and former Chief of the General Staff Marshal Nikolai Ogarkov's call in the early to mid-1980s for a high-tech revolution in military affairs. Although both dictate a radical streamlining of the Soviet Armed Forces and a substantially greater dependence on quality over quantity, where Ogarkov sought a new force structure bent on immediately carrying the offensive deep into enemy territory, Gorbachev seems predisposed to making Soviet forces structurally incapable of sustained offensive power.[2]

Or so it would seem. The ambiguity over precisely where Gorbachev stands between reform-minded civilians and a conservative military hierarchy should come as no surprise. Given the precarious state of the Soviet economy and the nationalist ferment brewing in several of the country's outlying regions, Gorbachev has every reason not to alienate the military by definitively declaring his opposition to certain interpretations of military strategy. Nevertheless, the Soviet leader's fence-

sitting has highlighted the issue of just how permanent a transformation is taking place in Soviet national security policy. The
differences between civilian reformers and military specialists
represent much more than just idiosyncratic fussing. For, while
Soviet willingness to accede to huge asymmetrical reductions as
part of a formal CFE agreement will effectively eliminate the
threat of a standing-start surprise attack by the Warsaw Pact, it
is still very much in the West's security interests to remove or
reduce those Soviet military capabilities that would be most
likely to generate instability if Central European political
conditions should change immoderately in the longer-term
future.

The radical transformation of East European politics alone
has made progress toward parity in East–West conventional
forces appear obsolescent. While negotiators' chores will
be many and demanding before a so-called CFE I agreement
can be reached, attention has necessarily turned to broader
concerns about the future of military alliances; the continuing
role, if any, of European-based nuclear weapons; and the far
more substantial cuts in conventional forces than the now
seemingly insignificant ones that CFE will likely exact. CFE II
– or the set of negotiations that will seek to go beyond CFE I's
aim of reducing Warsaw Pact superiorities in tanks, artillery,
and troop carriers to levels just below NATO's current ones –
will inevitably have as its mandate a virtual restructuring of the
European security framework.[3] Its objective must be the
maintenance of military stability in a period of rapid political
and economic change.

Carefully negotiated reductions could produce a more stable
military balance, but the urge to reach a quick outcome or to
demobilize could instead lead to a fundamentally unstable
military situation in Central Europe: one in which the military
balance is measured in mobilisation and reinforcement potential. In this regard, the West faces several unalterable military
realities *vis à vis* a potentially adversarial Soviet Union – the
foremost being much longer lines of reinforcement, principally
by sea from North America to continental Europe, and an
inherently more vulnerable reinforcement infrastructure,

dependent on a few air and sea points of debarkation and a lamentably small number of useful air bases, all located within a Central Region that has little strategic depth. Although no arms control agreement can alter geostrategic reality, CFE II could rectify the fact that current negotiations – in order to avoid any serious restrictions on Western dual-capable missiles and aircraft – fail seriously to constrain the destabilising potential of the Soviet air operation. Aircraft can become especially destabilizing when – as in the Soviet air operation – they are wedded to the prompt use of ballistic missiles for the purpose of rapidly achieving fire and air superiority at the start of conflict. Indeed, as ground forces are radically thinned out in the region from the Atlantic to the Urals, long-range air and missile capabilities will become significantly more influential determinants of military power in Central Europe.[4] How and to what extent these military instruments are controlled will largely set the conditions for future European military stability.

Soviet Views of Military Stability

No longer is the Soviet military, as it was under Mikhail Gorbachev's predecessors, the sole source of wisdom and insight on all national security matters. The role of civilian defence analysts of the Soviet Academy of Sciences has increased at least to the point where alternative analytical inputs are available to the political leadership to support defence decision-making. Andrei Kokoshin describes this process as the "deep politicisation of traditionally military questions," resulting in the creation of a new discipline, "military-political research."[5] But there probably remains a substantial difference between Gorbachev using the products of "military-political research" to rationalise defence planning – thereby helping to produce the non-threatening posture so essential to Soviet foreign policy – and his using such civilian analyses to influence doctrinal shifts at the military-technical level of defence decision-making. Responsibility for the latter area has traditionally been the exclusive domain of the General Staff and, despite much speculation to the contrary, there has probably been little reduction in the General Staff's military-technical role. Nonetheless, the role of the civilians has sharpened the debate markedly within and outside the Soviet Union. This is especially true in regard to the relationship between force structure and military stability.

Perhaps the most analytically useful Soviet contribution on stability is a July 1988 article by Kokoshin and his retired military colleague at the Institute for the USA and Canada, Major-General Valentin Larionov.[6] Kokoshin and Larionov offer four alternative force postures, progressing from the lowest to the highest state of stability. What makes the contribution particularly insightful is that the authors' models of stability accommodate the respective viewpoints and distinctions between and amongst the various civilian and military participants in the ongoing security debate.

The first and most destabilising force posture is one in which both alliances are poised to initiate offensive operations from the very start of conflict, penetrating deep into the opposition's strategic rear area to effect a collapse of both the will and capability to resist. Although Soviet military specialists view NATO as having the wherewithal to conduct such operations, this force posture palpably mirrors the objectives of the Soviet conventional-only contingency analysed in Chapters 3 and 4 of this book. Pre-emption and exploitation of massive conventional fires dominate this force posture, because the chief goal is to take advantage of NATO's severe vulnerabilities before the Alliance has had sufficient time to complete its mobilisation and dispersal of air, ground, and nuclear forces. Soviet military and civilian analysts alike have strongly supported moving away from such a force posture, while Soviet unilateral withdrawals from Eastern Europe have materially allayed Western concern about short-warning pre-emptive attacks. Still, despite the strong prospect of even more radical reductions in Soviet tanks, artillery, and troop carriers, it is notable that the major instruments of pre-emption remain relatively untouched (dual-capable missiles not at all and aircraft not enough) by current CFE proposals.

Kokoshin and Larionov's second paradigm closely mimics

the ostensible shift in Soviet military doctrine toward its current emphasis on war prevention and defensive operations. Most favoured by the Soviet military, this force posture spurns initial offensive operations but not at the expense of failing to maintain a strong counter-offensive potential essentially no different from that of the first force posture. Conflict termination would take place only after the routing of the aggressor on his own territory. According to former Chief of the General Staff, Marshal Sergei Akhromeyev, currently a close military adviser to President Gorbachev, the Soviet military now intends to remain on the defensive for three to four weeks before conducting a decisive counter-offensive.[7] Kokoshin and Larionov express concern that the simple forswearing of offensive intent at the outset of conflict may not eliminate worrisome crisis ambiguities that come with the retention of significant offensive forces, even though they may be less ready in comparison with today's force dispositions.

The third force posture model also abjures initial offensive intent but rejects as well the taking and holding of enemy territory, making it similar to NATO's declared policy of restoring the *status quo ante*. Thus, offensive capability would be adequate only to repulse the aggressor with an operational-level counter-stroke; strategic reserves, presumably, would not be sufficient to exploit the initial repulsion through the seizure of the aggressor's territory. Kokoshin and Larionov worry that a major incentive to violate the model's declaratory intent could result should the defender suffer much greater territorial damage than the aggressor. Unmentioned by the authors are the offensive incentives that would flow from unequal force postures due to differences in mobilisation schedules.

Representing the civilian specialists' notion of truly "defensive defence," the fourth and final force posture model depends on the co-ordinated restructuring of the military forces of both alliance systems to the point where only tactical-level operations are possible. Particularly high on Kokoshin and Larionov's list of offensively oriented forces requiring elimination are attack aircraft, tactical and operational-tactical ballistic missiles (especially when tied to automated target acquisition means, making them "reconnaissance-strike complexes"), and large tank and air-assault formations. A less radical variation on the theme of reducing attack potential in tactical-level formations is the proposal by Kokoshin and Larionov's colleague, Alexander Konovalov, to create three 50-km corridors on each side of the inter-German border with severe limits on tanks, bridging equipment, artillery, ammunition storage, and tactical ballistic missiles (a maximum range cap of 50 km).[8] Naturally, negotiating any of these more radical force postures would be fraught with definition problems relating to weapons and doctrine, not to speak of the enormous institutional turmoil associated with substantive change. Thus, Kokoshin and Larionov envisage a multi-stage process that could accommodate such delicate issues as the inclusion of naval and space strike weapons and the progressive denuclearisation of both alliance systems.

The Soviet Military's Perspective: Making a Virtue of Necessity

Although much of the work of the Soviet academics lacks rich military-technical detail, it is nonetheless important because of its clear influence on the Soviet political leadership's unilateral and declaratory arms control initiatives. To the extent that an alternative source of national security thinking truly informs the decision process, understanding its make-up can shed light on plausible boundary conditions of current and follow-on CFE negotiations. Still, it remains as important as ever to gauge the perspectives of the General Staff and military services on alternative future force postures. The Soviet military has yet to shed its atavistic interest in the virtues of offensive action; it instinctively clings to the second variant of Kokoshin and Larionov's four models, because it affords them the most operational flexibility in an otherwise constrained planning framework. For the political leadership to take arms control positions consistent with Kokoshin and Larionov's fourth (defensive defence) model would require unprecedented intervention into military planning.

In my view, the Soviet military planning framework will

continue to narrow as a natural by-product of CFE negotiations. But radical departures from the norm – especially of the
type that would render Soviet forces structurally incapable of
offensive operations – are so fraught with political risk and
negotiating dispute that their principal impact will be felt more
in the realm of public than East–West diplomacy. The real
issue is the extent to which negotiations can move the Soviet
military away from its predisposition to retain strong counter-
offensive potential and towards an increasingly stable – if not
entirely defensive – force disposition. Gaining insight into just
how this might be accomplished requires not only an understanding of Soviet military views about future warfare but also
an awareness of how potential Soviet strengths interact with
current and prospective Western weaknesses.

At first blush, the consequences for the Soviet military
of accepting parity with NATO in several major weapon
categories appear profound. Accepting parity and thereby
forsaking favourable force ratios ought to shake severely
General Staff confidence in meeting traditional Soviet time-
lines for a theatre-strategic campaign in Western Europe,
even if one were to put aside any notion of Warsaw Pact
cohesion. But such a view is far too narrow from a Soviet
planning perspective; it deals with only a portion of the "beans"
that comprise combined-arms warfare – especially future
warfare fought with thinned-out formations and a vastly
circumscribed role for nuclear weapons. Nor does it deal
seriously with the role of airpower (in its broadest combined-
arms sense) as the primary contributor to success on the
ground. As noted earlier, a CFE treaty will leave the tools
of the Soviet air operation relatively unchecked, while the
targets against which the air operation is planned will shrink
both as a result of CFE reductions and unilateral NATO
actions. And, finally, a future marked by radically reduced
forward-based forces underscores the growing importance of
rapid strategic redeployment. Much shorter lines of communication and a cadre mobilisation system could offer Soviet
planners distinct advantages in executing either a major re-
entry into Eastern Europe or a strategic reinforcement to

support conventional conflict with the West. Each of the three foregoing issues – ground operations under conditions of force parity, the role of airpower, and mobilisation and strategic redeployment – deserves closer scrutiny.

Coping with Conventional Force Parity
A full appreciation of Soviet military views of future conventional warfare cannot be gained without keeping in mind the long-standing Soviet political goal of crippling the nuclear component of NATO's Flexible Response strategy. As Chapter 6 notes, the most critical uncertainty facing Soviet defence planners today relates to the adverse operational consequences of even a relatively confined level of nculear use on the battlefield – let alone escalation to nuclear strikes on the Soviet homeland. Of course, one consequence of parity is reduction in the threat of a Warsaw Pact short-warning attack and the provision of additional warning time. More warning time could be used to disperse battlefield nuclear weapons to safer havens than the few vulnerable garrisons that make Soviet pre-emption so inviting an operational concept. Alternatively, however, the future is more likely to bring a dangerous weakening of nuclear deterrence, continuing a trend strongly evident in the 1980s and likely only to worsen in the 1990s.[9] Thus, as nuclear deterrence diminishes as a prominent variable in the force balance, Soviet planners may find life with essentially equal force ratios quite tolerable – particularly in view of the urgent need to restructure the economy.

Perhaps the most salient motive for Soviet force restructuring is the way that Western trends in advanced conventional technologies have strongly increased Soviet incentives to emphasise manoeuvre warfare. Indeed, since the late 1970s Soviet planners have stressed the importance of a more effective single echelon as a potential counter to the Western notion of second-echelon targeting (as now exemplified by NATO's Follow-On Forces Attack or FOFA strategy). Rather than presenting lucrative second-echelon targets to NATO's increasingly effective high-tech weapons, Soviet planners began to concentrate on multiple operational and tactical manoeuvres that would permit a rapid penetration and inter-mingling of Soviet with Western forces.[10] Equally influential in Soviet calculations is the effect of terrain on force require-ments. Germany has become heavily urbanised; nearly half of West Germany is now considered urban (or close terrain).[11] Moreover, while many of the West's advanced conventional weapons work well against tanks in open terrain, their effective-ness is seriously degraded when employed against units in close terrain. Urbanised terrain affords military units partial protec-tion against sensor eyes and munition effects. It also means that fewer tanks and artillery and more infantry may represent a better force mix.

The historical antecedents of the current Soviet restructuring date back to the last days of the Great Patriotic War. Soviet military theoreticians then began to appreciate that their force structure was too tank-heavy to fight well in the heavily forested, urbanised, and hilly terrain of Central Europe. A speech given by General P.A. Rotmistrov in 1945 emphasized just these limitations and their effect on the 1st Belorussian Front during the Berlin operation. That the speech was re-published in 1985 strongly signifies that contemporary Soviet planners appreciate well the need for better combined-arms balance in the current Soviet force structure.[12]

Soviet interest in developing more independent force group-ings (tank, mechanised and combined-arms) configured for tactical and operational manoeuvre is reflected in several years of experimentation in the western military districts with corps made up of mixed brigades.[13] If the Soviet military adopts the corps structure – or a similar one – it will be adaptable to the particular threat opposing it and the unique characteristics of the local terrain. The corps structure' adaptability comes from the lack of a fixed table of organisation and equipment, suggesting an orientation much more suitable for fast-moving conventional warfare than for nuclear warfare. Thus, the recent consolidation of SS-21 missile battalions (formerly organic to divisions) into brigades controlled at army level makes good sense; these units are too cumbersome to accom-pany highly manoeuvrable brigades and corps.[14] Nevertheless, the SS-21's increased range and precision accuracy still permit it an important role in direct support of manoeuvring units. Conversely, restructuring could force some devolution – perhaps of anti-tank, self-propelled artillery, armed helicopters or tactical bridging – from armies to corps and brigades to furnish them with elements of independent operation. Just as the creation of High Commands in the theatres of military operation and the reorganisation of the Soviet air forces streamlined the Soviet military system to move more efficiently from peace to war, so too would the restructuring of the Ground Forces. To the extent that tailored combined-arms formations are manned, equipped, and disposed in peacetime to reflect their specific wartime operational missions, they would be far more ready for commitment to combat in case of war.

Chapter 1 noted that Soviet military writers see the introduction of highly accurate long-range firepower as compelling virtually a complete re-evaluation of the relationship between offence and defence. Conventionally armed ballistic missiles and aircraft will permit even the defence to cross immediately over to the offensive. As weapon ranges increase and tactical and operational manoeuvre becomes the standard, achieving firepower norms will no longer be accomplished by concentrated artillery. A new concept, known as "manoeuvre by fire," is meant to offset the physical vulnerability of concentrated artillery through a greater reliance on long-range strike assets (missiles and aircraft, presumably) to furnish integrated fire support.[15] The consolidation of SS-21 missile battalions into brigades controlled at the army level supports the "manoeuvre by fire" concept by permitting more effective control and greater employment flexibility at a higher command echelon.

Soviet planners expect that meeting engagements – where combatants encounter each other on the offensive – will dominate the future battlefield.[16] Such a form of warfare implies an essential convergence of offence and defence. Indeed, defensive operations create the conditions for taking the offensive. Soviet adoption of the notion of defence activeness, which appeared in the 1986 Soviet *Military Encyclopaedic*

Dictionary, does not differ conceptually from the major tenets of the US Army's AirLand Battle doctrine or the NATO Northern Army Group's so-called "Bagnall concept" (named after its principal author, General Sir Nigel Bagnall). The following description of the Bagnall concept offers a striking parallel with Soviet Defence Minister Yazov's dictum that "it is impossible . . . to destroy the aggressor only with defence:"[17]

> The revised concept places greater emphasis on the selection and defence of vital areas; on co-operation between ground and air forces; on tactical flexibility and mobility; and on the employment of reserves . . . It is important to recognise that the concept does not mark any abandonment of the principle of forward defence . . . But it does recognise that force improvements permit the adoption of a more mobile tactical concept. Static defence can lead only to a war of attrition, while the new concept would allow defenders to seize the initiative from the aggressor.[18]

Convergence of Western and Soviet operational doctrines somewhere in the neighbourhood of Kokoshin and Larionov's second and third models is surely preferable to today's comparatively unstable force sizes and dispositions. But if we are to identify just how arms control can reduce instabilities to a minimum, we need a more meaningful picture of competitive counter-offensive doctrines under conditions of relative force parity. Many Western analysts anticipate that Soviet acceptance of rough force parity precludes them from achieving the required local force ratios to achieve success at least at the operational level of warfare. Yet a closer look at the Soviet view of required force ratios suggests otherwise.

An over-simplistic, but nonetheless frequently used, index of the conventional balance is the theatre-wide force ratio model, which helps analysts make judgements about probable war outcomes. The standard threshold – or force ratio below which the attacker would have difficulty obtaining success – has become 1.5:1. The assumption is that an attacker with less than this force ratio across the theatre would be unable to produce needed local superiorities of 3:1, which are believed to be essential to penetrate successfully along a narrow sector of the front.

Among the numerous shortcomings of the theatre-wide force ratio model are its assumptions about the threshold of success. The 1.5:1 threshold is derived from assuming that while the attacker achieves a 3:1 advantage in one penetration sector, he must also maintain a 1:1 ratio in all other sectors. Soviet military theoreticians point out that secondary sectors can be defended in a variety of ways with force ratios of much less than 1:1.[19] Simply put, more efficient use of defensive tactics in one or more sectors permits higher force ratios in others. For example, Soviet specialists indicate that the most active defence sectors might entail force ratios of 2:1, which would permit some tactical encirclement. Less active or even passive sectors would find force ratios of 1:1 or 1:1.5. But to configure appropriately sized counter-offensive groupings (with a minimum ratio of 3:1, and 4:1 preferred), Soviet commanders would be called upon to borrow from less active or even passive defence sectors. Such borrowing could lead to force ratios in the most passive sectors of 1:2.

Despite such a disadvantageous force ratio, Soviet military observers still believe that the defender could contribute critically to operational success. By attracting NATO's strongest forces to commit themselves in the hope of success and then by inflicting losses on them sufficient to reduce their reserve capacity to protect vulnerable flanks and rear areas, defence sectors give leverage to sectors on the offensive. Using a historical analogy, one Soviet military commentator noted that, despite a 1:1 force ratio at Stalingrad and great risk in the type of tactics employed, Soviet forces defeated 22 enemy divisions – a force larger than today's German III Corps and US V and VII Corps in NATO's Central Region.[20] The Soviet military's heightened attention to the effective use of field fortifications and other defensive techniques has to be seen in the light not just of its obvious political appeal but also of its important contribution to offensive success.

Enlarging the Role of Airpower as a Balance Variable
Western techniques for conducting balance assessments are notoriously weak in considering the contribution of airpower to

war outcomes. For NATO's part there is a tendency to assume that the West's qualitative edge in airpower (superior aircraft, avionics, and pilot skill) affords the Alliance the luxury of living with force ratios that might exceed 1.5:1 in the Warsaw Pact's favour. On the Soviet side, military planners freely admit that independent manoeuvre operations entail high risks, the foremost being the susceptibility of penetrating units to Western air attack if Soviet air superiority (local if not theatre-wide) is not obtained. Without air superiority, airpower in the minimum essential strike groupings would not be available to interdict NATO reserves attempting to break out from successful Soviet encirclement operations.

The Soviet air operation's role in furnishing shock firepower at the start of conflict also plays into Soviet methods for determining required force ratios on the main axes of penetration. Instead of simply calculating available forces in Soviet strike groupings compared with NATO forces along the adjacent sector to their tactical depth, Soviet planners consider opposing forces to the full depth of the attacking Front's mission, or out to a distance to 250 to 350 km – nearly the full strategic depth of the Alliance's Central Region.[21] Moreover, Soviet planners weigh the effects of initial preparatory fires; their fire support systems "adjust the force ratio" through attrition of NATO forces in the intended attack sectors.

This book (especially Chapters 3, 4, and 6) has focused heavily on the role of the Soviet air operation in exploiting NATO vulnerabilities. As new Soviet declaratory doctrine moves away from the mechanics of pre-emption toward ways of "preventing war," we ought to continue monitoring closely what is said and done regarding the air operation's future character. Monitoring is needed because CFE will leave the dual-capable missile and air components of the air operation relatively intact, and NATO's extant vulnerabilities are only likely to worsen as threat perceptions fade and prudent survivability measures are abandoned. Indeed, even if all Soviet forces are removed from Eastern Europe, missiles and aircraft would still furnish the cutting edge of any Soviet projection of military power back into that region or anywhere else along the USSR's vast periphery.

Soviet military theoreticians have only hesitantly relinquished the rhetoric of pre-emption. In the 1986 Soviet *Military Encyclopaedic Dictionary*, edited by the then Chief of the General Staff, Marshal Sergei Akhromeyev, the term "defence activeness" was used to describe air and artillery fire "during the
times the adversary is preparing for an attack."[22] Since the announcement of the Warsaw Pact's new defensive military doctrine in May 1987, Soviet treatment of the role of firepower has been carefully toned down, primarily by casting it in the context of measures to prevent war. For example, in the lead article of the December 1988 issue of the restricted journal *Military Thought*, General of the Army G.I. Salmanov spends considerable time on the political aspects of war prevention and arms control before turning to a discussion of the conduct of war.[23] But once into that discussion he raises some familiar themes, the defensive thrust notwithstanding. Salmanov believes that the initial period of war still remains as important as ever in setting the conditions for subsequent success. During this period Soviet forces must be prepared to conduct "active defensive" operations, which permit the launching of decisive counter-attacks to rout the enemy. Where offence and defence become most indistinguishable is in Salmanov's description of a system of fire to be employed at the outset of war:

> We must be able quickly to establish a system of fire, with which, in response to the initiation of aggression, the enemy will receive an immediate and overwhelming answering fire strike that is capable of sharply weakening the enemy's offensive potential even before his second echelon strike groups are committed to conflict. It follows that in the planning and developing of the Ground Forces, Air Forces and Air Defence Forces special attention must be devoted to their capability to achieve fire and air supremacy *from the very beginning of a war.*[24]

The urge to usurp control at the outset of conflict could generate great instability during tense periods of political and economic change in Eastern Europe and the Soviet Union. From NATO's standpoint, the tools of the air operation are most worrisome when, as now, they are based in Eastern

Europe, within easy reach of critical Western airpower and reinforcement targets. Yet, even if Soviet missiles and aircraft are ultimately removed from Eastern Europe along with ground forces, they would still generate instability by furnishing the Soviet military with a decisive firepower edge, which would make re-entry into Eastern Europe a much more attractive option than it would have been if these weapons had been reduced through arms control.

Oddly enough, despite reduced threat perceptions and defence budgets within both alliance systems, there is a good chance that NATO's planned deployment of the conventionally armed US Army Tactical Missile System (ATACMS) in late 1990 will legitimize the Soviet military's need for a new missile to replace the Scud-B.[25] With over 700 launchers facing NATO, the Scud-B was originally slated to be replaced by the SS-23 missile. But to the great consternation of the Soviet military, Mikhail Gorbachev, wishing not to complicate INF negotiations, acceded to US insistence that constraints be placed on SS-23s by including them in his "double zero" solution in April 1987. Since that time, Scud missile units have replaced SS-23 units as they were removed from their garrisons for elimination under the treaty's provisions – as this book predicted would occur.[26] Hints that the Soviet military might be pressuring the political leadership on missile modernisation arose in May 1989, when Soviet Foreign Minister Shevardnadze surprisingly warned that the Soviet Union might deploy a new missile or stop the INF Treaty's elimination of SS-23 missiles if NATO proceeded with plans to deploy a follow-on to the Lance (FOTL) missile having a range similar to the SS-23.[27] Although Shevardnadze backed off his threat a week later, it is difficult to imagine the Soviet military reacting benignly to the proliferation of conventionally armed ATACMS missiles, even if NATO – as now appears likely – fails to deploy a follow-on to the nuclear-armed Lance.

There certainly is a legitimate military need to modernize the ageing Scud missile force, just as there was a sound military requirement in the 1970s to replace the ageing, vulnerable, liquid-fuelled SS-4 and SS-5 with the modern, mobile, solid-fuelled SS-20. Yet, as the Soviet military is so frequently reminded today by its civilian critics, the massive deployment of SS-20s may have produced military confidence in contingency planning, but only at great political and, with NATO's successful INF deployments, military costs. The Soviet military's relative quiescence hitherto about replacing its Scud inventory is probably related in part to fear of repeating "the SS-20 mistake." Rouble cost constraints certainly add to the political costs of taking the initiative to replace Scud now. What is needed is a pretext of sufficient magnitude to soften these costs.

ATACMS deployments will very likely furnish such a pretext. Measured in terms of launchers, eventual numbers of ATACMS could reportedly go as high as 1000 – simply because ATACMS is launched from the M-270 Multiple Launch Rocket System (MLRS), which could end up deployed in several NATO countries. At least in theory, the number of ATACMS launchers could significantly reduce the Warsaw Pact's current 14:1 advantage over NATO in ballistic missile launchers in the Atlantic to the Urals region.[28] Moreover, the Soviet military sees the widespread deployment of ATACMS as signalling the effective implementation of AirLand Battle and FOFA, especially as ATACMS is integrated with much-improved reconnaissance and target acquisition systems. Thus, it is unlikely that the Soviet military will lightly countenance NATO's deploying modernised fire support elements to help implement its doctrine while a major component of the Soviet air operation passes into deep obsolescence.[29]

Although ATACMS is advertised as a conventionally armed missile system, the US Army has fought hard all along to make ATACMS dual capable. That would at once proliferate conventionally armed missiles to support AirLand Battle doctrine, accommodate the FOTL requirement, enhance FOTL survivability by masking nuclear-armed ATACMS within a large MLRS population, and save on the costs of developing a completely separate launcher and missile for the FOTL mission. Complicating such an apparently efficient approach is the anticipated verification requirement to distinguish nuclear from conventional missiles, which is sure to come up in future negotiations on short-range nuclear forces. But even if political circumstances preclude future FOTL deployments in Western Europe, US Army and Department of Defense officials are nonetheless likely to press ahead on a US-based FOTL – probably using ATACMS/MLAS with a functionally related observable difference between the nuclear and conventional versions. If Congress permits such a course, it too will help legitimate the Soviet military's rationale for a follow-on to Scud.

NATO ought to be concerned about a Soviet decision to deploy a new missile to replace the Scud-B for several reasons. The influence of airpower in its larger combined-arms sense will increase roughly in proportion to reductions in land power. Land power reductions mean fewer ground targets, and this is especially true for the highest-priority targets of the Soviet air operation: NATO's in-theatre nuclear weapons. The INF Treaty eliminated the most survivable and militarily most significant targets – Pershing II and ground-launched cruise missiles. Revolutionary political changes in Eastern Europe have virtually doomed the FOTL programme, as well as any prospect of retaining modernised nuclear artillery shells in the Federal Republic of Germany. Dual-capable air bases may become the heart of NATO's residual nuclear capability, but their relatively small number in the context of the above target shrinkage makes them an even more inviting target for prompt missile attack than ever before.

From a Soviet targeteer's perspective, CFE's intrusive verification provisions will inevitably force NATO to sacrifice some aspects of its survivability for the sake of increased transparency. As just one example, on-site inspections of POMCUS reinforcement facilities create opportunities for the Soviet Union to collect valuable information on the specific location of equipment, internal storage configuration, potential bottlenecks in dispersing equipment, and the like. Without access inside large area targets, such as POMCUS facilities, targeting them effectively with conventional munitions is a daunting task. Though seemingly unimportant on the surface, information from inspections could figure heavily in the selection of appropriate munitions, attack size, aim-points, and timing with other strike assets. As Chapter 3 discussed in detail, Soviet planners never treat targets in a generic sense; they identify what is uniquely vulnerable about each target. To be sure, CFE's transparency will cut both ways, opening up the Warsaw Pact and exposing their vulnerabilities as well as NATO's. But geographic reality suggests a critical difference: because NATO Europe has little strategic depth, most of NATO's newly transparent facilities will be within relatively close striking distance of missiles and aircraft.

As pointed out in Chapter 6, NATO has several options designed to blunt the effectiveness of a sharpened air operation. But even the most modest of measures could cost the Alliance significant sums – an unlikely proposition during a period of shrinking budgets. The most important counter to the combined use of missiles (particularly a new Scud follow-on) and aircraft – a dual-mode Patriot air defence system – involves more than simply the deployment of an upgraded radar (involving software changes to permit tracking high-angle missile threats), which is currently programmed and being deployed at modest cost.[30] More costly and problematical, given today's political circumstances, is the acquisition of additional missiles and radars beyond the number needed just to conduct the air defence mission. This could cost roughly half a billion dollars per year over a ten-year period. What's more, the burden could get even heavier were the Soviet military to develop a follow-on to the SS-23 with a significantly reduced radar cross section and perhaps some terminal manoeuvrability. Overall, it is difficult to foresee the kind of sustained political support needed to implement an effective set of counters to improvements in the Soviet air operation.

The Growing Importance of Rapid Strategic Deployment
A future marked by thinned-out forces in Central Europe underscores the importance of rapid strategic deployment. The Soviet military system may be better geared than the US one to generate force groupings from reserve formations. Soviet

military strategy has a long-standing emphasis on seizing the initiative in the first operations of war and then developing initial success by committing forces from the interior of the Soviet Union along shorter lines of communications. To this end the Soviet cadre mobilisation system may be well suited to deal with the consequences of a major reduction in conventional forces, while still maintaining the infrastructure to generate forces quickly.

The Soviet cadre system allows Soviet planners to field large forces at considerably less cost than in Western armies. Built along the lines of the Israeli mobilisation system, it has a ratio of mobilised (regular) to reserve of 1:1.[31] The amount of equipment in regular and reserve units is about the same, although equipment in Soviet reserve units today is not of the same quality as that of regular units. Nevertheless, if CFE verification protocols do not manage to forestall the continued production of treaty-limited items both inside and outside the area of the Atlantic to the Urals, then the cadre system could provide future Soviet planners with a useful framework for reserve mobilisation. Even though additional time would be needed to fill out and prepare cadre units for wartime, the fact that the command structure remains intact in peacetime permits the retention of an efficient means of preparing for war.

The implications of Soviet force restructuring could also sharpen Soviet readiness to cope more effectively than NATO with conventional force reductions. A restructuring that focuses on creating corps, brigades, and battalions (the last being the principal building block formation) would enhance the use of reinforcement by battalion increment – a much more flexible method of force commitment than Soviet planners use today. This would at once speed strategic deployment and reduce Soviet vulnerability to interdiction. It would not be surprising to find the Soviet military emphasising in the future heavy-lift units for strategic deployment and perhaps some form of POMCUS sets, even if only kept in the peripheral military districts of the Soviet Union.[32] While Western negotiators should be sensitive to ways of constraining rapid Soviet

xl

mobilisation and strategic deployment potential, they should be equally aware of the reciprocal implications of such measures for a Western Alliance beset by longer strategic lines of communications.

Some Final Thoughts

In a world bewilderingly short of constants, no matter who leads the Soviet Union, it will remain a military superpower after the implementation of the CFE and START treaties – indeed, even if political change in Eastern Europe results in a total withdrawal of Soviet forces from that region. Never have opportunities to deal with the constant of Soviet military power been so conspicuous. This fortunate coincidence of Western security interests and Soviet necessities requires careful thought yet prompt action. Nowhere is this more true than in the area of controlling dual-capable delivery systems.

When I completed the hardback edition of this book just after the signing of the INF Treaty, I concluded in the final chapter that the elimination of all dual-capable ballistic missiles would at once rectify important conventional imbalances favouring the Warsaw Pact and materially enhance future crisis stability.[33] Although several analysts have recognised both the military and political value of such a negotiating strategy, it was perhaps inevitable that the proposal would be overtaken by yet another of NATO's nuclear crises – this time over modernising short-range nuclear forces (SNF).[34] What lay behind my call for eliminating all dual-capable missiles – while retaining a modernized but reduced stockpile of artillery shells and improved air-delivered nuclear weapons – was a concern about their future use as *conventional*, rather than nuclear, means of delivery. As argued earlier, there is reason to remain concerned about the contribution of missiles to the instability of air power in the aftermath of a CFE agreement. What has changed as a consequence of Eastern Europe's political liberalisation is that the prospects for SNF modernisation have receded sufficiently to recreate a more appropriate analytic

xli

framework for considering the question of who fares better if conventionally armed ballistic missiles are eliminated. But before turning to that question, we need to consider SNF's future contribution to NATO defence strategy.

Radical political change in Eastern Europe, together with potential political instability in the Soviet Union, underscores the need for NATO to retain some in-theatre nuclear weapons. What seems clear, however, is that requirements for NATO's nuclear stockpile will be determined far less through the application of military operations research and increasingly through the political process. Perhaps the most important politico-military function of NATO's future nuclear stockpile will be to provide a hedge against the uncertainty of radically thinned-out forces in a Europe rife with political change. Moreover, as this book has reminded the reader, the Soviet Union still retains a modern stockpile of nuclear artillery, missile and air-delivered warheads based in the area from the Atlantic to the Urals. Its military planners pay serious attention to contingency plans for nuclear use. For these reasons alone, NATO should carefully consider how to deal with future reductions that will come from SNF negotiations after the implementation of a CFE agreement.

Although they have not foresworn their goal of complete elimination of nuclear weapons, Soviet political authorities have begun to temper their insistence on a nuclear-free Europe by the year 2000. Both President Gorbachev and Foreign Minister Shevardnadze have indicated a willingness to work instead towards the goal of "minimum nuclear deterrence."[35] Just what a minimum nuclear deterrent force would look like would depend for the most part on how many Soviet and US troops remain in Central Europe. If follow-on CFE negotiations were to produce cuts to a level 50% below existing NATO figures, it is difficult to foresee a stockpile (exclusive of British and French nuclear weapons) of more than 1500 to 2000 warheads, consisting exclusively of air-delivered missiles and bombs. This number would begin to move closer to the 500 to 1000 warheads mentioned by Soviet civilian analysts as representing the Soviet notion of minimum nuclear deterrence.[36]

As for the specific prescriptions for refurbishing NATO's nuclear stockpile offered in Chapter 6, those that have to do with ways of compensating for INF weapons (using SLCMs and aircraft-delivered weapons) continue to have strong merit. Threatening to use nuclear-armed SLCMs against Soviet territory (should the Soviet military attempt to alter the conventional balance radically through covert mobilisation and attack) carries far greater deterrent value than threatening the destruction of East European countries with SNF weapons (should Soviet troops pass along lines of communication). FOTL and nuclear artillery are simply politically untenable in today's radically changed environment; nuclear missiles and artillery shells should be prime candidates for elimination in future SNF negotiations. That leaves dual-capable aircraft to carry the burden – albeit a reduced one – of NATO's in-theatre nuclear mission.

The fates of ballistic missiles in the 0 to 500-km range category and dual-capable aircraft are intertwined in several important ways. During the height of NATO's SNF crisis in the spring of 1989, US government officials argued that if FOTL were not deployed, NATO would have to rely too heavily on increasingly vulnerable dual-capable air bases.[37] Ironically, by pushing the deployment of dual-capable missiles, the Administration helps to justify the replacement of Scud-B missiles with versions that promise to render more vulnerable not only air bases but also critical NATO reinforcement facilities, upon which the Alliance's future mobilisation potential will depend. Not surprisingly, the threat to air bases was cast in terms of Soviet tactical air-to-surface missiles (TASMs). Although Soviet TASMs are indeed likely to grow as a threat, they possess few of the operational advantages of ballistic missiles when used against airfields. As discussed in Chapter 4, aircraft delivering TASMs can be detected taking off from their airfields in Eastern Europe, thereby furnishing NATO with time to sortie aircraft and avoid being pinned down on air bases. By contrast, ballistic missiles provide very little warning time, and so greatly increase the chances that aircraft will be pinned down. Follow-up aircraft strikes against pinned down aircraft would deliver a far more telling blow than those preceded by TASM strikes. TASMs simply cannot leverage the effectiveness of aircraft in the worrisome way that ballistic missiles can.[38]

To return to the question posed earlier: who fares better if conventionally armed ballistic missiles are eliminated? According to the US Army's program manager for ATACMS, "[Without ATACMS] the Army does not have the capability to influence the deep battle." Should ATACMS be eliminated, "We are asking battlefield commanders to fight a war with one hand tied behind their back."[39] US Department of Defense planners also believe that FOFA and AirLand Battle's deep-attack capabilities will be even more necessary after CFE cuts because Soviet reserves will be critically important to attack success.[40] But, viewed from a broader perspective, missiles are by no means the only deep-attack assets available to NATO. In fact, aircraft have traditionally been counted on to play the most significant deep-attack role through their battlefield air and deep interdiction missions. And because aircraft – especially those equipped with stand-off weapons – can attack Soviet targets much beyond ATACMS' range of 150 km, they are more capable than missiles of stemming the tide of Soviet operational and strategic reserves.[41] Indeed, were NATO aircraft seriously attrited in the initial hours of a combined-arms air operation, the odds on ATACMS and other ground force units performing their missions as originally planned would be substantially reduced, due to the Soviet achievement of air superiority.

But the biggest disadvantage of missiles is the danger that they may provoke an arms race that will substantially degrade the effectiveness of aircraft at a time when NATO can least afford it. Operationally NATO cannot afford it, because a combination of geography and CFE cuts means that it will become increasingly vulnerable to combined missile and air attacks. This could become particularly grave as political events compel the Alliance to depend exclusively on dual-capable aircraft for its in-theatre nuclear mission. Politically, with revolutionary change occurring in Eastern Europe, now is clearly not the time to begin a contentious security debate, even one confined largely to intra-alliance squabbling within senior policy-making fora. Financially, NATO is ill-prepared to pay for active and passive defences against both missile and aircraft threats. And, while ATACMS may make good sense for dealing with mid- to high-intensity conflicts, the USA would be better off spending its shrinking defence resources on weapons more flexibly designed to cope with contingencies not only in Central Europe but worldwide. Finally, to the broader question of who fares better if ballistic missiles are eliminated, the answer is manifestly the West.

In view of the prominent role ballistic missiles play in both the air operation and emerging manoeuvre concepts, the Soviet military is unlikely to take kindly to the elimination of all remaining ballistic missiles. But the West holds great leverage over the pressure the Soviet military can bring to bear on its political leadership. By proposing to eliminate all remaining ballistic missiles globally, the West could remove any remaining pretext for the Soviet Union to replace its huge Scud inventory. True, the West would gain a net military advantage, but even the Soviet military probably sees some benefit in removing important reconnaissance strike complexes from AirLand Battle doctrine. Overall, however, if the two alliances succeed in negotiating missile elimination – whether in expanded CFE II or SNF negotiations – European crisis stability will benefit most.[42] Ironically, as the alliances step away from hair-trigger, short-warning attack postures, decision-makers may be more willing to risk a show of force in uncertain crises.[43] By figuratively tying one hand behind the backs of their battlefield commanders through missile elimination, the two alliance systems will have succeeded in moving their respective force postures toward more truly stable instruments of security. Any additional benefits that might flow from the two alliances taking the political high ground on the matter of controlling ballistic missile proliferation worldwide would only add to the inter-alliance rationale for eliminating ballistic missiles below 500 km in range.[44]

Notes

1. Fear that the Soviet Union's "new political thinking" may represent only a breathing spell (*peredyshka*), essential to prepare for inevitably conflictual relations with the West, is perhaps best manifested in the expectation that, should Gorbachev fail or be ousted, it is likely that he would be replaced by a neo-conservative leadership that has yet to rid itself of the class perspective. Such a neo-conservative leadership would probably base its political support on more favourable relations with the Defence Ministry and the KGB, although for tactical reasons its foreign policy would not change demonstrably from Gorbachev's in the near-term future. For a perceptive treatment of alternative Soviet political futures, see William P. Murphy, *Whither the USSR? An Estimate of the Likely Direction of Soviet Policy over the Next 3 to 5 Years* (Arlington, VA: Pacific-Sierra Research Corporation, August 1989).

2. It is also too simplistic to think that the Soviet military willingly accepts radical cuts in force structure based on *perestroika's* promises of a brighter technological future. Indeed, tension existed between the Ogarkov-led General Staff's revolutionary approach to technology innovation and the services' (in particular, the Ground Forces') desire for a more considered, evolutionary approach to change. For a perceptive treatment of conflicts over modernization within the Soviet military, see Rose E. Gottemoeller, *Conflict and Consensus in the Soviet Armed Forces* (Santa Monica, CA: Rand Corporation, October 1989).

3. CFE I would also set ceilings on combat aircraft and US and Soviet out-of-country manpower.

4. The point about airpower taking on a proportionately more important role in a post-CFE setting is made forcefully in Air Vice-Marshal R.A. Mason, "Airpower in Conventional Arms Control," *Survival*, September/October 1989, pp. 397–413. Mason also properly points out that a weakness in NATO's current proposal is the exclusion of any consideration of air-base infrastructure and global constraints on aircraft. The Warsaw Pact has a huge asymmetric advantage in the number of air

bases, which increases sortie rates and enhances aircraft survivability. Moreover, geography dictates that it will be much quicker for the Soviet Union to return aircraft for combat in Central Europe from east of the Urals than for the USA to do so from North America.

5. Andrei Kokoshin, "The Development of Military Affairs and the Reduction of Armed Forces and Conventional Arms," *Mirovaya ekonomika i mezhdunarodnyye otnosheniya*, January 1988, p. 20.

6. "Counterpositioning Conventional Forces in the Context of Furnishing Strategic Stability," *Mirovaya ekonomika i mezhdunarodnyye otnosheniya*, July 1988, pp. 23–31.

7. As reported in an interview with Pierre Darcourt in *Le Figaro*, 13 June 1989, p. 3.

8. Konovalov's proposal was presented at a conference on conventional arms control sponsored by the Mosher Institute at Texas A&M University in February 1989. Details are in Don Oberdorfer, "NATO, Soviets Set for Force Cut Talks," *Washington Post*, 5 March 1989, p. A34. A handwritten copy of Konovalov's proposal was handed out at the conference and later obtained by the author.

9. Contributing to this phenomenon – at least in the eyes of many Europeans – were President Reagan's Strategic Defense Initiative, which questioned both the morality and utility of nuclear deterrence; the Reykjavik Summit, which toyed with the notion of a nuclear-free world; the "double-zero" solution to the INF Treaty, which created significant conceptual and operational gaps in the continuum of nuclear deterrence; the Montebello decision, which reduced the NATO nuclear stockpile from its all-time high of 7200 warheads to around 4000; the prospect of a START treaty, which would further erode any idea of gaining perceptual or operational advantage from any conceivable set of strategic nuclear attack options; and finally, and most importantly, the almost certain failure of NATO to modernise – perhaps even over the long run to retain – its short-range nuclear forces in the aftermath of political changes in Eastern Europe and conventional force parity with the Warsaw Pact.

10. For an analysis of changes in Soviet operational art and tactics, see David M. Glantz, *Soviet Operational Art and Tactics in an Era of Reform* (Fort Leavenworth, KS: Soviet Army Studies Office, April 1989).

11. Soviet Notebook, *International Defense Review*, July 1989, p. 889.
12. The re-publication of Rotmistrov's speech is noted and discussed in Colonel David M. Glantz, "Force Structure: Meting Contemporary Requirements," *Military Review*, December 1988, pp. 64–5. It is standard Soviet practice to allude to historical examples to make a point about current conditions.
13. The best treatment of Soviet force restructuring is found in *ibid.*, pp. 58–70. Also see Christopher N. Donnelly, *Red Banner* (London: Jane's, 1988), p. 232.
14. *Soviet Military Power 1989* (Washington, D.C.: USGPO, 1989), pp. 49–50.
15. Glantz, *op. cit.*, in Note 10, pp. 13–14.
16. Mary C. FitGerald, "The Dilemma in Moscow's Defensive Force Posture," *Arms Control Today*, November 1989, p. 17.
17. D.T. Yazov, *On Guard of Socialism and Peace* (Moscow: Voyenizdat, 1987), p. 33.
18. Taken from the 1986 UK Statement on the Defence Estimates, as quoted in Diego A. Ruiz Palmer, "Countering Soviet Encirclement Operations: Emerging NATO Concepts'" *International Defense Review*, November 1988, p. 1415.
19. Information on the Soviet approach to required force ratios is taken from John G. Hines, *Soviet Front Operations: Planning for Encirclement* (Sandhurst: Soviet Studies Research Centre, Royal Military Academy, April 1985).
20. *Ibid.*
21. *Ibid.*, p. 17. Hines cites the Voroshilov General Staff Academy lecture materials as his source for information on the role of fire support in operational planning.
22. S.F. Akhromeyev, ed., *Voennyi entsiklopedicheskii slovar'* (Moscow: Voyenizdat, 1986), pp. 496–497.
23. "Soviet Military Doctrine and Several Views on the Character of Wars in Defence of Socialism," *Voyennaya mysl'*, No. 12, December 1988, pp. 3–13. I am indebted to my colleague Kerry Hines for bringing this article to my attention.
24. *Ibid.*, p. 10 (emphasis added).
25. ATACMS deployment plans are outlined in Caleb Baker, "Late 1990 Deployment Planned for ATACMS Missile," *Defense News*, 11 December 1989, p. 39.
26. *Soviet Military Power 1989, op. cit.*, in Note 14, p. 49.
27. "Soviets Threaten to Violate INF Treaty Over SNF, But

Quickly Back Down," *Arms Control Today*, June/July 1989, pp. 23, 27. Reports that elements of the Soviet military were upset over Gorbachev's decision to include the SS-23 in the INF treaty come from personal interviews by the author.

28. The Pact has nearly a 20:1 launcher advantage today in the global inventory.

29. This does not mean that the Soviet Union is prohibited from making product improvements in the Scud family of missiles. The possible existence of a more accurate and longer-range Scud-C is discussed in Chapter 2.

30. The cost of the programme to upgrade the Patriot radar is reportedly less than half a billion dollars in research and development funding and $100 million for warhead modification and procurement. See Chapter 6 for more details on Patriot dual-mode options.

31. According to Christopher Donnelly, for every dollar spent to maintain a battalion in the Israeli army, it costs the UK 3.9 times as much and the USA 11.1. See Donnelly, *op. cit.*, in Note 13, pp. 122 and 158–61 for details of the Soviet cadre mobilization system.

32. For an elaboration of Soviet trends in strategic deployment capabilities, see Graham H. Turbiville, Jr., "Strategic Deployment: Mobilizing and Moving the Force," *Military Review*, December 1988, pp. 41–49.

33. The proposal for a "missiles-only" triple zero agreement first appeared in an article adapted from this book. See Dennis M. Gormley, "Triple Zero and Soviet Military Strategy," *Arms Control Today*, January/February 1988, pp. 17–20.

34. Among the several analysts who recognised the merits of a missiles-only third zero, as distinct from the elimination of all remaining SNF weapons, were Arnold Kanter, *Nuclear Modernization and Arms Control in NATO* (Santa Monica, CA: Rand Corporation, December 1988) and Sir Hugh Beach, "The Case for the Third Zero," *Bulletin of the Atomic Scientists*, December 1989, pp. 14–15.

35. Gorbachev's mention of such a goal came in his July 1989 speech to the European Parliament in Strasbourg. Shevardnadze repeated the call for minimum nuclear deterrence in his September 1989 speech to the United Nations in New York.

36. Obtained from personal interviews by the author.

37. Michael R. Gordon, "NATO Dispute: Tug-of-War Over

Limited Arsenal," *New York Times*, 24 May 1989, p. 4.

38. An interesting question is whether stealthy aircraft could achieve the same prompt pin-down effects as ballistic missiles. In all likelihood, they could not do so when used in large numbers, as are ballistic missiles. Instead, stealthy vehicles will be much more adept at achieving local tactical surprise against units in the field. The same will probably hold true for air engagements where a favourable angle of attack is achieved through tactical surprise. For more on stealth tactics, see Jasper Welch, "Assessing the Value of Stealthy Aircraft and Cruise Missiles," *International Security*, Fall 1989, pp. 47–63.

39. As quoted in Baker *op. cit.*, in Note 25.

40. Based on personal interviews by the author.

41. In fact, for deep-attack strike missions (both conventional and nuclear), stealthy aircraft will grow in importance because of their increased chances of penetrating enemy air defences.

42. See Mason, *op. cit.*, in Note 4 for some useful ways of dealing with aircraft in current and future negotiations.

43. Jeffrey W. Legro, "Soviet Crisis Decision-Making and the Gorbachev Reforms," *Survival*, July/August 1989, p. 353.

44. The effect of such an agreement should not be overstated however. Serious follow-up work in various diplomatic fora will be needed to achieve any practical results.

1

Changing Soviet views on theatre warfare: from Stalin to Gorbachev

The Soviet accumulation of military power over the past 35 years has prompted a continuing search in the West for insight into the underlying motivations for Moscow's huge defence expenditures. Explanations range from an innate desire on the Kremlin's part to alter the international environment through actual use of military force, to the USSR's obsessive fear of potential American-led aggression fuelled by its perceived inferiority *vis-à-vis* Western technological prowess. Analysts are even more uncertain about the future course of Soviet military power under Mikhail Gorbachev's stewardship. However one judges these complex matters, what seems palpably clear is that the Soviet Union has already procured sufficient military power to challenge both the operational utility of Western strategy (under conceivable military circumstances) and the political consensus needed to sustain its credibility within an alliance context.

Attention to the changing nature of Soviet views on modern warfare is especially important in appraising the role of dual-capable Soviet theatre forces that remain after INF treaty implementation. All too frequently, Western views of Soviet concepts of warfare are tied exclusively to the role of nuclear weapons as developed under Nikita Khrushchev in the late 1950s. The historical antecedents of contemporary Soviet military thought are indeed relevant; Soviet military theoreticians are loath to discard anything that has stood the test of time. Nevertheless, the Soviet predilection to retain time-honoured traditions should not lead us to ignore Moscow's acceptance of new military options. History reveals rather abrupt changes in

1

Soviet military-intellectual thought over the past 35 years. After first appearing to eschew analysing the implications of nuclear weapons for combat under Stalin, Soviet military theoreticians shifted emphasis to a virtually exclusive nuclear orientation in the first half of the 1960s. From about 1965 to the present, Soviet military thought and action reflect a more even-handed approach to assessing threats and to establishing requirements for military procurement. Indeed, the last two decades of Soviet military thought and development represent a persistent search for, and, in large measure, the achievement of, increasingly more flexible means of employing military power.

The last three and a half decades of military thought and force development have produced a consistent set of Soviet views about the most probable theatre warfare contingencies that might confront the Soviet Union today. Broadly outlined, they include three major courses of conflict.

1. *Massive nuclear strikes used at the outset of conflict to the full depth of relevant theatres of military operations (TVDs).*[1] Such a contingency would immediately involve using Soviet homeland-based strategic nuclear forces against European targets, with follow-up exploitation by Warsaw Pact ground and air forces.

2. *An escalatory conflict in which an initial (and relatively short) period of conventional operations precedes an increasingly more widespread use of nuclear weapons.* The nuclear phase of such a conflict could proceed immediately to the use of Soviet homeland-based forces or, more likely, would begin with tactical nuclear weapons and thereupon escalate rapidly to general nuclear warfare. A different version of such an escalatory conflict might include nuclear operations in one TVD during which only conventional operations were conducted in another TVD.

3. *A conventional-only conflict in which major strategic operations are successfully carried out within one or more TVDs without recourse to nuclear weapons.*

Naturally, each major contingency calls for a different mix of nuclear and conventional forces. Under the first contingency, theatre-based nuclear systems would play only a secondary role to strategic nuclear forces. The second, by contrast, would require greater numbers and vastly more flexible dual-capable forces to cope with the more varied circumstances of escalation. And the third could not hope to succeed without dramatic improvements in the quantity and effectiveness of conventionally armed theatre missiles and aircraft.

There appears to be a relationship between the changing nature of Soviet doctrinal views and the acquisition of supporting theatre forces. It is unclear precisely what factors most influence the development of new Soviet doctrine and supporting military instruments. Nonetheless, the general outlines of the reciprocal relationship between doctrine and technology are evident in the Soviet force development process. In this regard, the force development process reflects a complex, interactive association between doctrine and technology in which, as David Holloway writes, "technological change exerts a determining influence on the methods of warfare, but doctrine has a significant role in adapting those methods to new weapons."[22]

Within this interdependent relationship, other factors impinge upon the force development process.[3] Soviet perceptions of potential adversary doctrinal and technological challenges surely play an important role. Doctrinally, the Soviet Union has witnessed several abrupt post-war shifts in US military policy; Eisenhower's "massive retaliation" and Kennedy's "flexible response" are only the most glaring examples. Technologically, the Soviet military must cope with high levels of innovation and technical virtuosity in Western military developments. Finally, the bureaucratic politics of the Soviet military-industrial complex obviously affect the force development process. Khrushchev (and perhaps now Gorbachev) used military doctrine to divert resources from the military into the civilian sector of the Soviet economy. Between and within branches of the Soviet armed forces, there have been numerous struggles for power and resources, which condition the process of force development.[4]

Former Chief of the Soviet General Staff Marshal Nikolai V. Ogarkov views the creation and production of sufficient quantities of new weapons as the starting point of the force development process.[5] Once the process is begun, this "new qualitative condition" influences the development of new forms and methods of combat, as well as the organisational structure of the armed forces. Quantitative and qualitative improvements in dual-capable theatre forces have occasioned a radical shift in Soviet views on the use of these weapons as instruments of theatre strategy. The Soviets no longer see them as just a follow-up force to strategic and long-range theatre nuclear forces. Instead, highly accurate conventional missiles and aircraft are now regarded as a means to achieve the decisive results hitherto thought possible only with nuclear weapons.

The 1950s: Early Temporising

Although the genesis of the first contingency (massive nuclear strikes) lies in Khrushchev's reappraisal of the role of the nuclear-missile weapon in decisively affecting the outcome of future wars, we must briefly survey the 1950s to reveal the origin of Soviet theatre nuclear forces.

The temporising attitude of Soviet military theoreticians toward nuclear weapons had less to do with Stalin's reputed hammerlock on doctrinal formulation than with what appears, in retrospect, to be a reasoned assessment of the limited impact on military operations of available nuclear weapons.[6] Stalin clearly appreciated the need to develop and produce atomic weapons and suitable delivery means; however, he saw little reason to downgrade his "permanently operating factors" of warfare as determinants of the course and outcome of future wars, for simply too few atomic weapons were then available to influence warfare *decisively*. In fact, it is doubtful that more than a few atomic weapons were available for use before Stalin's death in 1953. Stalin had only set the stage for producing large numbers of regional delivery systems (primarily by commissioning the Tupolev TU-4 and TU-16 bombers and the Yangel SS-4 medium-range ballistic missile), the most important of which would not be deployed in militarily significant numbers until the mid- to late 1950s. The Soviet Union's principal adversaries (in the late 1940s and early 1950s) confronted Soviet planners with a substantial conventional threat, together with a maturing, but nonetheless small, stockpile of atomic weapons.[7] In retrospect, it does not seem odd that Stalin and his theoreticians should have managed only to *study* nuclear-related problems rather than to comprehend fully the implications of, and prepare for, nuclear warfare.[8]

Most Western analysts view Stalin's passing as unleashing a flood of changes in the Soviet approach to nuclear warfare. Equally important were developments in US nuclear strategy and force structure. The Eisenhower Administration placed nuclear weapons, strategic and tactical alike, at the centre of its declaratory and operational policies. The force structure consequences included a ring of B-47 bomber bases around the periphery of the Soviet Union, with decreased emphasis on conventional ground forces.

But perhaps of greater significance to Soviet shorter-range nuclear developments were US decisions on tactical nuclear weapons.[9] In 1949, the USA decided to develop and acquire tactical nuclear weapons to counter Soviet conventional advantages in Europe. By 1951, the USA had tested the first sub-kiloton atomic weapons. That same year, Project Vista, hosted by the California Institute of Technology, drew attention to the role of nuclear weapons in land warfare. Two years later, the USA deployed the first nuclear-capable artillery weapon, followed the next year by the Honest John rocket system and the Matador cruise missile. Deployments of shorter-range nuclear weapons complemented those required by the doctrine of "massive retaliation." To that end, NATO's Political Directive of 1956 called for early initial use of tactical nuclear weapons to counter a Warsaw Pact invasion while the USA was launching a strategic nuclear attack against the Soviet Union.[10]

The Soviets were impressed by these developments.[11] Although they continued to deny that strategic nuclear weapons would decisively influence warfare, they acknowledged that shorter-range nuclear weapons enabled the defender to thwart the offence's effectiveness. Indeed, NATO's deployment of a tactical nuclear arsenal directly imperilled the Soviet concept of offensive operations based on the traditional principles of mass and concentration of force. The response to this challenge entailed a massive effort to mechanise the ground forces and to modify the principles of mass and concentration through the adoption of new dispersal norms. Mechanisation of the ground forces, of course, concurrently afforded Soviet units the resources to exploit their own nuclear strikes. Recognition of this development provided for integrating shorter-range nuclear weapons into the Soviet force structure.

Soviet developmental efforts in shorter-range nuclear weapons in Stalin's last years were not entirely dormant. At least two variants of an operational-tactical rocket were tested by 1950.[12] Stalin probably initiated development of the Scud operational-tactical missile and the Frog tactical rocket a year or two before his death. Before the deployment of Scud (1957) and Frog (1958), Soviet ground forces could probably count on limited nuclear support from short- and medium-range bombers. In fact, by 1954, Soviet military exercises began to include air-delivered atomic weapons in support of the ground forces. This attempt was the first to incorporate nuclear weapons into the fire support available to front and army commanders. Interestingly, this front and army support consisted of nuclear strikes into the operational-tactical depth of the enemy against such targets as enemy airfields and air command and control facilities[13] – a targeting theme wholly consistent with contemporary Soviet nuclear *and* conventional strike planning.

The Soviet developmental approach to artillery-fired atomic projectiles illustrates the dilemmas that confronted the Soviet military in integrating shorter-range nuclear weapons into the ground forces. According to Khrushchev, the deployment of Soviet nuclear artillery represented "pointless imitation" of the

US 280-mm atomic gun. Deployed in 1955, the Soviet counterparts consisted of 310-mm guns and 420-mm mortars mounted on heavy truck chassis. Khrushchev's memoirs describe his disappointment, especially in the light of the need for "huge quantities of raw (fissionable) material to make one small warhead."[14]

The Soviets decided to develop nuclear artillery even though their military theoreticians remained unconvinced that nuclear weapons would decisively influence the course and outcome of warfare. They saw these weapons as mere supplements to traditional forms of firepower – artillery, small arms, tanks, and aircraft.[15] At the same time, however, the Soviets built a large force of medium-range bombers and began developing medium-, intermediate-, and intercontinental-range ballistic missiles to counter the forward deployment of US and British strategic aircraft. Given priority requirements in the strategic area, it seems plausible that critical shortages in raw (fissionable) material impeded further development of Soviet nuclear artillery at this stage. Indeed, such shortages may well have delayed a rapid build-up in tactical and operational-tactical missiles, which Soviet planners evidently found to be more in tune with Khrushchev's budding "revolution in military affairs" than cumbersome artillery pieces.

Despite the slow build-up of Soviet nuclear capability, sufficient quantities of nuclear weapons were beginning to change Soviet views on the role of these weapons. By early 1958, the Soviet General Staff had decided that military doctrine and strategy required fundamental revision to reconcile the implications of nuclear weapons – especially the nuclear missile weapon.[16]

1960–1964: Khrushchev and the Massive-Use Option

Creation of the Strategic Rocket Forces (SRF) in December 1959, and Khrushchev's announcement of a new military doctrine before the fourth session of the Supreme Soviet in January 1960, represented no abrupt change in Soviet military thought. To be sure, the resolution of internal military debates in the late

1950s was important in this transformation; but of critical importance to this new stage in force development was the availability of sufficient quantities of nuclear weapons. From 1957 to 1960, the Soviets deployed no fewer than seven new theatre nuclear weapons.[17] This new quantitative condition significantly influenced the development of new forms and methods of combat and corresponding changes in force structure.

Khrushchev's new military doctrine specified that a future war involving the USSR would be an all-out, coalitional conflict in which nuclear escalation would be inevitable. In fact, massive nuclear strikes would occur immediately, or almost immediately, upon the breakout of war. The new nuclear missiles of the SRF would decisively determine the course and outcome of such a conflict.

The campaign in European TVDs would be fought within the framework of a general war opening with massive nuclear exchanges. The Soviets pictured the West initiating the war with a surprise nuclear attack to which the SRF would respond with rapid strategic nuclear strikes followed by a full-scale theatre offensive against NATO Europe. Soviet ground forces were to exploit the nuclear strikes of the theatre component of the SRF (SS-4 medium-range missiles and Badger medium-range bombers); moreover, the ground forces now could depend upon and exploit the nuclear strikes of the Rocket Troops and Artillery. The latter organisation, transformed out of the old artillery arm of service, consisted of new tactical rocket (Frog) and operational-tactical missile (Scud) units organic to Soviet ground-force divisions, and armies and fronts, respectively.

Absent from the new military doctrine was the notion that any restraints could be imposed on the conduct of war. A doctrine espousing global nuclear war and the rapid seizure of objectives to the full depth of TVDs was unsuited to graduated or discrete operational concepts. The theatre campaign would begin with strikes conducted by homeland-based strategic forces *followed*, rather than *preceded*, by massive nuclear strikes of the Rocket Troops and Artillery of the Ground Forces. Of course, such a reverse-escalation notion was equally fundamental to the then current US strategy of "massive retaliation."

Despite relative symmetry at the strategic doctrinal level, US and Soviet military planners charted divergent approaches to shorter-range theatre nuclear forces. In general, each nation viewed the role of these forces in a distinctly different way, a difference that concomitantly affected the means of controlling nuclear weapons designed to support the ground forces.

In 1962, the USA began large-scale introduction of dual-capable nuclear artillery systems into NATO forces. The basic deployment approach integrated both delivery means and nuclear warheads at the lowest level possible: the artillery firing battery of a conventional artillery unit, once properly certified, became a nuclear-capable unit. Artillery-fired atomic projectiles – under US control – were dispersed throughout NATO forces. By 1969, some 7000 US theatre nuclear warheads would be stored on European soil, over half earmarked for battlefield use. Operationally, NATO planners envisaged using nuclear-capable artillery and rockets in much the same manner as conventional fire support. Targets for nuclear artillery and rockets were essentially those struck by conventional artillery: infantry or armoured manoeuvre units, artillery, command and control, and air defence deployed primarily along the line of contact.

By contrast, the USSR avoided blurring the distinction between conventional and nuclear systems. Soviet tactical and operational-tactical nuclear delivery systems did not replace or augment existing fire support systems (conventional rocket and tube artillery) of the Ground Forces; they performed independent, albeit coordinated, missions that enabled the ground forces to exploit the results of their success. The following extract from a November 1965 Soviet military journal suitably captures the role of operational-tactical nuclear forces:

Technical progress has also produced serious changes in the Ground Forces. Although earlier their basic firepower was artillery, now the chief means of firepower has become the rocket units, able to carry to the enemy decisive defeat with nuclear attacks on enormous areas, and at great depth. Such possibilities of nuclear rocket weapons determine their role in the Ground Forces. *This is not a support means as was, and remains, cannon-type field artillery.* The team of the launch position of tactical or operational-tactical rockets is able to *independently* decide combat operations.[18] (Emphasis added.)

The Soviets created the Rocket Troops and Artillery, a new and separate service within the Ground Forces to control what they believed was a qualitatively new weapon. Soviet planners did not integrate nuclear weapons into conventional artillery units; rather, they dedicated nuclear rocket and missile units exclusively to nuclear missions. Organised as dedicated and independent units, the Rocket Troops and Artillery could undertake such complex and burdensome tasks as positive control, care, and maintenance of nuclear weapons, thus avoiding having these problems imposed on conventional artillery units.

Shifting Priorities in Force Development
Khrushchev's "new military doctrine" prompted a major re-evaluation of defence priorities and service roles in the overall context of a nuclear-missile war. The centrality of nuclear-missile weapons in the institutional debates over resource allocation signified much more than simplistic fascination with the absolute qualities of nuclear missiles or an imperative to respond to the Kennedy Administration's plan to modernise and expand the land- and naval-based components of US strategic nuclear forces. Equally important (especially to military planners), nuclear missiles permitted the achievement of military objectives that, in the past, could be obtained only through time-consuming, sequential operations of vast human and materiel proportion. Soviet military theoreticians recognised that the unique properties and characteristics of the nuclear missile radically altered these conditions. According to an article in the General Staff's restricted journal in early 1966,

> only with the development of nuclear rocket weapons and other long-range weapons has it become possible to conduct, *in a short period of time,* direct and very effective deep attacks and achieve results not only of operational, but also strategic significance.... At the end of World War I, attacks on the enemy were limited to tactical

scales; in the course of World War II, such attacks already had an operational and, in a number of cases, even strategic scale. In modern conditions – if nuclear arms are used – *attacks can be carried out in the whole depth of the theatre of military operations within strategic limits.*[19] (Emphasis added.)

Striking to the full depth of the TVD in the shortest possible time became the foundation upon which requirements for the massive theatre nuclear option were, and continue to be, formulated.

The qualitatively new nuclear-missile weapon, one deployed in sufficient numbers, substantially influenced the articulation of new forms and methods of combat (captured in Sokolovsky's *Military Strategy*), as well as the organisational structure of the armed forces (with the creation of the SRF, Rocket Troops and Artillery, and corresponding reductions in resources for other general-purpose forces). Technology and force procurement initiated the force development process; its offspring, doctrine, conditioned it.

As is well known, Khrushchev exploited the opportunity to reduce defence spending for large ground, air, and naval surface forces. Of particular interest here is the consequent decline in importance of aircraft-delivered nuclear weapons. At the operational-tactical level, the new Rocket Troops and Artillery service assumed the missions of Frontal Aviation. Aircraft suffered from several disadvantages compared to missiles and rockets: they lacked assured target penetration because of growing enemy air defences; they were weather-sensitive; they needed comparatively large and costly base support, which was vulnerable to attack; and their effective employment required special pilot skills requiring expensive training programmes.[20] The unique characteristics of aircraft in conducting strikes against mobile targets and in following up missile strikes would remain underappreciated until a more accommodating doctrinal framework evolved. Quite simply, a doctrine and strategy that foresaw massive strategic nuclear missile strikes that were able to achieve war's basic objectives at the beginning of conflict left little room for nuclear-capable Frontal Aviation.

Even though the Ground Force's Rocket Troops and Artillery fared much better than Frontal Aviation in resource and mission allocation, it by no means received a blank cheque. Khrushchev's memoirs illustrate relative priorities in this regard:

> There were incidents when Marshal Grechko insisted that we develop a tactical missile with a small nuclear warhead that could be used by our infantry against an advancing army. I agreed with Grechko that it would be good to arm our troops with tactical nuclear weapons at the platoon and regiment level or even at the division level, but I had to explain to him that the smaller the explosive charge of a warhead, the more raw material you need – and we simply didn't have enough raw material to go around. Therefore, we had to concentrate first and foremost on intercontinental – that is, strategic rather than tactical – missiles.[21]

Expansion of nascent artillery-fired atomic projectiles was probably curtailed by 1962.

Khrushchev's concentration on deterrence in strategic force allocation obscures the underlying military rationale for deploying large numbers of long-range theatre nuclear missiles. Certainly, in relation to the USA, Khrushchev saw great deterrent value in deploying SS-4s and SS-5s (from 200 in 1960, to 705 by 1965)[22] to perform the role large ground forces previously played: holding Western Europe hostage. But seeing this role exclusively as a stop-gap until sufficient Soviet ICBMs could be deployed is short-sighted. Indeed, this myopic view of the rationale for Soviet long-range theatre missiles partly accounts for the surprise in some Western circles surrounding the Soviet SS-20 deployment in 1977. Unquestionably, strong motivations in the European TVDs underlie the historic and continuing Soviet need for long-range theatre nuclear forces. The most important are the following:

- Military requirements in the Western TVD were, and are today, equally important to those in the transoceanic TVD. Simply put, from the late 1950s to the present, robust nuclear and conventional capabilities have faced Soviet military planners along the USSR's geographic periphery, especially in Western Europe.

- The paramount theme in Soviet military strategy at the origin of the massive theatre-wide attack option was the necessity to attack priority targets to the strategic rear of the TVD. Aside from changes in notions of escalation, the deep-attack theme remains a principal feature of contemporary Soviet strategy.

- A prime design criterion in Soviet ballistic missile development has been "range to target."[23] It was decidedly less costly for the Soviets to threaten deep targets in the Western TVD with medium- and intermediate-range missiles and bombers than exclusively with intercontinental-range systems.

- Deciding on the specific number of long-range theatre nuclear systems arose primarily from warfighting, rather than just political or deterrent, considerations. Therefore, understanding these warfighting considerations provides important insights into essential Soviet theatre nuclear requirements, particularly in the framework of the unique targeting demands of each individual TVD.

The Brezhnev Years: The Search for New Military Options

The genesis of the second contingency (an escalating conflict) that shapes Soviet military requirements for dual-capable theatre forces grew out of the post-Khrushchev reaction of the Soviet military to an over-reliance on nuclear weapons. The constituents of this reaction and consequent search for new options consisted of three elements: the re-emergence of the military as the dominant force in the development of military science; the implications of the Soviet achievement of strategic nuclear parity with the USA, which hastened the search for new forms and methods of combat; and recognition that NATO had eschewed sole reliance on massive retaliation and sought more flexible forms of response.

The Soviet armed forces, especially the ground, air, and naval surface forces, exploited a more pliable political leadership to resurrect those traditional Soviet military themes (especially the combined-arms approach to warfare) more conducive to a balanced force development process. Indeed, the Soviet military began to re-evaluate the course of military development immediately after Khrushchev was ousted.[24]

Soviet achievement of strategic nuclear parity with the USA strongly conditioned cracks in the monolith of the single-variant notion of warfare. Although the signing of SALT I in 1972 represented formal recognition of this new strategic reality, Soviet military authorities, by 1965, could already foresee that parity would probably change the "objective conditions" affecting the outbreak of war. In other words, while a future world war might possibly start with massive exchanges of nuclear weapons, the existence of emerging Soviet retaliatory forces altered US calculations of such a strike's effectiveness; consequently, the West would be compelled to seek alternative methods and forms for starting and conducting future wars. Out of this dilemma, Soviet military theoreticians saw the USA forge the doctrine of "flexible response," which "combined the most varied methods and means of waging armed conflicts, with and without nuclear weapons."[25]

By late 1968, several authoritative Soviet military figures had acknowledged the USSR's intent to base planning requirements on a more flexible view of potential conflict contingencies. Perhaps the most prominent example is an article published in the restricted journal of the General Staff by V. D. Sokolovsky, former Chief of the Soviet General Staff, and editor of *Military Strategy*, and Maj Gen M. Cherednichenko. In it, the authors reached the following conclusion:

> The possibility is not excluded of wars occurring with the use of conventional weapons as well as the limited use of nuclear means in one of several theatres of military operations, or of a relatively protracted nuclear war with the use of capabilities of all types of armed forces.[26]

Interestingly, this admission covers each of the three contingencies under discussion but lacks the rich detail needed to shed light on such issues as the prospects for a conventional war or limited use of nuclear weapons occurring in the Western TVD. Nonetheless, this and other statements implied the need to prepare Soviet shorter-range nuclear forces for possible "tactical nuclear wars" preceding escalation to theatre-wide and general nuclear war.[27] Only with the passage of time and with the creation of the necessary military instruments would Soviet planners gain sufficient confidence to clarify these matters. By the end of the decade, however, Soviet military theoreticians had charted a clear course foreshadowing (indeed, stimulating) the large-scale conventional and nuclear build-up of the 1970s. That course had few inherent limitations with respect to procurement guidance, given the reality that there was now

> ... too great a risk on the destruction of one's own government and the responsibility to humanity for the fatal consequences of the nuclear war is too heavy ... to make an easy decision on the immediate employment of nuclear weapons from the very beginning of a war without having used all other means for the attainment of its objectives.[28]

Force Requirements and Planning for an Escalating Contingency
Soviet design and procurement of sufficient numbers of theatre nuclear systems merely to satisfy the needs of the massive-use contingency was unquestionably less exacting than the need to fulfil the requirements of the escalating contingency; moreover, the latter introduced complex uncertainties into the force planning process. Planning for the massive-use contingency could be carried out in peacetime. It consisted of a relatively straightforward application of operational-strategic and operational-tactical nuclear forces against a largely fixed target set. To that extent, Soviet force-sizing analysis was also comparatively simple: given a known number of high-priority targets combined with damage expectancy requirements, Soviet military planners could easily stipulate nuclear force requirements and provide for the deconfliction of strategic and operational strikes based primarily on the range capabilities of strike assets. But an escalating contingency and the acceptance of an uncertain phase of conventional operations, followed, perhaps, by nuclear strikes limited to a front's nuclear forces, presented enormously complex problems for force sizing and planning.

The difficulty of predicting precisely when a conflict would escalate to nuclear operations confronted Soviet planners with a taxing dilemma: not abandoning a conventional advantage too soon and not exercising a nuclear option too late. By the late 1960s, Soviet planners foresaw the conventional phase of a major European campaign lasting no more than four or five days.[29] During this phase, Soviet planners placed highest priority on destroying the enemy's theatre nuclear weapons by conventional means. But success in this endeavour was highly uncertain, given the difficulty of locating large numbers of mobile nuclear launchers. An even more complex task involved preparing Soviet forces to make a smooth transition from conventional to nuclear operations. The Soviet military saw a decisive advantage accruing to the side that successfully pre-empted the other's effective use of nuclear weapons. Pre-emption hinged critically on at least three interdependent conditions: (1) detecting the enemy's preparations to use nuclear weapons; (2) locating enemy nuclear forces; and (3) having an adequate number of one's own nuclear weapons in constant readiness to respond.

The dilemma of not abandoning a conventional advantage too soon, while not exercising a nuclear strike too late, is perhaps most manifest in the requirement to detect the enemy's intention to use nuclear weapons. Unfortunately, Soviet military literature has not divulged precisely what conditions must prevail in the enemy's force posture to convince the Soviet political leadership of the urgency to pre-empt the enemy's first-use plans. But given the Soviet Union's heavy investment in electronic reconnaissance means, together with the expected "noise" associated with NATO's decision to escalate, it appears safe to assume that the Soviets would attempt to base their pre-emptive actions on relatively precise information.[30] Such precision would help reduce the chances of a premature abandonment of successful conventional operations; it would also lower the probability of inadvertent Soviet escalation based on such preliminary (but, from NATO's standpoint, precautionary) steps as the West's dispersal of nuclear weapons. The only evidence implying a Soviet intention to pre-empt based on indirect indicators consists of analyses reported in the military literature of situations that could induce NATO to use nuclear weapons. These conditions or thresholds have included disruption of NATO's strategic command and control, loss of a certain percentage of NATO conventional forces, and the loss of NATO territory.[31] But these examples may represent only an effort to sensitise Soviet planners to the circumstances that would create strong escalatory incentives rather than to define a precise threshold set of conditions that would convince Soviet political authorities to release nuclear weapons.

The second condition upon which effective pre-emption depends is target acquisition. The Soviets conceived the massive-attack contingency when NATO's nuclear capability was largely confined to airfields. The advent of mobility, co-incident with the Soviet acceptance of an escalatory contingency, presented Soviet planners with enormous difficulties. No longer could they depend on using surprise to lull NATO into not dispersing its nuclear weapons for as long as possible. In a contingency in which massive strikes of long-range nuclear weapons occur from the very start of conflict, surprise could produce devastating results. But in a contingency in which several days of conventional fighting precede nuclear escalation, Soviet planners could not be certain that massive conventional air strikes (without the benefit of timely and accurate conventional missile strikes) would succeed significantly. Moreover, the complexity of the target-location problem was further compounded by the need to converge this highly perishable information with the proper mix of fully prepared nuclear strike systems, all within the narrow warning window provided by Soviet intelligence.

It is in the third condition of effective pre-emption (readiness to conduct a nuclear strike) that Soviet planners fell especially short in the late 1960s, particularly with respect to theatre nuclear forces based in Eastern Europe. Readiness to conduct a pre-emptive nuclear strike was measured in two ways: first, readiness to make a rapid transition from conventional to nuclear combat; and second, possession of sufficient quantities of ready nuclear weapons to meet mission needs.[32]

The readiness problem was more complex than simply coping with slow reactions of nuclear forces. In fact, the conventional phase of operations afforded nuclear forces adequate time to reach an advanced readiness state, if such a condition had not already been attained before the onset of hostilities. Most important was the need to switch rapidly from conventional to nuclear combat. In this regard, the Soviet military planned, in effect, an operational *coup de théâtre*. Soviet tactical rockets (Frog) and operational-tactical missiles (Scud and Scaleboard) were only nominally dual-capable; system accuracies did not justify expending expensive missiles on ineffective conventional strikes.[33] Soviet planners turned this weakness into a strength by planning to keep short-range missiles and rockets passive (and thus more survivable) during conventional hostilities; further, nuclear warheads could be mated to missiles to permit a rapid transition to nuclear combat once the decision was made to pre-empt. But the same could not be said for aircraft organic to a front commander. Here, Soviet planners fully intended to employ aircraft during the conventional phase of operations. By doing so, however, they might not have sufficient aircraft ready to meet the needs of pre-emption, and earmarking a certain percentage of dual-capable aircraft for a nuclear withhold only reduced Soviet air resources for the conventional campaign.[34]

Accepting a conventional phase of operations also allowed anticipating an uncertain loss of missile and rocket launchers and aircraft before the transition to nuclear combat. Restricted Soviet military writings similarly drew attention to the over-committed nature of missile and rocket operations. Soviet planners discussed strategies for distributing scarce missile resources to a diverse target set. Such topics as whether to withhold a portion of the missile and rocket forces for known but unlocated priority targets (enemy nuclear missile launchers) or to employ available assets to destroy enemy manoeuvre units illustrate the dilemmas that underscored the need for short-range force expansion.[35] By 1970, improvements in quality and quantity of shorter-range nuclear systems were clearly mandated, if Soviet military planners were to be the least bit sanguine about conducting effective pre-emptive strikes with front nuclear forces before proceeding to theatre-wide and general nuclear conflict.

Growth in Shorter-Range Forces
Limitations in frontal nuclear forces were tolerable under a contingency that foresaw operational-tactical nuclear systems as merely a follow-up force to SRF and Long-Range Aviation medium- and intermediate-range nuclear forces. Indeed, severe limits in frontal nuclear forces compelled Soviet planners throughout the 1960s to depend heavily on SRF support to front targeting chores.[36] But an escalating contingency meant an expanded role and, therefore, expansion in the front commander's organic nuclear assets.

The Soviet force development process was already improving military instruments by the mid-1960s; the Scud-B demonstrated a 87% increase in range over its predecessor, while the Frog-7 showed a 40% range increase. Additionally, by the late 1960s or early 1970s, rocket and missile units began to augment their force structure; Frog battalions expanded from three to four launchers per battalion, while Scud brigades added a launcher to each of its three battalions, thus increasing the brigade from 9 to 12 launchers.[37]

The most substantial improvement in front-organic nuclear delivery came in tactical aviation. What had been, in the 1960s, a force limited in both numbers and range became, in the 1970s, a force of considerable means. From 1965 to 1977, the offensive load capacity of Soviet Frontal Aviation in Eastern Europe grew by 90%.[38] The SU-7, the workhorse of Frontal Aviation's nuclear delivery capability during the 1960s, was limited to 20% of the payload capacity and 60% of the range capability of its 1972 replacement, the SU-17 Fitter C. Many analysts see the enormous growth in dual-capable Frontal Aviation as the product of three new aircraft designs deployed initially from 1972 to 1974: the SU-17 Fitter C, the MIG-27 Flogger, and the SU-24 Fencer.[39] They overlook the contribution of improved versions of earlier designs, such as the MIG-21 Fishbed J, K, and L ground-attack series of aircraft. First deployed in 1970, the Fishbed J, for example, represented a 100% increase over the Fishbed D in maximum combat radius and offensive load carrying capacity.[40]

Surely, these dramatic improvements in Soviet ground-attack aircraft relate closely to the change in Soviet views from single-variant warfare to one foreseeing escalatory stages. The escalating contingency, opening with conventional operations, required a conventional surrogate for the massive nuclear strikes previously assigned to medium- and intermediate-range ballistic missiles and bombers. An indeterminate phase of conventional operations would permit NATO to disperse nuclear weapons from fewer than a hundred storage sites and garrisons (or stationary targets) to several hundred field mobile sites. Each nuclear-capable artillery and missile firing battery, together with nuclear supply units, represented an individual, high-priority mobile target. The real-time reconnaissance feature of Frontal Aviation offered Soviet planners more flexibility in attack against mobile targets compared to missiles and rockets. Equally compelling was the need to cope with Frontal Aviation's transition dilemma. Given the requirement to maintain perhaps a third of frontal air's dual-capable aircraft in a nuclear withhold status, a substantially larger inventory of ground-attack aircraft became vital to fulfilling the enlarged mission requirements of the escalating contingency.

The Re-emergence of Nuclear Artillery

While the requirements of the massive-use contingency had provided little support for nuclear artillery, Soviet interest in option enhancement and the escalating contingency led to the reappearance of nuclear artillery after a hiatus of about ten years. By the late 1970s, Soviet ground forces had reportedly deployed some 300 towed 203-mm guns and 240-mm mortars, organised as heavy artillery brigades and earmarked to deliver nuclear artillery rounds in a 30-km range.[41]

The first signs of renewed Soviet interest in nuclear artillery appeared in a series of advocacy articles in the restricted and open military press in the early 1970s.[42] In addition to favourably reviewing use of nuclear artillery in modern combat, the authors frequently employed an often-used Soviet tool: allusion to similar military circumstances during World War II. Overall, these articles provide important insights into motivating factors that apparently influenced the Soviets to deploy nuclear artillery. For example, in 1973, Soviet General I. Pavlovsky noted in the restricted journal *Military Thought* that "nuclear ammunition has become a close combat weapon" in the US Army, a fact which suggested the utility of nuclear artillery for line-of-contact targeting to aid offensive or defensive operation of manoeuvre units.[43] Six months later, in the same journal, Col Gen of the Artillery G. Peredel'sky implied that Soviet ground forces needed nuclear artillery to combat that of NATO. He claimed that NATO's nuclear artillery had to be destroyed, not merely neutralised. He suggested that Soviet conventional artillery fires might be an inadequate means of countering enemy nuclear artillery.[44] In fact, Soviet calculations indicated that destruction of an enemy artillery unit required 50–100% more conventional than nuclear artillery rounds and a 3 to 1 superiority over the enemy in conventional artillery tubes.[45] Also, such concentrations of conventional artillery fire could increase the Soviet artillery's vulnerability to nuclear counterattack.

Another problem facing Soviet nuclear planners may have been the absence of a relatively discrete (low-yield) nuclear targeting means for close-in combat. The lowest nuclear yield for the Frog tactical rocket may have created friendly troop safety problems; lower-yield nuclear artillery perhaps offered a better alternative than high concentrations of conventional artillery fire in attacking close-in enemy units.

By 1975, Marshal of Artillery Peredel'sky suggested a specific set of artillery missions, consisting of the following elements:

- Counter-battery operations against enemy nuclear-capable artillery and tactical missile units.
- Line-of-contact strikes to support breakthrough operations
- Strongpoint destruction and support to river crossings
- Destruction of surrounded enemy forces.[46]

Several articles in the Soviet press in the mid-1970s seem to confirm Western reports that the Soviets initially deployed nuclear artillery with heavy artillery brigades.[47] The articles discussed the role in the Great Patriotic War of artillery units as reserves of the Supreme High Command (RVGH). Some were "separate artillery and mortar brigades."[48] The weapons in the RVGK units "included artillery of great and special power."[49] RVGK units were attached to fronts operating in critical sectors of the campaign, thereby providing increased flexibility and manoeuverability of fire support for ground-force operations. Though no nuclear artillery was available in World War II, the RVGK artillery performed the missions suggested for Soviet nuclear artillery.

In retrospect, Soviet military writings suggest that the military re-introduced nuclear artillery in the early to mid-1970s, but in a deployment mode substantially different from the Western-preferred manner. Rather than commingling nuclear artillery with division-level conventional artillery units, the Soviets, instead, reconstituted World War II heavy artillery brigades and subordinated them to the General Staff in peacetime. In war, they probably constituted reserves of the VGK; the VGK could then assign firing battalions to front commanders for use in critical sectors. The asymmetrical approach may have represented a preliminary, experimental phase, which signalled a more widespread deployment of truly dual-capable artillery. Indeed, such a deployment is well underway with new dual-capable towed and self-propelled 152-mm guns and the 203-mm self-propelled guns stationed for the first time outside the Soviet Union.[50]

Command and Control

Command and control considerations also apparently sparked Soviet interest in acquiring a wider range of nuclear options under the escalating contingency. Soviet military theoreticians made it unambiguously clear (that is, there was no debate in the literature) that the political leadership of the Communist Party of the Soviet Union (CPSU) would completely control the decision to use nuclear weapons. In a

1970 book, a senior instructor at the Voroshilov General Staff Academy clarified the CPSU's role.

> The decision on the employment of such devastating weapons as nuclear weapons has become the exclusive prerogative of the political leadership. It is the political leadership, and not the military leadership, who determines the need for employment of weapons of mass destruction, who selects the primary targets and the moment of the infliction of a strike on these targets.[51]

By no means did the political leadership's absolute role apply only to the use of strategic nuclear weapons. In the second edition of the important book *Methodological Problems of Military Theory and Practise*, published in 1969, the military author notes that

> the selection of the main targets of military operations and the methods of their destruction is in many respects conditioned by political considerations. At the present time the question of whether or not to employ nuclear weapons *not only at the strategic but also at the tactical level* is a political question.[52] (Emphasis added.)

Implicit is the CPSU's desire to maintain flexible military options while controlling nuclear decisions and selecting targets and timing of strikes. Thus, both the military (who were expected to formulate and develop options) and political leadership (who, perhaps felt that options gave them some decision latitude) had persuasive reasons to support expansion of operational-tactical nuclear forces.

The Soviets needed a system to assure political control of this expanded force of operational-tactical weapons, where the potential loss of control appeared more probable than at the strategic level. Maintaining weapon systems at low readiness levels within the comparatively safe Soviet homeland environs afforded control of strategic nuclear forces. By contrast, operational-tactical nuclear forces were more closely integrated into a conventional force structure deployed on the territories of the Soviet Union's capricious allies. One available means of control was to maintain operational-tactical nuclear forces at low levels of readiness; this reportedly was the case for Eastern European Soviet nuclear forces throughout the 1970s.[53] Large, heavily secured Soviet main operating bases for nuclear-capable Frontal Aviation were reasonably safe havens for maintaining control of air-delivered nuclear weapons. For operational-tactical missiles and rockets, however, Soviet planners apparently relied on the Rocket Troops and Artillery to furnish an extra measure of positive command and control.

> The fact that a missile [unit] is separated as an independent element of the combat formation of troops is based on the following reasons: in view of the great range of missiles it is usually positioned at a greater distance from the enemy than [conventional] artillery and outside the areas of disposition of the artillery, and it moves in the course of combat considerably less in comparison with artillery; *it has specific features in fire control, supply of munitions, preparation of weapons for launch, and maintenance.* Consequently, the simultaneous control of artillery and missile [units] as a single element of the combat formation is hindered.[54] (Emphasis added.)

Thus, although the missile and rocket units of the Rocket Troops and Artillery were integrated into the Soviet Ground Forces by their organic relationship to fronts, armies, and divisions, the RTA's organisational framework furnished a means to secure control, maintenance, and preparation for launch of nuclear weapons in a system separate from the conventional ground force component.

Of perhaps even greater importance to nuclear command and control is the fundamental role of *maskirovka*, or deception, in Soviet planning for the deployment of a front's nuclear weapons. To appreciate this element, we must recognise the fundamentally different US and Soviet approaches to deploying nuclear weapons in their respective forward areas. These contrasting approaches result from each nation's relationship with its allies, differing perceptions of the use of nuclear weapons, and fears about safety of nuclear stockpiles in peacetime and their survivability in war.

US nuclear weapons in Europe serve the primarily political purposes of Alliance cohesion and deterrence of war. In the early 1950s, the USA began to deploy tactical nuclear weapons in Western Europe to symbolise its commitment to NATO and to compensate for perceived conventional force weaknesses. NATO Alliance members have always viewed theatre nuclear weapons primarily as a deterrent force, linking the defence of Europe to US strategic nuclear weapons based in the American homeland. To serve the twin goals of Alliance commitment and deterrence through the threat of escalation, US nuclear deployments in Europe have been widespread and visible. The locations of roughly 100 US-controlled nuclear storage sites are known to interested European publics and certainly well known to Warsaw Pact intelligence sources. The tension and security concerns induced by widespread Western European nuclear deployments, such as potential terrorist attacks in peacetime and the overrunning of nuclear storage sites early in wartime, are longstanding matters of serious concern in Alliance councils.

In marked contrast, the Soviet Union determined its nuclear presence in Eastern Europe by the needs of a warfighting strategy. The USSR has relied on its massive ground force presence in Eastern Europe, supported by medium- and intermediate-range nuclear forces based in the Soviet homeland, to underscore deterrence of war. Soviet planners did not require a widespread and visible nuclear presence in Eastern Europe to deter NATO. Indeed, there were strong reasons for just the opposite approach.

Soviet deployments of nuclear weapons in Eastern Europe have been intentionally obscure for two reasons. The first relates to Soviet military strategy which stresses the importance of surprise – achieved through deception among other ways. A nuclear deployment scheme like NATO's is simply counter-productive, because its visibility significantly increases the chances of both losing surprise (in a covert transition to a war footing) and being surprised (enemy attacks on nuclear storage sites before dispersal).

The second – and perhaps more important – reason for secrecy surrounding the Soviet nuclear presence in Eastern Europe stems from Moscow's lack of confidence in the allegiance of its Warsaw Pact allies. Soviet planners have more to worry about than just NATO threats to the security of their nuclear weapons: the location of nuclear deployments in Eastern Europe must be protected from both Western intelligence and the populations of the USSR's restive allies.

Soviet nuclear weapon deployments in Eastern Europe were used overtly as a political tool when Moscow announced, in October 1983, that the USSR would retaliate against NATO's planned Pershing and cruise missile deployments by stationing nuclear missiles on the territory of its Eastern European allies. That declaration drew a US response that the Soviet Union had stationed nuclear weapons on Warsaw Pact territory for years.[55] The consequences of these revelations will be explored in greater detail later on.

The Role of Shorter-Range Forces in an Escalating Contingency
In the mid-1970s the Soviet military's goal appeared to be the attainment of a diverse set of military options, backed up by qualitatively and quantitatively improved military forces. Success in attaining this optimistic goal would carry enormous coercive value in peacetime. Should war occur, however, the Soviets intended to prevail at the lowest level of conflict by dominating the escalation process, thereby diminishing the risk of nuclear strikes on Soviet soil. As early as 1973, the Soviet General Staff's journal *Military Thought* assumed that the Warsaw Pact could prevail at the level of operational-tactical nuclear warfare.[56] In about a decade, the Soviet inventory of operational-tactical nuclear delivery systems (Frogs, Scuds, dual-capable aircraft, and nuclear artillery) doubled in size and represented roughly a 2.5 to 1 advantage over equivalent NATO systems by the mid-1970s.[57]

Soviet planners in the mid-1970s anticipated that war with NATO would probably begin with conventional weapons and then escalate to the limited employment of nuclear weapons initiated by NATO to forestall the collapse of its defences. According to lecture materials from the Voroshilov General Staff Academy, the Soviets would try to pre-empt NATO's limited use of nuclear weapons with strikes by "operational and tactical nuclear delivery means."[58] In other words,

NATO's limited nuclear use would not automatically engender massive Soviet nuclear strikes by several fronts' operational-tactical nuclear forces and Soviet homeland-based theatre-strategic nuclear forces.

Apparently, the output side of the Soviet force development process (more operational-tactical systems with greater range), together with NATO's expressions of interest in more graduated strategies of warfare, raised Soviet confidence in the prospects of prevailing under such less-than-massive conditions. Achieving decisive results against the enemy's highest priority targets would guide Soviet planners in sizing attack options. No evidence suggests the Soviet use of limited nuclear attacks as devices for intra-war bargaining or signalling.

Despite applying the tag "limited" to operational-tactical nuclear pre-emption, such an attack could be quite large, depending primarily on when after the commencement of hostilities it occurred. In shaping baseline requirements for operational-tactical nuclear forces, Soviet planners would, of course, be driven by worst-case assumptions. For example, escalation to operational-tactical nuclear pre-emption could develop shortly after hostilities began; under such conditions, nearly all the enemy's high-priority targets would need to be struck. The extent to which NATO responds to warning through dispersal and reinforcement largely dictates the size of the target set. A longer conventional phase, during which Warsaw Pact forces would target NATO nuclear systems and other priority targets, might reduce the size of operational-tactical pre-emption considerably. The uncertain length of conventional operations, the relative success of NATO's efforts, if any, to attack Warsaw Pact nuclear forces, and the operational condition of friendly nuclear forces make sizing such attacks fraught with uncertainty. The important point is that the Soviet notion of limitations entailed counter-military strikes (as distinct from strikes against military industry and political-administrative centres) conducted initially by the nuclear forces organic to Warsaw Pact fronts, armies, and divisions in one or several TVDs, rather than by virtually all

Soviet theatre and strategic nuclear forces as under the massive-use contingency.

The 1980s: Conventional Solutions for Nuclear Problems

The third contingency (conventional-only) culminated an evolutionary process that began in the mid-1960s with the Soviet search for operational flexibility. Soviet military planners initially saw the conventional phase of a major war as brief, lasting a few days at best, during which time preparation for operational-tactical, then strategic nuclear phases would occur. By the mid-1970s, however, they saw the conventional stage expanded to a strategic operation (an ascription previously reserved for nuclear-related operations) lasting up to 30 days.[59] By 1982, Soviet military writers were discussing entire wars between major coalitions conducted without nuclear weapons.[60] In the important 1982 book *Military-Technical Progress and the Armed Forces of the USSR*, Maj Gen M.M. Kir'yan expressed confidence that the Soviet armed forces had perfected appropriate methods and a force structure capable of conducting warfare "both with the use of nuclear weapons and with the use of only conventional means. . . ."[61] Further on, Kir'yan depicts the West's "theory of war's escalation" and the implications it holds for shaping Soviet military requirements as including the

> unleashing and for some time waging [of war] using only conventional means and then shifting at a certain point to the use of nuclear weapons, first with tactical and later on with possibly even more powerful weapons. Use of only conventional weapons has not been excluded in waging armed conflict. Under these conditions Soviet military thought developed the means to wage military operations with and without the use of nuclear weapons.[62]

The above description makes clear the continuing Soviet need for nuclear options at the tactical, theatre, and strategic levels. Indeed, the Soviet notions of conventional strategic operations and entire wars fought only with conventional weapons were developed in the context of constraints imposed on all combatants by rough nuclear parity. Nonetheless, the efficacy of plausible nuclear options for Soviet planners lies in the coercive power these options hold in peacetime and the intra-war deterrent leverage they provide should war occur. And despite the Soviet unilateral declaration of no-first-use of nuclear weapons, there remains an unremitting requirement for Soviet unclear forces. The Soviet

> contemporary concept of non-nuclear war envisions the combination of the achievement of strategic results by conventional weapons with the readiness to repel nuclear attacks.[63]

Optimism in Soviet military commentaries of the early 1980s was, no doubt, based on a combination of politico-military factors. Politically, Soviet foreign policy successes during the 1970s were seen as the product of the restraining influence of strategic parity on US influence around the globe. Militarily, emerging conventional technologies – longer-range, highly accurate, dual-capable delivery systems in particular – began to foreshadow the capacity to furnish conventional solutions for nuclear problems. Preventing NATO from employing nuclear weapons, the threat of which constitutes the heart of NATO's deterrent strategy, formed the crux of the Soviet problem. The solution to this operational conundrum lies in the Soviet force development process. The deployment of enough new weapons in the 1960s enabled Soviet military theoreticians to perfect new forms and methods of combat operations, giving hope that a war could be conducted by stages; a new phase in the dialectical process of force development then offered the prospect of conducting decisive missions (such as preventing NATO's nuclear riposte) without using nuclear weapons. The then Minister of Defence A. A. Grechko reflected on the process in his 1975 book when he suggested that

> due to a qualitative improvement in conventional means of destruction and the increase in units and formations, there has been a great improvement in the fire, shock and manoeuvre capabilities of troops, which permits assigning them very decisive

missions on the battlefield which they are capable of accomplishing without resorting to nuclear weapons.[64]

Yet, the quality and quantity of new conventional weapons were not the only conditions necessary to bring the latest phase in the force development process full cycle. At least two additional conditions seemed in order: the necessity, first, to modify and improve operational concepts of war that would materially capitalise on the availability of new and better conventional weapons and, second, to reshape the Soviet armed forces to enable them to execute these newly accommodated operational concepts.

The following examples illustrate a few of the many operational and organisational changes instituted in the mid- to late 1970s:

- Soviet planners reorganised the air force and air defence force to provide greater flexibility in employing long-range strike aircraft, organic close-air support, and air defence of the ground forces. Consistent with these changes, they refined the air operation, which, in effect, substitutes for an initial mass nuclear strike against high-value military targets throughout the depth of NATO's defence.

- They revised the World War II "mobile group" concept in the guise of the operational manoeuvre group (OMG). Broadly speaking, the function of the OMG is to penetrate NATO lines rapidly, create paralysis and eventually complete collapse before NATO can employ nuclear weapons.

- They streamlined logistics command and control and prestocked large quantities of ammunition (60–90 days), fuel (90 days), and other war supplies in forward areas. In the past, NATO could count on detecting an impending offensive by monitoring the movement of supplies from rear-area dumps to forward positions. Such an expectation is no longer the case.[65]

- Major improvements in the mobility and firepower of

Soviet airborne divisions coupled with helicopter-borne air-assault brigades suggested a highly co-ordinated approach to deep-penetration attacks against NATO high-value targets.

- Now that front commanders possessed weapons with ranges capable of influence well beyond a front's area of interest, the General Staff saw the need to co-ordinate the activities of several fronts. To that end, Soviet planners re-established the concept of the High Command in the TVD, which is designed to control the complex timing and execution of multi-front air, missile, airborne, and ground activity of a conventional strategic offensive in a continental TVD. This command and control feature, together with the restructuring of air and air defence forces, places Soviet and Warsaw Pact forces in a more streamlined posture to respond to modern war conditions. Principally, those conditions dictate surprise and pre-emptive action.

The operational objectives of the conventional-only contingency are simple to conceive but complex to execute. The massive nuclear and escalating contingencies held a straightforward solution to the problem of disrupting NATO's nuclear weapons, air forces, and command and control centres: massive missile- and air-delivered nuclear weapons employed pre-emptively at the start of war or soon after. A conventional solution to a nuclear problem would require a qualitatively new role for operational-tactical delivery systems (especially missiles) if Soviet planners were to be confident in the success of the conventional-only contingency.

Force Requirements and Planning under a Conventional-Only Contingency
Soviet strategy for a conventional strategic operation in the Western TVD envisions a decisive conventional operations' period to cause a rapid collapse of NATO defences, especially NATO's ability to escalate to the nuclear level. Soviet

expectations of executing such a bold strategy hinge on employment of a formula that not only exploits the technical virtues of improved mobility, firepower, and weapon accuracy but also denies NATO the ability to capitalise on its own improved military capabilities.

The Soviet operational concept entails employment of division- and perhaps army-size OMGs to prevent NATO from organising a coherent in-depth defence. Emphasising surprise and high-speed advances, OMGs would attempt to penetrate deep into NATO's rear to disrupt or destroy nuclear weapons, aircraft, logistic support, command and control centres, and reserve and withdrawal forces. Success would depend on important variables, the most critical of which is winning the counter-air campaign.[66] The effective commitment of OMGs early in a threatre-wide campaign presupposes a successful air operation against NATO to reduce the chance of air attacks on OMGs before, during, and after their insertion. Soviet planners view NATO's air assets as having the requisite speed and firepower to react decisively to OMG penetrations. Equally important, the air operation would be expected to disrupt NATO's air defence network to enable friendly fighter-bombers, helicopters, and transport aircraft to accompany or follow-up OMG penetrations. Airborne and helicopter assault operations simply cannot be executed until the air battle is won.

Many Western analysts are sceptical about Soviet capabilities to execute a conventionally oriented strategic operation in the Western theatre. They question whether the Warsaw Pact could achieve the air superiority needed to enable deep raids behind NATO's forward lines and whether they could locate and attack NATO nuclear forces once they have dispersed to relatively secure field positions. However legitimate, these questions focus on the contingency in which the Soviet Union would least like to be involved: one where NATO has had sufficient time to disperse its in-theatre nuclear and conventional forces and to mobilise its superior military potential. Such a Western-preferred scenario is founded on the canonical 10- to 14-day mobilisation sequence in which NATO detects a Warsaw Pact mobilisation four days after its start, and responds with ten days of its own mobilisation before the Warsaw Pact begins an offensive.

Conservative Soviet planners share the sceptics' doubts over Warsaw Pact prospects under Western-preferred conditions. Despite recent improvements in long-war preparations (such as logistics stockpiling), Soviet military authorities are sensitive to several prominent Warsaw Pact weaknesses, among them the questionable reliability of the USSR's allies, command and control inflexibility under rapidly changing circumstances, and shortcomings in theatre reconnaissance capabilities. Such a combination of shortcomings would probably render any Soviet prospects for a sustained offensive against a prepared NATO highly dubious. Yet, the convergence of these vulnerabilities with the Soviet Union's emerging conventional attack options makes the Warsaw Pact more, not less, worrisome an adversary, especially in uncertain crisis situations. Perhaps the best way for Soviet planners to reconcile Warsaw Pact weaknesses is through achieving decisive results pre-emptively in the first campaign of a future war, before events get completely out of hand.

Clearly, the opening stage of war is of decisive importance to strategic success. During this period the number of installations (targets) that must be attacked to achieve decisive results is relatively small compared with the targeting requirements of the post-mobilisation period. In his 1974 book *Initial Period of War*, Gen S.P. Ivanov describes the role of surprise:

> to inflict a decisive defeat on the enemy's first strategic echelon; and then, by continuing with a speedy offensive into the depths of his territory, to complete his total defeat before he was able to mobilise and make use of his military and economic potential.[67]

Exploiting the initial period by no means requires the execution of a "bolt from the blue" surprise attack. In light of modern reconnaissance means, Soviet planners recognise the low probability of ever catching NATO completely by surprise. Yet, NATO's politico-military decision process offers much room for Soviet crisis manipulation. Once a decision to go to war is reached, the chief Soviet goal is to exploit NATO's severe vulnerabilities before the Alliance is able to complete its mobilisation and dispersal of air, ground, and nuclear forces.

Increasing the weight of the initial pre-emptive blow could compound the inherent tendency for NATO airpower to operate with reduced efficiency in the initial stages of a war. One of the major consequences of NATO's lack of realistic pilot training is the expectation that the critical first few days of conflict will be characterised by higher aircraft attrition and reduced sortie effectiveness. Moreover, Western historical experience underscores the deleterious consequences that a short-term but significant increase in the rate of aircraft attrition can have on the overall course of war. In World War II, for example, the attrition rate for B-17s and B-24s was an acceptable 2%, but it was so high for one particular day that strategic daylight bombing was suspended until enough escort fighters were available.[68] Of course, the reduced efficiency of airpower during the initial period could cut both ways. But, as noted in a recent Soviet historical account of the initial period of war,

> even where both opposing sides had considerable forces and means but one of them pre-empted the other in deploying and launching an attack, the outcome of operations in the initial period placed the nation subjected to surprise attack in an extremely difficult situation.[69]

By no means does pre-emptive success hinge on the use of nuclear weapons. The above cited Soviet author, after discussing how the long-range nuclear missile has dramatically shortened the duration of the initial period of war, imparts the same decisive potential to new conventional weapons.[70] At first blush Soviet conventional payloads delivered by ballistic missiles seem rather unattractive when compared to aircraft-delivered payloads, which can outweigh the former by at least 2 to 1. If we put aside for the moment the synergistic effects of co-ordinated missile/air attacks, it is critical to point out the contribution missiles make (especially large salvos) to achieving pre-emptive surprise and increasing the weight and shock effect of the initial blow. It should come as no surprise that Soviet military planners, so many of whom are steeped in the artillery tradition, see great advantage in overwhelming priority enemy targets with a large fraction of their own offensive firepower, the application of which is invariably compressed in time.[71] Soviet theatre strategy thus places a premium on avoiding lengthy gaps in the intensity of attack. To illustrate using an historical example, one Soviet analyst notes that "losses . . . up to 80%, but inflicted over the course of a long time, may not deprive a unit of its capacity for combat, but even . . . allow it to be victorious. In contrast, even losses of a mere 10%, inflicted within minutes, demoralise a unit to such an extent that it may remain incapable of combat for a long time."[72]

What are the constituents of this decisive, pre-emptive attack during the initial period of war? In the late 1970s, Western analysts accorded much attention to the role of Soviet Frontal Aviation in conducting a massive conventional air operation against NATO's nuclear forces, command posts, and airfields at the beginning of hostilities. To be sure, the 1970s brought dramatic improvements to Frontal Aviation's assets: nearly a doubling in offensive load capacity and 70% more versatility in comparison with the predecessor generation of aircraft.[73] By 1978, the Central Intelligence Agency estimated that Frontal Aviation's share of Soviet defence spending was about twice that of the Strategic Rocket Forces, a figure aptly reflecting the increased burden assumed by the operational front commander for furnishing pre-emptive shock power at the commencement of hostilities.[74]

But it is short-sighted to view Frontal Aviation as the linchpin of the Soviet conventional-only contingency.[75] Although the air operation does substitute for the initial mass nuclear strike of the massive nuclear and escalatory contingencies, its constituents are far more varied and complex than is implied by its name. Indeed, before Frontal Aviation's attack through selected NATO air defence sectors to open up several penetration corridors, tactical and operational-tactical missile forces would attack NATO air bases and air defences with improved conventional munitions while electronic warfare aircraft would disrupt NATO air defence radar and communications networks. After Frontal Aviation's attack to open penetration corridors, longer-range aircraft of the Supreme High Command (including SU-24 Fencers and TU-26 Backfires, for example) would attack high-priority targets to the depth of the theatre. This panoply of missile and air activity would precede and thereby enable, by virtue of achieving air superiority, the initiation of warfare on the ground by an equally varied mix of airborne, air assault, and OMG formations.[76] If any part of the air operation merits the epithet "linchpin," it belongs to the emerging force of highly accurate tactical and operational-tactical ballistic missiles deployed with Warsaw Pact ground forces in Eastern Europe. The extent to which the INF treaty incapacitates the contribution of conventionally armed missiles to the air operation is, therefore, a topic of key concern, which we shall turn to in detail later on.

An Uncertain Future: Soviet Defence Planning Under Gorbachev

In reviewing the last 35 years of Soviet military developments, one is struck by the consistent, even-handed Soviet approach to assessing threats inherent in Western strategy and to establishing requirements for military procurement. This stands in contrast to the history of abrupt swings in Western national security planning, where decisions about the size of defence budgets seem less realistically adapted to fundamental national security goals and plans. Yet, the enormous accumulation of military capabilities needed to cope with the three contingencies described above may represent an aberration of sorts, unnatural in the sense that most of the military instruments and supporting operational concepts were largely amassed during the Soviet military's unprecedented position of authority under the Brezhnev regime.

The special status accorded the military, especially in the

early Brezhnev years, was formed in reaction to Khrushchev's interference in the military-technical aspects of military doctrine and the Soviet Union's quest, in the wake of the Cuban missile crisis, to build sufficient military power to challenge the credibility of the USA's extended deterrence strategy. The military's special status meant priority treatment in budgetary matters and unparalleled control of the national security decision-making apparatus.

The Soviet military literature describes military doctrine as consisting of two parts: the socio-political and military-technical. The socio-political component is the domain of the Communist Party of the Soviet Union, which broadly defines the dominant threats to the nation's interests. Reacting, as it must, to capitalist threats to socialism, the socio-political component of Soviet military doctrine is *defensive* in nature. By contrast, the Soviet High Command and military services dominate the military-technical component, or that side of military doctrine that must wrestle with the details of military strategy, operational art, tactics, and force structure. Where the political component of doctrine is defensive, the military-technical side is unabashedly *offensive* in nature.

Naturally, shifts in the relative influence of the various institutional players have occurred over time in Soviet civil-military relations. Both Stalin and Khrushchev not only controlled the socio-political but frequently interfered with the military-technical component of military doctrine. Under Brezhnev, however, the Soviet military became virtually the sole repository for the sinews of national security decision-making: information, especially that needed to make threat assessments upon which fundamental defence and arms control decisions rest.

But there were signs of a breakdown in the military's unprecedented autonomy as early as the mid-1970s. In the area of military spending, the sustained annual growth rates of 4–5% over a decade came to a halt in 1976, with strategic offensive and defensive forces actually experiencing a drop in real growth, while conventional forces would continue to grow, but at the reduced level of 1.5% annually.[77] Moreover, the political

leadership probably began to affect military morale and training adversely through such declarations as Brezhnev's, at Tula
in January 1977, where he declared that the Soviet Union did
not seek military superiority over its opponents.

Soviet military planners faced new challenges with the
advent of the Reagan Administration. Although the pro-
fessional Soviet military seemed confident in the early 1980s
about their ability to operate successfully in either nuclear or
conventional contingencies, many senior military officials
began to express doubts about managing the future military
competition with the West. The West's fascination with such
doctrines as AirLand Battle, Follow-On Forces Attack or Deep
Attack, and several counter-air initiatives (such as NATO's
Counterair-90) impressed and worried Soviet planners. They
respect these more offensively oriented strategies; in contrast to
the seriousness with which Soviet military planners greeted
AirLand Battle in the early 1980s, they were virtually mute in
their reaction to the US Army's promulgation of an "active
defence" doctrine in the Field Manual 100-5 of 1976.[78] They
were especially impressed with the potential of the West's
emerging conventional technologies to achieve decisive results
at the start of any military campaign. These near-term Western
initiatives tended to reinforce longstanding Soviet offensive
proclivities by compelling Soviet planners to emphasise even
more the critical need to achieve surprise and to exploit the
initial period of war.[79]

At the strategic level, Moscow saw new challenges to its
military gains in a number of US initiatives. Offensive modernisation programmes (MX, Trident D-5) were viewed as yet
another attempt to impose "unilateral deterrence" on the
socialist community. Even more worrisome for the long-term
competition is the US Strategic Defence Initiative (SDI). SDI's
technological challenge cannot simply be dealt with by
increases in defence expenditures. In fact, SDI raises the more
fundamental question of whether or not the Soviet technological
base is capable of keeping pace with Western military developments in the 21st century.[80]

Manifestations of Soviet military concern about the implications of Western defence initiatives were evident in the early 1980s. Marshal Ogarkov's views are generally well known in the West, but by no means is he the only senior military official who has expressed concern about the long-term military competition and the changing character of future war.[81] Indeed, after Ogarkov was relieved of his position as Chief of the General Staff for being perhaps too vociferous about his concerns, his replacement, Marshal Akhromeyev, more delicately called attention to the same issues by challenging Soviet military scientists to produce a "correct forecast of the development of the military-strategic situation and the methods of the conduct of war."[82] But the most explicit reflection of disquietude is found in the work of Col Gen M. A. Gareyev who generally asserts that the answers Soviet military science had fashioned in the late 1970s are relevant to neither contemporary or future circumstances facing the Soviet Union.[83]

While senior military leaders worry about the future military competition, the political leadership has broader concerns. They have probably evaluated with increasing concern the insubstantial return on their huge investment in military capabilities. The military's satisfaction that they could cope successfully with the three contingencies discussed above is, very likely, an insufficient measure of investment success from a political standpoint. Surely, the force development process furnished the political leadership with enough military power, practically and formally, to be declared an equal to the USA at the level of strategic nuclear forces. Yet, the achievement of strategic parity failed to deliver on the Soviet claim to global equality with the USA in political as well as military terms. Aside from some political gains in Africa, which later soured, and the invasion of Afghanistan, which might be interpreted as a geostrategic if not a geopolitical gain, the Soviet record seems spotty at best. Indeed, to the extent it was seen to be successful in the West, it fuelled a hostile political and military reaction, beginning in the last years of the Carter Administration and culminating in the election of Ronald Reagan and dramatic increases in US defence expenditures, including, most notably, SDI.

Although their long-term goals and priorities may not be quite the same, Soviet political and military leaders share a common concern over the adverse implications of economic stagnation. Perhaps of most concern within the military is the highly suspect capacity of defence industries to produce increasingly high-tech components for weapon systems in the 1990s and beyond. Just as Stalin decided, in the late 1920s, to invest in heavy industry before rearmament, Gorbachev's plan is to restructure the economic system to create the basis for future civilian and military competition with the West.[84] In a sense, the gravest threat to the Soviet Union is seen as internal stagnation rather than external aggression.

What remains uncertain is the extent to which the Soviet military has signed on to the Gorbachev reforms, especially in light of the belt tightening that is bound to take place. If the current investment rate remains intact, the military's existing force modernisation programmes will be completed by the early 1990s, after which critical decisions must be made on new plant investment. But there are already tenuous signs of a reduction in the growth of the military budget in the form of cuts in conscript manpower, a slowing of conventional weapons production, and a shift of key defence industry personnel into the civilian economy.[85]

Another reason to question the extent of the military's support of the Gorbachev's reforms is the apparent decreasing role of the military in defence and arms control decision-making. Even during the last stages of the Brezhnev regime, there was evidence of differences of view between the political and military leaderships about the nature of the threat and the party's attendant responsibilities.[86] It has become even more apparent that the Gorbachev leadership and the military have not settled these differences over the appropriate approach to defence management. In fact, General Secretary Gorbachev's remarks at the 27th Party Congress in February 1986 at least suggest that the Party does not share the military's threat viewpoint. There, he referred to "limitations on military potential with the boundaries of reasonable sufficiency." Even more to the point, Gorbachev asserted that "the task of ensuring security is increasingly seen as a political problem, and it can only be resolved by political means."[87] Not just coincidentally, a mixed civilian-military group in the International Department of the Central Committee under Anatoly Dobrynin shows signs of becoming an alternative centre of military threat definition. What seems certain, however, is that the military no longer maintains exclusive control over information pertinent to arms control and defence analysis.

At least on the surface, surely the most dramatic turn in Soviet military debate is reflected in suggestions of a new defensive orientation to the military-technical component of military doctrine. Not surprisingly, this antithetical advocacy is prominently led by Soviet civilian defence intellectuals. Given Western Europe's concern over Soviet conventional superiority after the elimination of INF missiles, it is difficult to give much credence to the notion that the Soviet military might adopt a strategy and force structure similar in nature to the "non-provocative defence" proposals of the European left. As a tool of public diplomacy, the Soviet foreign ministry has already noted that "the proclamation of the [defensive conventional] doctrine is having a salutary effect on the climate and the situation in the world."[88]

But there is more to discussions of a defensive Soviet military doctrine than just public diplomacy. Even so prominent a military spokesman as Col Gen Gareyev has declared that one of the "main tenets of the military-technical aspect of military doctrine" is its "profoundly defensive direction."[89] On the other hand, General Secretary Gorbachev's handpicked Minister of Defence, Gen D. T. Yazov, recently re-emphasised the primacy of the offensive in a new book. There, he stated that "[it] is impossible ... to destroy the aggressor only with defence. Therefore, after the attack has been repelled, the army and navy must be capable of conducting a decisive offensive."[90] Certainly such a requirement would justify the recent declaration by the Chief of Staff of the Warsaw Pact, Army General A. I. Gribkov, that the Soviet Union's new defensive military doctrine dictated no restructuring of Soviet conventional forces.[91]

Thus, within military circles there is no inherent contradiction between discussions of a so-called "defensive" military doctrine and the traditional Soviet focus on the offensive. In fact, Soviet military planners see the introduction of highly accurate long-range conventional firepower influencing an even greater attention to the relationship between offence and defence. The proliferation of such weapons on both sides has led Warsaw Pact military analysts to begin "a complete re-evaluation of the very essence of the defence on the future battlefield."[92] Prior to the introduction of long-range conventional firepower, defensive operations could only be conducted with any effect along the forward line of engagement. Now highly accurate battlefield missiles and aircraft armed with conventional submunitions permit even the defence to seize the initiative from the attacker. To cite a contemporary Warsaw Pact view:

> Now the defender, being able to reach the enemy at distant pre-battle positions, on march routes, and in assembly regions, does not have to only wait for the blow, for the strike. He himself can make the decision about the beginning of the battle. The choice of time of the encounter has ceased to be an exclusive attribute of the attacker.[93]

The above commentary aptly describes the tyranny of pre-emption in which defence and offence are indistinguishable.

Finding light in the midst of controversy and debate in Soviet politico-military circles is likely to become even more difficult in the wake of INF ratification and implementation. Developing a broad popular consensus on the nature of the Warsaw Pact threat is essential to rational defence planning in an age of shrinking resources. If Western consensus-building on the nature of the threat was difficult under the comparatively straightforward circumstances of the Brezhnev regime, achieving that goal in a period of rapid (and perhaps only apparent) change under Gorbachev will be even more problematic but more important than ever before, given the stakes for the Western Alliance. This chapter has introduced a suggested analytic framework of representative Soviet planning contingencies. The remaining chapters of the book examine the consequences of the INF treaty provisions for Soviet and Western security in the context of these contingencies.

Notes

1. Soviet military authors define the TVD as a large geographic area that "permits the concentration and deployment of strategic groupings of forces and the carrying out by them of military operations in accomplishment of strategic missions." This definition is cited and discussed in Dennis M. Gormley, "Understanding Soviet Motivations for Deploying Long-Range Theater Nuclear Forces," *Military Review*, Vol. LXI, No. 9, September 1981, pp. 20–34.
2. David Holloway, "Doctrine and Technology in Soviet Armaments Policy," in Derek Leebaert, ed., *Soviet Military Thinking* (London: George Allen and Unwin, 1981), p. 266.
3. For a detailed discussion of these factors, see Dennis M. Gormley *et al., Soviet Perceptions of and Responses to U.S. Nuclear Weapon Development and Deployment*, Pacific-Sierra Research Corporation, PSR Report 1211, June 1982.
4. Edward L. Warner, *The Military in Contemporary Soviet Politics* (New York: Praeger, 1977), pp. 153–155, 175–188.
5. N. V. Ogarkov, *Always in Readiness to Defend the Fatherland* (Moscow: Voyenizdat, 1982), p. 38.
6. For a thoughtful treatment of this issue, see Notra Trulock III, "Weapons of Mass Destruction in Soviet Military Strategy," an unpublished paper presented at the Joint Conference on Soviet Military Strategy in Europe, sponsored by the Boston Foreign Affairs Group and the Royal United Services Institute for Defence Studies on 24–25 September 1984, Oxford, England, pp. 10–30.
7. *Ibid.,* p. 14.
8. *Ibid.,* p. 15.
9. For a discussion of the influence of these events on Soviet decision-making, see Douglas M. Hart and Dennis M. Gormley, "The Evolution of Soviet Interest in Atomic Artillery," *Journal of the Royal United Services Institute for Defence Studies*, June 1983, pp. 25–34.
10. Robert C. Richardson, "NATO Nuclear Strategy: A Look Back," *Strategic Review*, Spring 1981, pp. 40–41.

11. Hart and Gormley, *op. cit.* in Note 9, pp. 28–30.

12. Trulock, *op. cit.* in Note 6, p. 13.

13. P. Galin, "Aircraft and Rocket-Carriers of Tactical Nuclear Weapons," in P. T. Astaskenkov, ed., *Atomic Energy in Aviation and Rocket Technology* (Moscow: Voyenizdat, 1959), p. 48, as cited in Trulock, *op. cit.* in Note 6, p. 24.

14. Nikita Khrushchev, *Khrushchev Remembers: The Last Testament*, ed. and trans. by Strobe Talbott (Boston: Little, Brown, and Co., 1974), pp. 52–53.

15. G. Pokrovsky, "Weapons in a Modern Army," *Marxism-Leninism on War and the Army* (Moscow: Voyenizdat, 1955), p. 168, as cited in Thomas W. Wolfe, *Soviet Strategy at the Crossroads* (Cambridge: Harvard University Press, 1964), p. 155.

16. Oleg Penkovsky, *The Penkovsky Papers* (New York: Ballantine Books, 1982), p. 162.

17. Included were the SU-7 ground-attack aircraft, the AS-2 air-to-surface missile, the SS-N-3 sea-launched cruise missile, the SS-N-4 submarine-launched ballistic missile, the SS-4 medium-range ballistic missile, the Scud-A operational-tactical ballistic missile, and the Frog-1 rocket.

18. S. U. Malyanchikov, "The Character and Features of Nuclear Rocket War," *Kommunist Vooruzhennykh Sil*, November 1965, p. 178, as cited in Joseph D. Douglass, Jr., *The Soviet Theater Nuclear Offensive* (Washington, D.C.: USGPO, 1976), p. 20.

19. Kh. Dzhelaukhov, "The Infliction of Deep Strikes," *Voyennaya Mysl'* No. 2, February 1966, trans. FBIS FPD 0763/67, 8 August 1967, pp. 14–15.

20. Stephen M. Meyer, "Soviet Theatre Nuclear Forces, Part I: Development of Doctrine and Objectives," *Adelphi Papers*, No. 187 (London: IISS, 1983/84), p. 20.

21. Khrushchev, *op. cit.* in Note 14, p. 52.

22. Robert P. Berman and John C. Baker, *Soviet Strategic Forces: Requirements and Responses* (Washington, D.C.: The Brookings Institution, 1982), p. 42.

23. For a detailed discussion of Soviet ballistic missile design considerations, see *The Theory of Flight and Construction of Ballistic Missiles* (Moscow: Voyenizdat, 1974), trans. by I. N. Pentsak, FTD-ID(RS) T-1605-75 and *Design of Guided Ballistic Missiles* (Moscow: Voyenizdat, 1969), trans. by the US Air Force, FTD-MT-24-10-70.

24. S. A. Tyushkevich, *The Soviet Armed Forces: The History of Their*

Development (Moscow: Voyenizdat, 1978), p. 476 as cited in Trulock, *op. cit.* in Note 6, p. 45.

25. A. Kvitnitsiky and Yu. Nepodayev, "The Theory of the Escalation of War," *Voyennaya Mysl'*, No. 9, September 1965, trans. FBIS FDD 952, 2 March 1966, p. 14. For a Western view of Soviet perceptions of escalation, see Dennis M. Gormley and Douglas M. Hart, "Soviet Views on Escalation: Implications for Alliance Strategy," *The EAI Papers*, No. 8 (Marina del Rey, CA: European American Institute for Security Research, Summer 1984).

26. V. D. Sokolovsky and M. Cherednichenko, "Military Strategy and Its Problems," *Voyennaya Msyl'*, No. 10, October 1968, p. 156.

27. N. A. Lomov, "The Influence of Soviet Military Doctrine on the Development of Military Art," *Kommunist Vooruzhennykh Sil*, November 1965, pp. 16–18.

28. Tyushkevich, *op. cit.* in Note 24.

29. B. Samorukov, "Combat Operation is Involving Conventional Means of Destruction," *Voyennaya Mysl'*, No. 8, August 1967, trans. FBIS FPD 0125/68, 26 August 1968, as cited in "Selected Readings from *Soviet Military Thought* (1963–1973)," System Planning Corporation, SPC Report 584, April 1980, p. 263.

30. Or the plethora of messages filling NATO communications nets requesting release of nuclear weapons.

31. See, for example, Yu. Nepodayev, "On the 'Nuclear Threshold' in NATO Strategy," *Voyennaya Mysl'*, No. 6, June 1966, trans. CIA FPIR 0503/67, 26 May 1967, pp. 70–79.

32. See, for example, Samorukov, *op. cit.* in Note 29.

33. System inaccuracies, of course, would not have precluded use of chemical munitions, which the Soviets consider weapons of mass destruction alongside nuclear and biological weapons.

34. The existence of a nuclear withhold for Frontal Aviation is ascribed to in N. Semenov, "Gaining Supremacy in the Air," *Voyennaya Mysl'*, No. 4, April 1968, trans. FBIS FPD 0052/69, 27 May 1969, p. 44.

35. This example is taken from D. Samorukov and L. Semeyko, "The Increase in Efforts in Nuclear Warfare Operations," *Voyennaya Mysl'*, No. 10, October 1968, trans. FBIS FPD 0084/69,4 September 1969, p. 48.

36. See, for example, Douglass, *op. cit.* in Note 18, pp. 73–74.

37. Donald R. Cotter, James H. Hansen, and Kirk McConnell, "The Nuclear 'Balance' in Europe: Status, Trends, Implications,"

USSI Report 83-1 (Washington, D.C.: United States Strategic Institute, 1983), pp. 41–45; FM 100-2-3, Soviet Army Troops Organization and Equipment, Coordinating Draft, August 1982, pp. IV-88 and IV-164.

38. Robert P. Berman, *Soviet Air Power in Transition* (Washington, D.C.: The Brookings Institution, 1978), p. 54.
39. See Stephen M. Meyer, "Soviet Theatre Nuclear Forces, Part II: Capabilities and Implications," *Adelphi Papers*, No. 188 (London: IISS, 1983/84), pp. 22 and 56.
40. Berman, *op. cit.* in Note 38, p. 32.
41. Jeffrey Record, *NATO's Theater Nuclear Modernization Program: The Real Issues* (Washington, D.C. and Cambridge, MA: Institute for Foreign Policy Analysis, Inc., 1981), p. 44.
42. These articles, since they appear to have been written coincident with or just before initial deployment of modern Soviet nuclear-capable artillery, do not include the development process. Research and development probably began some seven to ten years before deployment. However, advocacy articles were still necessary to influence where the weapons would be deployed, how many systems would be deployed, their roles and missions, and the organizational relationships governing their employment in wartime. As such, these writings provide a useful barometer of Soviet intent.
43. I. Pavlovsky, "The Ground Forces," *Voyennaya Mysl'*, 4 April 1973, p. 33.
44. G. Peredel'sky, "Artillery in the Struggle to Attain Fire Superiority," *Voyennaya Mysl'*, 10 October 1973, pp. 39–62.
45. V. Kolesov, "Massing of Artillery under Contemporary Conditions," *Voyennaya Mysl'*, 11 November 1972, pp. 70–71.
46. G. Peredel'sky, "Soviet Artillery Main Assault Force in War," *Voyenno-istoricheskiy Zhurnal*, 4 April 1975, p. 66.
47. Western reports include David L. Isby, *Weapons and Tactics of the Soviet Army* (Jane's: New York, 1981), p. 194 and Harold Brown, *DoD Annual Report FY 1981* (Washington, D.C.: USGPO, 29 January 1980), p. 91.
48. A. Simonenko, "Artillery of the Reserve of the Supreme High Command," *Krasnaya Zvezda*, 12 February 1978, p. 68.
49. *Ibid.*
50. *Soviet Military Power*, 2nd edition (Washington, D.C.: USGPO, 1983), p. 40 and *Soviet Military Power 1986* (Washington, D.C.: USGPO, 1986), p. 39.

51. M. P. Skirdo, *The People, The Army, The Commander* (Moscow: Voyenizdat, 1970), p. 121.
52. V. Krupnov, "Dialectics of the Development of Methods and Forms of Armed Conflict," in A. S. Zheltov, ed., *Methodological Problems of Military Theory and Practise* (Moscow: Voyenizdat, 1969), p. 344.
53. Meyer, *op. cit.* in Note 39, p. 31.
54. A. A. Sidorenko, *The Offensive (A Soviet View)* (Moscow: 1970), trans. U.S. Air Force (Washington, D.C.: USGPO, 1974), p. 100.
55. Eltran Bronner, "U.S. Says Soviet Has A-Arms in E. Europe," *International Herald Tribune*, 2 June 1983, p. 1. For an official acknowledgement, see *Soviet Military Power 1984* (Washington, D.C.: USGPO, 1984), p. 81.
56. M. I. Cherednichenko, "Military Strategy and Military Technology,' *Voyennaya Mysl'*, No. 4, April 1973. Trans. FBIS FPD 0043/73, 12 November 1973, p. 53.
57. J. J. Martin, "How the Soviet Union Came to Gain Escalation Dominance – Trends and Asymmetries in the Theater Nuclear Balance," in Uwe Nerlich, ed., *The Soviet Asset, Military Power in the Competition over Europe* (Cambridge, MA: Ballinger Publishing Co., 1983), pp., 110–111 and 114–115.
58. As cited in Trulock, *op. cit.* in Note 6, p. 72.
59. James McConnell, "The Interacting Evolution of Soviet and American Military Doctrines," Center for Naval Analyses Memorandum No. 80-1313.00, 17 September 1980, pp. 96–97.
60. M. M. Kir'yan, ed., *Military-Technical Progress and the Armed Forces of the USSR* (Moscow: Voyenizdat, 1982), pp. 312–313.
61. *Ibid.*, p. 312.
62. *Ibid.*, p. 313.
63. L. Ol'Shtynsky, *Cooperation of the Army and Navy* (Moscow: Voyenizdat, 1983, p. 89.
64. A. A. Grechko, *The Armed Forces of the Soviet State* (Moscow: Voyenizdat, 1975), trans. U.S. Air Force, Soviet Military Thought series, No. 12 (Washington, D.C.: USGPO, no date), pp. 147–148.
65. Changes in the Warsaw Pact logistics structure are reported in *Soviet Military Power 1985* (Washington, D.C.: USGPO, 1985), pp. 65–66. The value of Warsaw Pact logistics activity as a warning indicator is discussed in William J. Lewis, *The Warsaw Pact: Arms, Doctrine, and Strategy* (Cambridge, MA: Institute for

Policy Analysis, 1982), p. 234.

66.   P. Lashchenko, "Perfection of Methods of Encirclement and Destruction of Large Enemy Groupings Based on the Experience of the Great Patriotic War," *Voyenno-istoricheskiy Zhurnal*, No. 2, February 1985, pp. 21–31.

67.   S. P. Ivanov, *Initial Period of War* (Moscow: Voyenizdat, 1974) as cited in P. H. Vigor, *Soviet Blitzkrieg Theory* (New York: St. Martin's Press, 1983), p. viii.

68.   Lt Col. D. J. Alberts, "Deterrence in the 1980s, Part II: The Role of Conventional Air Power," *Adelphi Papers*, No. 193 (London: IISS, 1984), pp. 18–19.

69.   A. I. Eiseev, "On Certain Trends in Changes in the Content and Nature of the Initial Period of War," *Voyenno-istoricheskiy Zhurnal*, November 1985, p. 15.

70.   *Ibid.*, p. 17.

71.   Nathan Leites, *Soviet Style of War* (New York: Crane Russak, 1982), p. xviii.

72.   V. Tokarevskii, quoted by V. Ye. Savkin, *The Basic Principles of Operational Art and Tactics* (Moscow: Voyenizdat, 1972), p. 18, as cited *ibid.*, p. 39.

73.   Berman, *op. cit.* in Note 38, p. 31.

74.   Central Intelligence Agency, National Foreign Assessment Center, *Estimated Soviet Defense Spending: Trends and Prospects* (Washington, D.C.: USGPO, 1978), pp. 3–4.

75.   For example, see Joshua Epstein, *Measuring Military Power: The Soviet Air Threat to Europe* (Princeton: Princeton University Press, 1984), pp. 5–7.

76.   For a more detailed discussion, see Phillip A. Petersen and John G. Hines, "The Conventional Offensive in Soviet Theater Strategy," *Orbis*, Fall 1983, pp. 695–739.

77.   *Allocation of Resources in the Soviet Union and China – 1984*, Hearings before the Subcommittee on International Trade, Finance, and Security Economics of the Joint Economic Committee (Washington, D.C.: USGPO, 1985), p. 14.

78.   Col Frederick C. Turner, *Comments on FM 100-5 from a Soviet Point of View*, Special Report of the US Army War College, Strategic Studies Institute, 15 March 1978.

79.   For more on the reinforcing nature of Soviet and Western military doctrines, see Dennis M. Gormley, "The Impact of NATO Doctrinal Choices on the Policies and Strategic Choices of Warsaw Pact States: Part II," in "Power and Policy: Doctrine,

the Alliance and Arms Control," *Adelphi Papers*, No. 206 (London: IISS, 1986), pp. 20–34.

80. For a good treatment of the implications of SDI for Soviet planning, see Benjamin S. Lambeth and Kevin N. Lewis, *The Strategic Defense Initiative in Soviet Planning and Policy* (Santa Monica, CA: The Rand Corporation, 1988).

81. For an illustration of Ogarkov's concerns, see "Military Leader's Thought," *Krasnaya Zvezda*, 2 October 1983, p. 3. The author is indebted to his colleague, Notra Trulock III, for drawing his attention to these internal debates within the Soviet military. For more, see Notra Trulock III, *Soviet Military Thought in Transition: Implications for the Long-Term Military Competition*, Pacific-Sierra Research Corporation, Interim Report, 22 May 1987.

82. S. Akhromeyev, "The Role of the Soviet Union and its Armed Forces in the Achievement of a Sharp Turn in the Second World War and its International Significance," *Voyenno-istoricheskiy Zhurnal*, February 1985, p. 24.

83. M. A. Gareyev, *The Views of M. V. Frunze and Contemporary Military Theory* (Moscow: Voyenizdat, 1985).

84. Christopher N. Donnelly, "The Soviet Military Under Gorbachev," Soviet Studies Research Centre, Royal Military Academy, Sandhurst, December 1986, p. 8.

85. *Ibid.*, p. 11.

86. The best account of these differences of viewpoint is found in Trulock, *op. cit.* in Note 81, *passim*.

87. "Political Report of the Central Committee of the CPSU to the XXVII, Congress of the Communist Party of the Soviet Union Report of the General Secretary of the CC CPSU Comrade M.S. Gorbachev," Stenographic Report, p. 90, as cited *ibid.*, p. 28.

88. Vladimir Petrovisky, Deputy Foreign Minister, as quoted by TASS, 22 June 1987, cited in FBIS, 23 June 1987, p. AA3.

89. M. A. Garayev, quoted in a Moscow television news conference, 22 June 1987, FBIS, 23 June, 1987, as cited in Jack Snyder, "The Gorbachev Revolution: A Waning of Soviet Expansionism?" *International Security*, Winter 1987/88, p. 122.

90. D. T. Yazov, *On Guard of Socialism and Peace* (Moscow: Voyenizdat, 1987), p. 33. The author is indebted to Notra Trulock for bringing this citation to his attention.

91. A. I. Gribkov, Interview in *Krasnaya Zvezda*, 25 September 1987, pp. 2–3, as cited in Snyder, *op. cit.* in Note 89, p. 123.

92. S. Koziej, "Anticipated Directions for Change in Tactics of Ground Troops," *Ground Forces Review*, September 1986, p. 1, as cited in Notra Trulock III and Dennis M. Gormley, *The Implications of Future Technology on Warfare*, Pacific-Sierra Research Corporation, PSR Report 1777, December 1987, p. 36.

93. *Ibid.*, pp. 36–37.

2

Soviet dual-capable theatre forces

Chapter 1 traced the prominent role of dual-capable theatre forces in enabling the Soviet military to plan with greater confidence for increasingly more flexible military contingencies, nuclear and non-nuclear alike. Today's front commander with the Soviet Group of Forces, Germany, possesses missile and air weapons dramatically superior to their predecessors. But clearly the most significant improvement lies in the increased range of these weapons. Strategically critical NATO targets, which over the past two decades could be struck only by medium- and intermediate-range nuclear systems based in the Soviet homeland, have become vulnerable to dual-capable missile and air forces based in Eastern Europe.

The implications of improvements in Soviet deep-strike means are portentous. They render planning and execution of military operations from a front's perspective obsolete. They raise questions about the integration of longer- and shorter-range nuclear forces in Soviet nuclear strike planning. And, to the extent that shorter-range and non-restricted longer-range forces could substitute for weapons banned by the INF treaty, there are important arms control implications as well. Finally, tied to an offensive strategy emphasising the pre-emptive employment of massive numbers of high-performance aircraft, conventionally armed short-range missiles presage an emerging set of Warsaw Pact attack options that could eventually turn currently debatable vulnerabilities in NATO's military infrastructure into dangerous deficiencies.

To begin an assessment of these implications, this chapter examines the current transitional state of Soviet dual-capable

51

theatre forces (artillery, strike aircraft, and short-range ballistic missiles), to include their delivery means, current and pro-jected deployment numbers, and payload options (nuclear, chemical, and conventional).

A Conceptual Framework

The Soviet elaboration of military art helps to explain the relationship between Soviet shorter- and longer-range forces. Each of the components of military art – strategy, operational art, and tactics – has an equivalent command level and organic weapons systems. The term *strategic* defines the highest levels: national and theatre. The *operational* level encompasses fronts[1] and armies, while the *tactical* level is associated with divisions and lower echelons. Operational commands plan and execute a series of separate battles unified by a single important objec-tive (either the destruction of a large enemy force or the capture of key terrain). Tactical echelons fight discrete engagements to accomplish operational objectives. Achieving one or more operational objectives, in turn, satisfies a strategic objective.

Beyond these theoretically distinct levels of authority for planning and execution, hybrid relationships emerge (operational-strategic and operational-tactical) which reflect the interdependent nature of Soviet military art. Theatre war-fare in Europe or Asia would involve both strategic and operational goals and forces. Consequently, medium- and intermediate-range ballistic missiles of the Strategic Rocket Forces are available to perform strategic strikes against high-value targets in the continental TVDs. Theatre warfare also embraces the operations of fronts, whose missions directly sup-port strategic objectives. But traditionally, a front's organic nuclear delivery means have not (until recently) possessed suf-ficient range to support the front's final objective, which can be more than 1000 km deep. Thus, missiles of the Strategic Rocket Forces directly support operational echelons (fronts). They perform, in effect, *operational-strategic* strikes.

Likewise, a hybrid category occurs between the operational and tactical levels. To illustrate, Soviet ballistic missiles are designed to achieve a certain minimum and maximum range. Thus, the minimum and maximum ranges of the Scud-B missile (80 and 300 km, respectively), which is a front and army delivery system, permit it to strike targets of interest to both operational and tactical command echelons. As such, the Soviet military refers to the Scud as an *operational-tactical* missile. Table 2.1 summarises a conceptual framework within which to discuss Soviet dual-capable theatre forces by relating delivery means to offensive depth and front objectives.

Dual-Capable Artillery

As discussed in Chapter 1, the Soviet development and deployment path to nuclear artillery differs notably from the approach taken by the USA and its Western allies. Rather than commingling nuclear artillery with division-level conventional artillery units, the Soviets at first chose to reconstitute World War II heavy artillery brigades consisting of towed 203-mm guns and 240-mm mortars. The fact that only some 300 of the latter towed pieces were reportedly deployed by the late 1970s suggested that this limited deployment represented a preliminary, experimental phase in the re-emergence of Soviet nuclear artillery.

Precisely when the more widespread deployment of truly dual-capable artillery began is uncertain, but it does appear to be linked in some fashion to the deployment of new self-propelled guns and howitzers in the mid-1970s. Indeed, the Soviets initiated a major improvement programme in their artillery arm to augment its capacity to keep pace with fast-moving manoeuvre forces. Only around 17% of Soviet artillery units in the Group of Forces, Germany, possessed self-propulsion by 1978; by the early 1980s, however, over 40% were so endowed.[2] Nuclear-capable SP versions now exist for the 152-mm howitzer and gun, as well as for the 203-mm gun and 240-mm mortar. The more numerous towed versions of the 152-mm gun are also believed to be nuclear capable.[3] Perhaps the most impressive capability of these artillery pieces is their range. The Soviet 152-mm guns and howitzers out-distance

Table 2.1   Conceptual framework.

Depths	Front Objectives	Inclusive Limits	Maximum Range of Objective	Delivery Systems	
Tactical		To enemy division rear boundaries	Forward edge of the battle area/battlefield	Nuclear artillery Frog, SS-21, Scud, SS-23, Frontal Air	Tactical
Immediate operational	Immediate	Into the enemy corps rear area	250-300 km	Scud, SS-23, SS-12/22, Frontal Air	Operational-Tactical
Operational	Long range	Into the enemy army group rear area	500-1000 km	SS-12/22, Strategic Aviation, SS-4, SS-20	Operational-Strategic
Strategic	Final	Remaining rear forces, logistical, political and economic centres	1000+ km	Strategic Aviation, SS-4, SS-20	

their nearest US equivalent (the 155–mm M109A2/A3) by nearly 60%, while the larger Soviet 203-mm guns have 30% greater range than the US M110A2 203-mm howitzer.[4] (See Table 2.2 for details.)

However impressive these figures may appear, it remains difficult to determine the extent to which the Soviets have deployed nuclear artillery throughout their ground forces. The difficulty lies in the distinction between truly certified nuclear artillery tubes, with nuclear rounds and trained crews readily available, and tubes for which there are no properly trained crews nor readily available ammunition. Numbers of Soviet nuclear-capable *delivery means* do not necessarily indicate an equivalent growth in nuclear artillery *shells* and properly trained crews. Nevertheless, the overall potential capability – especially the growth trend over the last decade – stands as most impressive. If we assume, for example, the availability of

Table 2.2   Soviet nuclear-capable artillery.

	2S3	2S5	M-1976	2S7	2S4
Location	Division	Army	Front	Front	Front
Propulsion	SP[b]	SP	Towed	SP	SP
Caliber	152-mm	152-mm	152-mm	203-mm	240-mm
Type	Howitzer	Gun	Gun	Gun	Mortar
Range (m)	27,000	28,500	28,500	30,000	9,700
IOC[a]	1972	1980	1978	1975	1975
Warhead yields	2-5 KT	2-5 KT	2-5 KT	2-5 KT	2-5 KT

[a]Initial operational capability
[b]Self-propelled

Sources: Soviet Military Power 1987 (Washington, D.C.: USGPO, 1987), p. 72 and *The Military Balance 1986–1987* (London: IISS, 1986), p. 205.

nuclear shells and appropriately trained troops, a Soviet wartime front – such as that formed out of the Soviet Group of Forces, Germany – would have well over 200 artillery pieces for
nuclear fire support.[5]

Strike Aircraft

The planned use of aircraft to deliver nuclear weapons in support of ground operations pre-dates the deployment of the first
Soviet short-range rockets and missiles. By 1954, Soviet
military exercises began to include air-delivered atomic
weapons in tactical operations. But aircraft, in general, and aircraft delivery of nuclear weapons, in particular, suffered a
serious decline in the Khrushchev years. At the operational and
tactical levels, the new Rocket Troops and Artillery service
assumed, for the most part, the missions of Frontal Aviation's
strike aircraft. Quite simply, a doctrine that foresaw massive
strategic nuclear missile strikes at the beginning of war left little
room for nuclear-capable Frontal Aviation.

A more balanced force development approach and the
acceptance of an escalating contingency in Soviet military
strategy during the early Brezhnev years furnished fertile
ground for substantial growth in Frontal Aviation's nuclear
role. As Chapter 1 notes, Frontal Aviation experienced a 90%
improvement in offensive load capacity between 1965 and
1977.

Although Fitter and Flogger make up the majority of the
current Soviet tactical ground-attack capability (over 1700
deployed), there are nearly 800 Fencer fighter-bombers now in
the Soviet Air Forces. First introduced in 1974, and still in production, the Fencer has over twice the combat radius (1300 km)
of Fitter and the same payload (3000 kg). More impressive is the
number of advanced air-to-surface missiles associated with
Fencer, to include the AS-10 through AS-14. Operating with
long-range navigation and electro-optical weapon delivery
capabilities, Fencers now provide Soviet theatre planners with

all-weather, day/night conventional and nuclear attack options to the full depth of the theatre. Indeed, the Fencer exemplifies the overall shift that has occurred in the Soviet Air Force's tactical force structure since 1978: the number of ground-attack regiments facing NATO has increased from 26 to 43, while fighter-interceptor units have declined by 14%.[6] What is more, Soviet fighter pilots are trained for both primary counter-air and secondary ground attack missions; thus, air superiority fighters like the new MIG-29/Fulcrum and SU-27/Flanker will not only be available to escort fighter-bombers on deep-penetration runs but also to conduct ground-attack missions. The technological sophistication of these latest additions to the Soviet air inventory challenges the notion that the West can rely on a qualitative edge in aircraft technology to offset the Warsaw Pact's 2.5 to 1 numerical superiority over NATO's air forces in Europe.[7]

More than half (450 of 800) of the Fencer fighter-bombers are assigned to the four theatre-oriented air armies of Soviet Strategic Aviation. It should be noted that the strike assets of these air armies also include 160 Backfire bombers and over 400 medium-range Blinder and Badger bombers. These aircraft, together with Fencer, provide primary deep-penetration aircraft support in theatre contingencies – nuclear and conventional alike.[8] Backfire production lines will probably remain open through the end of this decade, furnishing additional aircraft to create new units and to replace older models.

Estimates vary over just how many of what type of aircraft could be available for use in major hostilities in Central Europe. A conservative estimate suggests that around 1200 of over 2800 Soviet aircraft based in the Western TVD could be available for a conventional air operation, with over 200 aircraft reserved in a nuclear withhold status. This number of aircraft could be available without the need to sacrifice surprise by reinforcing forward bases in Eastern Europe before the beginning of hostilities. (See Table 2.3 for technical characteristics of aircraft, and Tables 2.4 and 2.5 for illustrations of aircraft availability.)

Table 2.3. Soviet dual-capable strike aircraft.

System	Service	Combat radius (km)	Max speed (Mach)	Armament weight (kg)
Medium-range bombers				
TU-16 Badger	1955	3100	.85	9000
TU-22 Blinder	1962	2900	1.4	5500
TU-26 Backfire	1974	4000	2.0	8000
Tactical Strike				
SU-7 Fitter A	1959	500	1.6	4000
MIG-21 Fishbed L	1970	750	2.0	1000
MIG-27 Flogger D/J	1971	600	1.7	3000
SU-17 Fitter D/H	1974	550	2.1	3000
SU-24 Fencer	1974	1300	2.0	3000

Sources: Soviet Military Power 1987 (Washington, D.C.: USGPO 1987), p. 36 and *The Military Balance 1986–1987* (London: IISS, 1986), p. 206.

Short-Range Ballistic Missiles

The first mobile short-range ballistic missile (Scud SS–1) and free rocket Frog (standing for *free rocket over ground*, which, technically, is not a ballistic missile) programmes were probably begun a year or two before Stalin's death. Although the new Rocket Troops and Artillery service fared much better than Frontal Aviation under Khrushchev, it by no means experienced unfettered growth. Limited quantities of Scud-A and Frog-1 were deployed, respectively, beginning in 1957 and 1958. Presumably, limits in short-range nuclear forces were tolerable under the then-dominant contingency, which foresaw such weapons as merely a mop-up force, not to be employed until after the execution of strategic nuclear attacks.

By the mid-1960s, however, the acceptance of an escalating contingency meant an expanded role for a front commander's

Table 2.4.   Soviet aircraft in the Western Theatre of
Military Operations.

Soviet Frontal Aviation		1671
Fighters	666	
Fighter-bombers	720	
Tactical bombers	90	
Recon/ECM	195	
Legnica Air Army		379
Fighters	135	
Tactical bombers	180	
Recon/ECM	64	
Smolensk Air Army		544
Bombers	416	
Recon/ECM	128	
Total		**2594**

Source: Phillip A. Petersen and Maj John R. Clark, "Soviet Air and
Antiair Operations," paper presented at the seminar, "New Technologies and the Economics of Defense," sponsored by the Hanns
Seidel Foundation and the Center for Strategic Concepts, LTD, 3–5
June 1987, Wildbad Kreuth, West Germany. Frontal Aviation figures
are based on fighter aviation regiments of 45 aircraft (ex-PVO
regiments at 36), fighter-bomber regiments of 45, tactical-bomber
regiments of 30, and reconnaissance electronic countermeasures
squadrons of 13. Reserve air army figures are based on fighter
regiments of 45 aircraft, tactical-bomber regiments of 30, and bomber
regiments (including reconnaissance aircraft) of 32.

short-range nuclear weapons. The product-improved Scud-B
and Frog-7, with increased range (300 and 70 km, respectively),
improved accuracy, and greater mobility, were introduced in
1961 and 1965, respectively. The anomalous SS-12 Scaleboard
short-range missile (900-km range) was deployed in 1967;
oddly, only in the Soviet Union. And by the late 1960s or early
1970s, Frog and Scud units began to increase in size; Frog battalions expanded from 3 to 4 launchers, while Scud brigades

Table 2.5.   Aircraft availability (without forward deployment) for the air operation in the Western Theatre of Military Operations.

	Total aircraft	Aircraft available	Nuclear withhold	First mass strike
Frontal Aviation				
Fighters	351	304	24	280
Fighter-bombers	405	351	27	324
Tactical bombers	60	48	10	38
Recon/ECM	117	100	9	91
Legnica Air Army				
Fighters	135	117	9	108
Tactical bombers	180	144	29	115
Recon/ECM	64	51	10	41
Smolensk Air Army				
Bombers	416	333	100	233
Recon/ECM	120	96	29	67
Total	1848	1544	247	1297

Source: Phillip A. Petersen and Maj John R. Clark, "Soviet Air and Antiair Operations," paper presented at the seminar, "New Technologies and the Economics of Defense," sponsored by the Hanns Seidel Foundation and the Center for Strategic Concepts, LTD, 3–5 June 1987, Wildbad Kreuth, West Germany. Frontal Aviation figures are based on fighter aviation regiments of 45 aircraft (ex-PVO regiments at 36), fighter-bomber regiments of 45, tactical-bomber regiments of 30, and reconnaissance electronic countermeasures squadrons of 13. Reserve air army figures are based on fighter regiments of 45 aircraft, tactical-bomber regiments of 30, and bomber regiments (including reconnaissance aircraft) of 32.

added an extra launcher to each of their three battalions, thereby increasing the brigade from 9 to 12 launchers.[9]

As previously discussed, an even greater expansion in dual-capable Frontal Aviation began to occur during this period. Not only was Frontal Aviation expected to play an increasingly important nuclear role, but a conventional one as well. Aircraft had to bear the brunt of strike missions during the conventional phase of war preceding nuclear escalation. By contrast, short-range missiles and rockets could contribute little to conventional fire support given their poor accuracies. They were simply too expensive a resource to be wasted on inefficient conventional fire missions.

In fact, the inability of Soviet military science to produce sufficiently accurate guidance systems for these missiles appears to have had a desultory effect on new missile development. A recent examination of Soviet land-based missile development programmes from 1950 to 1976 reveals a consistent growth pattern with one important exception: an interlude in new development activity from 1962 to 1971, during which Soviet defence decision-makers decided not to start any new short-range missile or rocket development programmes.[10] Without a solution to the accuracy problem – then, a technologically challenging task, indeed – Soviet defence officials apparently saw little purpose in further new development (versus modest product improvement as with the Frog 1-7 series) just to improve short-range missile range, reliability, and readiness, especially during a decade of dramatic resource allocation to the Strategic Rocket Forces and new tactical strike aircraft.

The Soviets initiated new development programmes in earnest, beginning in 1971 (SS-21) and continuing into the decade (SS-12/22 in 1973, and the SS-23 in 1975).[11] They even reportedly began a Scud product-improvement programme called the KY-3 (a temporary US designation for a missile test program at Kapustin Yar range), which seems to have culminated in the deployment of a 400-km range Scud-C toward the end of the decade.[12] It now appears that the initial versions of the three new missiles replacing Frog, Scud, and Scaleboard may not have possessed the kind of terminal effectiveness (a combination of high accuracy and tailored munitions) needed for broad-scale conventional use.[13] But by the end of the decade, follow-on versions apparently demonstrated major improvements in guidance and munition effectiveness. A 1979 partially declassified threat briefing by the US Tactical Air Command reports that

> previously, Soviet SRBMs [short-range ballistic missiles] were considered primarily a nuclear threat. However, recent evidence indicates the Soviets may be developing a credible conventional SRBM capability against a variety of threats, including airfields.[14]

The basis for the above concern about a truly dual-capable force of Soviet short-range ballistic missiles was revealed by a senior Pentagon official who disclosed that upgraded models of the SS-21, SS-22, and SS-23 have accuracies permitting their payloads to hit within 30 m of their targets.[15] Soviet military specialists claim that such accuracies are obtained by combining upgraded inertial guidance and either an in-flight update or terminal guidance.[16] By comparison, US terminal guidance systems for ballistic missiles such as Pershing II produce roughly the same accuracies as those reported for upgraded Soviet missiles. This improved accuracy for new Soviet missiles represents an advancement over their predecessors (Frog, Scaleboard, and Scud) by around a factor of 25.[17] And by no means would this mean a terminal point in development. In discussing general evolutionary improvements in conventional weapons, one senior Soviet military observer expects "that the new generation of armaments will be superior to the previous in terms of range several times over, in power tens of times, and in accuracy hundreds of times."[18] All in all, it seems prudent to assume that the earliest of the new generation of missiles (the SS-21) already possesses sufficient accuracy to deliver conventional submunitions effectively, and that by the end of this decade the longer-range SS-23 and SS-22 missiles could have been deployed with guidance systems roughly comparable to extant US technology (Pershing II).

Political circumstances surrounding the introduction of new missiles into Soviet forces in Eastern Europe have obscured their precise deployment status. In October 1983, Moscow announced that the Soviet Union intended to deploy "enhanced range operational-tactical missile complexes" in East Germany and Czechoslovakia in retaliation for NATO's deployment of Pershing II and cruise missiles.[19] Although the Western response mistakenly described the Soviet retaliation as including the SS-21, SS-22, and SS-23 missiles, it now appears certain that the counterdeployment consisted of precisely what Moscow announced: that is, an "enhanced range operational-tactical" missile refers to one with a range longer than a standard "operational-tactical" missile, such as Scud or its intended replacement, the SS-23. That could only mean the SS-12 Scaleboard or its product-improved cousin, the SS-22 (now officially called SS-12 mod), both of which have a 900-km range. Thus, Moscow's retaliatory measure consisted of moving the SS-12/22 Scaleboard from its sanctuary in the Soviet homeland into Eastern Europe, within closer range of its intended wartime targets. Replacing Scud missiles with the SS-23 represented an evolutionary modernisation of the Warsaw Pact operational-tactical missile inventory in Eastern Europe.

Current and Projected Deployments of Short-Range Ballistic Missiles

The 100-km range SS-21 Scarab, which is not affected by the INF treaty's provisions, has been replacing the 70-km range Frog-7 in Soviet tank and motorised rifle divisions since 1976. All of the 76 launchers with Soviet divisions in East Germany have been replaced by the new missile system at a reported rate of four per month.[20] To date, over 130 SS-21 launchers have been deployed in the Western TVD, with around 100 forward deployed with Soviet, East German, and Czech ground-force units.[21] Overall, approximately 800 Frog/SS-21 launchers face the NATO region, 200 of which are deployed with non-Soviet Warsaw Pact forces. Elsewhere, there are 215 deployed along the Chinese border and in the Soviet Far East; 100 facing South West Asia and eastern Turkey; and around 75 in strategic reserve.[22] The SS-21 missile is delivered by a launcher similar in design to the SA-8 surface-to-air missile transporter. It is a six-wheeled, lightly armoured, amphibious vehicle which furnishes the SS-21 system with better mobility than its predecessor.

According to official reports, the army- and front-level SS-23 missile system (nicknamed Spider) began to replace the SS-IC/ Scud-B missile during 1985 in one missile brigade in the Belorussian Military District.[23] In view of the fact that the SS-23 first became operational in 1980, it is curious that only 82 launchers and 200 missiles were deployed as of December 1987, as reported in the INF Memorandum of Understanding.[24] In fact, reports before the INF data base disclosures indicated as few as only two or three dozen deployed SS-23s.[25] Although the higher number of deployed SS-23s may have come as a surprise, it is still a small number given the large inventory of over 700 Scud launchers and several thousand missiles facing NATO, which the SS-23 was intended to replace.

Perhaps the unavailability in the early 1980s of a suitable guidance system promising accuracies sufficient for conventional weapon delivery was the constraining factor in the SS-23's slow deployment rate. Alternatively, given past Soviet problems with solid-fuel missiles, it would not be surprising for them to have encountered some problems with the solid-fuel SS-23.[26] Either one or both of these explanations may help rationalise the reported deployment of a product-improved Scud-C, which is said to have a range of 400 km, 100 km more than the Scud-B's range. Political events may also have combined with technical problems to slow the pace of SS-23 deployment. Soviet politico-military decision-makers have been aware since the first US draft INF treaty was tabled in 1981 that short-range ballistic missiles, with ranges between 500 and 1000 km, represented a potential obstacle to a treaty. Although this may not have been a factor until recently, it certainly could have dissuaded the Soviets from initiating a broadscale one-for-one (SS-23 for Scud) deployment program in the midst of delicate INF negotiations. Any technical problems associated with the SS-23 would have only reinforced such a decision.

Although the SS-23 will be eliminated under the INF agreement, there are no restrictions prohibiting the Soviets from testing and deploying a replacement for Scud-B/C missile units, as long as the new missile is not tested to a range of 500 km or more. Over 700 Scud launchers face NATO, with around 120 deployed in non-Soviet Warsaw Pact units. Elsewhere in the Soviet Union, 100 Scud launchers are deployed along the Chinese border and in the Soviet Far East; 75 are active in South West Asia; and 25 or so are maintained in strategic reserve.

The front-level, 900-km range SS-22 (now referred to in the West as the SS-12 mod) began replacing the SS-12 Scaleboard missile in 1979. A change in designation from SS-22 to SS-12 mod suggests that the new missile does not represent a wholesale generational change over its predecessor. In fact, it relies on the same transporter-erector-launcher as does the SS-12.[27] The modified SS-12 missile is probably an improved version of the original Scaleboard two-stage, solid-fuel missile, with perhaps the most substantial improvement manifested in the guidance system.[28]

The Scaleboard embodies the heart of the Soviet retaliation for Pershing and cruise missile deployments. The INF data base indicates that 58 Scaleboard launchers, probably configured into three or four brigades, were deployed into East Germany and Czechoslovakia beginning in late 1983 or early 1984. This was the first time that Soviet missiles of such an extended range (900 km) had been deployed outside Soviet borders. From launch locations in Eastern Europe, the Scaleboard extends Soviet missile coverage to more than half of the United Kingdom; its forward deployment also avoids the loss of surprise that would result from the 700-km trek from the western USSR into Eastern Europe during a delicate crisis period preceding war. Scaleboard's elimination under the INF treaty removes a key deep-strike capability from Soviet forces based forward in Eastern Europe.

What remains odd about the Scaleboard is its history of limited deployment. Only 115 launchers are deployed altogether – roughly half in East Germany and Czechoslovakia, and the other half scattered in various peripheral military districts in the Soviet homeland. What may help explain Scaleboard's limited deployment is its unusually long range (900 km) for a front-subordinated missile system. Although the standard front missile system (the Scud family and now the SS-23) has increasingly seen its range extended over the years, there is still a difference of 400 km between Spider and Scaleboard. Indeed, the Scaleboard stands just below the range – 1000 km – that would make it an asset of the Strategic Rocket Forces. In short, the maximum range of influence of a front commander and Scaleboard's range are not nearly compatible. Thus, Scaleboard, falls between the cracks, so to speak, as represented by the interests of a front commander and those of the SRF. In this respect, Scaleboard has always been a missile with a weak institutional footing within the Soviet Ground Forces. General Secretary Gorbachev may not have encountered much military opposition to his willingness to eliminate Scaleboard from the Ground Forces' missile inventory.

Missile and Launcher Growth
According to an official account, Soviet short-range ballistic missile units opposite the NATO region have as many as four reload missiles per launcher.[29] Given the dramatic improvement in accuracy for the new generation of Soviet short-range ballistic missiles, one should expect to see consequent growth in missile stockages in order to support the anticipated increase in the volume of conventional fire support. In fact, the estimated annual production rate for Soviet short-range ballistic missiles increased from 300 to 350 in 1983.[30] The supposition about growth in missile stockages to support conventional fire needs is borne out in the Soviet INF data base disclosure, especially and most surprisingly in the case of Scaleboard refire missiles. Generally, it is telling to note that the ratio of missiles to launchers (deployed and non-deployed) in the shorter-range category (SS-12 and SS-23) – nearly 4 to 1 – is significantly larger than the 1.3 to 1 ratio in the longer-range category (SS-20, SS-4, and SS-5). This supports the fact that shorter-range missiles would be involved in chemical and conventional as well as nuclear strike missions. But what was unexpected about the INF disclosure is the better than 5 to 1 ratio of missiles to launchers for the Scaleboard system. This

may suggest that the Soviets had an important non-nuclear fire mission in mind for the Scaleboard. If so, this missile could now have much better accuracy than is generally assumed to be the case.[31]

Soviet short-range missile units are also in the midst of a significant growth spurt. Army- and front-subordinated missile brigades are expanding from 12 to 18 launchers per unit; this increase represents the addition of another 2-launcher battery to each of the brigade's three battalions.[32] This growth appears similar to the incremental approach employed to expand Scud brigades from 6 to 9 launchers during the 1960s, and then from 9 to 12 launchers during the 1970s.[33] Such growth in short-range missile launchers would not only increase the number of launchers needed for conventional missions, where volume of fire delivered within a narrow timeframe is so important, but it could also compensate for the possible need to withhold some part of the force to enable a rapid change from conventional to nuclear warfare.

It is frequently assumed that virtually all of the total inventory of short-range missile launchers – around 1000 launchers – located throughout the western military districts of the Soviet Union and in Eastern Europe could be available for the first salvo in conventional or nuclear operations. But these launchers belong to Soviet and Warsaw Pact ground force formations. Because they have an organic support relationship to divisions (Frog and SS-21), armies (Scud and SS-23), and fronts (Scud, SS-23, and SS-12 mod), they have geographic boundaries within which they operate. Soviet missile units are echeloned in depth in the same fashion as the ground formations they support. Thus, even in the case where the Soviets decide to reinforce their existing units in Eastern Europe before war begins, armies from the Belorussian, Baltic, and Carpathian military districts and their supporting missile units would not participate in any significant way in initial operations. For example, a pre-war reinforcement might add one front to the northern, central, and south-western fronts; this would mean the addition of fewer than 70 launchers to the 350, or so, that now face NATO's Central Region from locations in East Germany and Czechoslovakia. (See Table 2.6 for technical characteristics of missiles. Tables 2.7 and 2.8 provide current and projected missile launchers organic to Warsaw Pact ground units in East Germany and Czechoslovakia.)

New Short-Range Ballistic Missile Development
With the elimination of the SS-23 under the INF treaty's provisions, the Soviet military will have strong incentives to deploy a new army- and front-level (operational-tactical) missile to replace the ageing Scud-B. It would not be surprising to see the Soviets begin testing a new missile with a range just under the 500-km lower limit of the treaty. In fact, according to a 1984 Department of Defence report, there was evidence that the Soviets were developing a new short-range ballistic missile that could possibly be ready for deployment by the end of this decade or the early 1990s.[34] A more recent report suggests the imminence of new testing.[35] Were testing to commence in 1988, a new SS-23 follow-on missile could probably become operational by 1994, if not sooner. One can safely expect the Soviets to borrow heavily from their investment in the SS-23 programme.

The Soviet military may already possess an interim solution to the ageing Scud-B problem – namely the product-improved Scud-C. Assuming that it has not already been deployed in significant numbers, the Soviets could decide to deploy it as a replacement for Scud-B pending the development of an entirely new missile. There is also no apparent technical barrier (nor an arms control one) preventing the Soviets from qualitatively upgrading the Scud-C (or Scud-B, for that matter) by replacing its existing guidance system with the SS-23's much improved version. The INF treaty's provisions permit each side to retain the "nuclear warhead device and guidance elements" of affected missiles, which could then be used in existing or future systems.[36] Some testing would naturally be required of any upgraded missile system, but as long as testing did not violate the 500-km lower limit provision, it would be permitted under the INF treaty. The Soviet military's incentive for such an interim solution and/or new follow-on missile programme is

Table 2.6. Soviet short-range ballistic missiles.

System	Location	Service	Max range (km)	CEP (m)	Warheads
Frog-7	Division	1965	70	800	HE nuclear chemical
SS-21 Scarab	Division	1976	100	30–50	ICM nuclear chemical
Scud-B	Army, Front	1961	300	570–900	HE nuclear chemical
Scud-C	Army, Front	1978	400	Unknown[a]	poss. ICM nuclear chemical
SS-23 Spider	Army, Front	1980	500	350 30–50 likely	ICM nuclear chemical
SS-12 Scaleboard	Front	1967	900	463–927	nuclear
SS-12 mod	Front	1979	900	300 30–50 likely	ICM nuclear

[a]Theoretically capable of incorporating advanced guidance to achieve 30 to 50 m CEP.

Sources: "The Effectiveness of United States Military Aid to Israel (ISMILAID)," Vol. 1, declasified (US Department of Defense, December 1974), p. IV 80; "Memorandum for the Verification Panel Working Groups, Subject: FBS and Other Non-Central Systems in Salt Two," declassified (US Department of State, October 1972), p. 23; Walter Andrews, "Allies' Weapons Said to be Inadequate to Threat of New Soviet Missile Power," *Washington Times*, 1 November 1984, p. 3; "Missile Deployment Strains U.S.-European Alliance, Tass Claims," *Washington Times*, 30 May 1984, p. 6; and *The Military Balance 1986–*

1987 (London: IISS, 1986), p. 205; Kerry L. Hines, "Short-Range Ballistic Missiles," *International Defense Review*, no. 12, 1985, p. 1913; and David C. Isby, *Weapons and Tactics of the Soviet Army* (New York: Jane's, 1981), p. 213.

straightforward: although Soviet planners might lose coverage of certain deep targets in NATO's Central Region with the elimination of SS-12/22 and SS-23, most critical airfields, nuclear storage sites, and air defence units could still be held at risk by an upgraded Scud-C or a new 450-km range ballistic missile.

Finally, there will always be ambiguity in verifying whether a new short-range ballistic missile, flight tested to just under the treaty threshold (500 km), actually has the capability to strike targets beyond the range threshold. Full-range testing is not essential to furnish confidence that a missile can reliably perform at ranges beyond what is reflected in a flight test programme.

Cruise Missiles

Noteworthy is the growing Soviet interest in cruise missiles, none of which are now assessed as dual-capable. Nor do they appear destined for deployment with Soviet forces in Eastern Europe. The 3000-km range AS-15, a clone of the US Tomahawk, became operational in 1984 with the long-range Bear H aircraft. It will probably also be employed with the new Blackjack strategic bomber once it becomes operational. The ground-mobile version of the AS-15, designated the SSC-X-4, will be eliminated under the provisions of the INF treaty. The INF data base disclosure indicated, somewhat surprisingly, that 84 SSC-X-4 cruise missiles have been produced but not yet deployed. Such non-deployed systems must be eliminated within the first six months after treaty ratification. Employment missions and deployment areas would probably have mirrored those of the SS-20 intermediate-range ballistic missile force. There is also a sea-launched cousin, the SS-NX-21, which is sufficiently small to be accommodated in standard

Table 2.7. Projection of Warsaw Pact short-range ballistic missile launchers facing NATO's Central Region in peacetime in 1990 to 1995.

Type	Country deploying	Location	Launcher total
SS-21	USSR	GDR	76
SS-21	USSR	CSSR	20
SS-21	GDR	GDR	24
SS-21	CSSR	CSSR	40
SS-23	USSR	GDR	144
SS-23	USSR	CSSR	36
Scud-B	GDR	GDR	24
Scud-B	CSSR	CSSR	27
SS-12 mod	USSR	GDR	36
SS-12 mod	USSR	CSSR	18
Total			**445**

Note: Projection is based on the following assumptions: (1) Each SS-21 battalion has 4 launchers. (2) Each SS-23 brigade at front and army has 18 launchers. (3) One SS-12 brigade each would support the northern, central, and south-western fronts facing NATO's Central Region in wartime. (4) By 1990, the SS-23 will not have replaced the 24 GDR and 27 CSSR Scud launchers. If we assume pressure by Moscow, these 51 additional launchers could be replaced with SS-23s by 1995.

Sources: Author's estimate is based on data in *Soviet Military Power 1986* (Washington, D.C.: USGPO, 1986); Kerry L. Hines, "Soviet Short-Range Ballistic Missile," *International Defense Review* No. 12, December 1985, pp. 1909–1914; *The Military Balance 1986–1987* (London: IISS, 1986); and Donald R. Cotter, James H. Hansen, and Kirk McConnell, "The Nuclear 'Balance' in Europe: Status, Trends, Implications," *USSR Review*, 83–1 (Washington, D.C.: United States Strategic Institute, 1983).

Table 2.8.   Post-INF projection of Warsaw Pact short-range ballistic missile launchers facing NATO's Central Region in peacetime in 1990 to 1995.

Type	Country deploying	Total	Launcher total
SS-21	USSR	GDR	76
SS-21	USSR	CSSR	20
SS-21	GDR	GDR	24
SS-21	CSSR	CSSR	40
Scud-B/C or SS-23 follow-on	USSR	GDR	144
Scud-B/C or SS-23 follow-on	USSR	CSSR	36
Scud-B	GDR	GDR	24
Scud-B	CSSR	CSSR	27
Total			391

Note: Projection is based on the following assumptions: (1) Each SS-21 battalion has 4 launchers. (2) Each Scud-B/C or SS-23 follow-on brigade at front and army has 18 launchers. (3) By 1990 to 1995, non-Soviet Pact missile units could have upgraded Scud-Cs as part of a normal modernisation programme. Although not indicated here, launcher growth is also a distinct possibility.

Sources: Author's estimate is based on data in *Soviet Military Power 1986* (Washington, D.C.: USGPO, 1986); Kerry L. Hines, "Soviet Short-Range Ballistic Missile," *International Defense Review*, No. 12, December 1985, pp. 1909–1914; *The Military Balance 1986–1987* (London: IISS, 1986); and Donald R. Cotter, James H. Hansen, and Kirk McConnell, "The Nuclear 'Balance' in Europe: Status, Trends, Implications," *USSR Review* 83–1 (Washington, D.C.: United States Strategic Institute, 1983).

Soviet torpedo tubes. The naval version is also expected to become operational in 1987. Much larger (roughly 12 m *vice* 7) sea- and possibly ground-launched cruise missiles (GLCMs) are under development. The naval version has already been tested from a specially configured Yankee-class cruise missile attack submarine. The range of these larger missiles is currently unknown.

Even though the Soviets could eventually furnish cruise missiles with sufficient accuracy to undertake conventional missions, it is doubtful that cruise missiles would supplant short-range ballistic missiles in the role of primary support to the conventional air operation. Cruise missiles simply do not possess many of the attributes Soviet planners find so compelling with ballistic missiles – primarily, prompt, assured penetration to the target, which enhances surprise, shock effect, and close co-ordination with subsequent aircraft attacks. Rather, in a conventional role, ground- and, possibly, sea-launched cruise missiles could supplement aircraft by increasing the weight and effectiveness of the dominant aerodynamic threat.

As far as nuclear missions are concerned, sea- and air-launched cruise missiles could, in theory, play an important role in a post-INF timeframe. The elimination of the mobile (and thus highly survivable) SS-20 force implies that Soviet planners will seek to replace at least a portion of the consequent lost target coverage. Intercontinental ballistic missiles and submarine-launched ballistic missiles could be allocated to theatre targeting missions, but a future strategic arms reduction agreement might constrain such an option. In this respect, cruise missiles may offer an attractive way of reconstituting the SS-20's most important mission: that of surviving a protracted conventional and possibly limited nuclear conflict to threaten massive theatre-wide nuclear escalation. The best choice for this mission would have been the SSC-X-4 ground-launched cruise missile because it could have been fully dedicated to perform the SS-20's reserve role. But its elimination under the INF treaty means that Soviet planners will have to rely on less-preferred choices like air- and sea-launched cruise missiles.

The latter are delivered by air and naval platforms that have multiple missions, which thereby compromise the extent of their contribution to replacing lost SS-20 target coverage.

Nuclear, Chemical, and Conventional Munitions

The prevailing notion, until recently, was that very few, if any, nuclear warheads for short-range forces were stored routinely in Eastern Europe. A masive nuclear-use contingency, in which longer-range, homeland-based forces are counted on for primary theatre strikes, furnishes a comforting logic to explain why Soviet planners would appear so unready to employ shorter-range forces.[37] But the logic of an escalating contingency, in which tactical and operational-tactical nuclear forces would be called upon before strategic nuclear forces, makes limited or no storage in Eastern Europe a risky proposition indeed for the Soviets.

Official Western reaction to Moscow's May 1983 threats to counterbalance NATO's INF deployments by basing similar weapons in Eastern Europe failed to clarify the ambiguity surrounding Soviet nuclear warheads in Eastern Europe. Wanting to downplay the military and political significance of Moscow's threats, Western officials acknowledged that both Soviet short-range delivery systems and their nuclear warheads have been based on Eastern European soil for many years.[38] Ironically, the Soviets probably had no desire to draw attention to the warhead storage issue; they merely sought to threaten a response in kind by deploying "enhanced-range operational-tactical missile complexes" to East Germany and Czechoslovakia. In the confusing aftermath of the threat, the nuclear warhead storage issue inevitably was raised in the many attempts to understand the precise nature of Moscow's retaliation. It was also inevitable that doubts would linger despite acknowledgement by US officials of Soviet nuclear warheads outside Soviet borders, as well as ambiguous references by Soviet officials.[39] Short of inspecting Soviet nuclear stockpile sites in Eastern Europe, which, according to a SHAPE report, contain approximately 4000 nuclear warheads,[40] ambiguity will always surround such a sensitive issue as nuclear stockpile locations and quantities. In retrospect, what is most surprising about the Soviet counterdeployments in Eastern Europe is Moscow's willingness to risk the internal consequences of drawing public attention to her nuclear presence on allied soil. Indeed, Moscow's new deployments produced more anxiety on the eastern side of the border than in Western Europe.

Although sound military reasons compel belief that the USSR has based a full complement of nuclear warheads for shorter-range forces in Eastern Europe, Moscow will continue to make its forward nuclear basing as opaque as possible. As long as Soviet planning authorities maintain an interest in an escalating contingency, in which Warsaw Pact nuclear forces would be required to pre-empt what remains of NATO's theatre nuclear forces after even a very short conventional phase, it seems safe to assume that the requisite number of nuclear warheads will be readily available to support Soviet tactical and operational-tactical force requirements.

Dramatic improvement in the accuracy of short-range delivery systems suggests a strong set of Soviet incentives to produce lower-yield nuclear warheads and bombs. Take, for example, the case of short-range ballistic missiles. Before the introduction of the new generation of missiles, Soviet planners could only contemplate rather high-yield weapons to achieve their attack objectives in Europe. Figure 2.1 illustrates the influence of improving accuracy on the size (number of strikes and total nuclear yield) of an attack. Most NATO targets are soft; that is, they are less than ten pounds per square inch (psi) in hardness. As Figure 2.1 shows, the relative inaccuracy of Frog, Scud, and Scaleboard missiles meant either the expenditure of several missiles per target if 10-KT warheads were desired or, more likely, a major increase in warhead yields. By contrast, the new generation missiles with 50-m or better accuracies could effectively destroy even much harder targets in a single strike using 10-KT warheads. In fact, assuming a missile accuracy of 50 m, the highest yield needed is 10 KT to destroy aircraft in shelters and to neutralise reinforcement operations at sea ports of debarkation. Overall, roughly 70% of

Figure 2.1.   Number of 10 KT weapons per 100 × 100 m target (10 psi hardness) to achieve a kill probability of one assuming a weapon reliability of one.

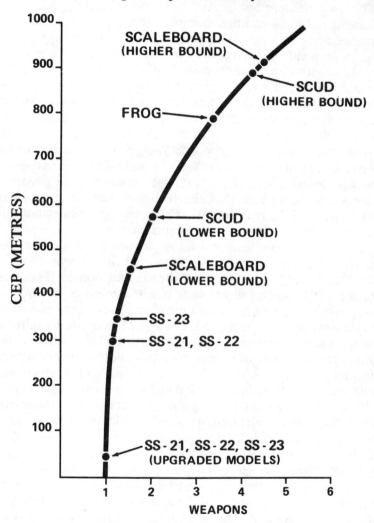

Sources: "The Effectiveness of United States Military Aid to Israel (ISMILAID)," Vol. 1, declassified (US Department of Defense,

December 1974), p. IV 80; "Memorandum for the Verification Panel Working Groups, Subject: FBS and Other Non-Central Systems in Salt Two," declassified (US Department of State, October 1972), p. 23; Walter Andrews, "Allies' Weapons Said to be Inadequate to Threat of New Soviet Missile Power," *Washington Times*, 1 November 1984, p. 3; "Missile Deployment Strains US–European Alliance, Tass Claims," *Washington Times*, 30 May 1984, p. 6; and *The Military Balance* (London: IISS, 1985–86), p. 162.

the entire fixed target set facing Soviet war planners could be effectively attacked with nuclear warheads of much less than a kiloton in yield.[41]

The above calculations are not meant to suggest the availability of sub-kiloton nuclear yields for current or projected Soviet short-range delivery systems. Rather, they only suggest the potential inherent in highly accurate delivery means. It is also important to note that Soviet targeteers have strong incentives to maintain higher yields in their nuclear inventory to deal with large manoeuvre targets (battalion-sized targets) and critical mobile targets that are imprecisely located.

Despite the purposeful ambiguity that surrounds Soviet offensive chemical warfare intent, Warsaw Pact artillery, missile, and air units reputedly are equipped with a vast stockpile of chemical agents, with US Department of Defense estimates ranging up to 700,000 agent tons. To counter these estimates, the Soviet Foreign Ministry released a statement in late December 1987 reporting that Soviet stockpiles "do not exceed 50,000 tons of poisonous substances."[42] Although the USA has not released the size of its stockpile, the Soviet Foreign Ministry statement indicated, not surprisingly, that the Soviet stockpile corresponds in size to the American one. Whatever the true size of the Soviet chemical stockpile, it is thought to contain a variety of nerve, blister, and choking agents in persistent and non-persistent forms. The Soviets are also investigating binary chemical weapons, which offer not only safer handling and storage potential, but also new possibilities for agent combinations.[43]

The Soviet military is served well by an active research and advanced development programme in the basic technologies supporting conventional munitions for short-range system delivery. In a recent US Department of Defense assessment of relative USA–USSR standing in 20 basic technology areas, the USA leads in 14 key technologies.[44] But in the area of conventional warhead technologies, the two countries stand even. Equally important, in the area of missile-delivered weapons, the proponent within the Soviet military (the Rocket Troops and Artillery) commands a powerful bureaucratic position. This strength contrasts sharply with the woeful state of conventional munitions proponency within the US military services, where platform procurement virtually eclipses systematic development and procurement of advanced conventional munitions.

Expressions of Soviet interest in developing tailored conventional munitions are not new. As long ago as 1968, when requirements were probably formulated and initial design work commenced for the new generation of dual-capable ballistic missiles, Soviet military specialists were discussing various ways missiles with 500 to 1000 kg of payload could be more effectively employed using submunitions.[45] Not surprisingly, NATO officials recently revealed that the Soviet military is developing submunition payloads for the SS-12 mod and SS-23 missiles, while the SS-21 is already deployed with such a conventional payload.[46]

A full panoply of conventional submunitions is being examined, and possibly developed and deployed, including high explosive, fragmentation, incendiary, shaped charge, and anti-armour bomblets and minelets, in both unguided and terminally guided packages.[47] An article in the Polish military literature notes the importance of "attacks by missile troops involving the use of cluster charges with conventional weapons."[48] Cluster munitions spread the available energy over a wide area by dividing the overall explosive weight into a number of smaller containers or submunitions. Area munitions of this sort appear ideally suited for attacks against soft targets, such as air defence batteries and handling and transport equipment at nuclear storage sites.

Another approach is to use fuel air explosives (FAEs), which disperse an aerosol that mixes with the air and then detonates by a burster charge. FAEs spread the energy uniformly over a large area and produce an explosive effect comparable to a very low-yield nuclear weapon. The Soviet military in Afghanistan has reportedly used FAEs delivered by SU-17 fighter-bombers. They are said to have created a crater 30 feet in diameter, and 18 feet in depth, and to have a 400-m radius of effect against personnel.[49]

Soviet military authors have also closely followed Western progress in specialised munitions for airfield attack.[50] Indeed, it appears that they already possess specialised munitions for attacking airfields. As one Warsaw Pact author noted in 1982, "the Rocket Troops would conduct attacks using warheads with submunitions against enemy air-base targets."[51] Although evidence is thin on the current availability of kinetic-energy penetrating munitions for aircraft or missile delivery, such weapons are likely to appear soon in the Soviet inventory, if they are not there already. But attacking runways is not the only method for suppressing air-base operations for short periods; the Soviet military has also investigated ways of temporarily limiting the manoeuvre capacity of targets (in this case aircraft) in cases when conventional munitions cannot meet optimal damage expectations.[52] An example of such an attack technique might involve "pin down" precursor missile attacks against NATO air bases designed to prevent the launching of aircraft until mass wave of bombers can follow up with more decisive attacks. Runway busting submunitions or anti-vehicle and anti-personnel mines – which are already in the Soviet inventory[53] – or a combintaion thereof would serve well in such short-duration (less than one hour) harassment and delay attacks.

Notes

1. A front does not exist in peacetime. It is a Soviet wartime organisation formed from armies in a military district or external group of forces. A front would be formed from armies in the

Group of Forces, Germany in case of war with NATO. NATO.

2. David C. Isby, *Weapons and Tactics of the Soviet Army* (New York: Jane's, 1981), p. 199. Also see Christopher Bellamy, *Red God of War* (London: Brassey's, 1986) for an excellent treatment of the role of artillery in Soviet operational art and tactics.

3. Official confirmation of these deployments is reported in *Soviet Military Power 1986* (Washington, D.C.: USGPO, 1986), p. 39. Also see Christopher Bellamy, "Soviet Artillery and Tactical Rocket Design," *Jane's Defence Review*, Vol. 4, No. 8, 1983, pp. 775–787.

4. *Soviet Military Power 1987* (Washington, D.C.: USGPO, 1987), p. 41.

5. For a breakdown of organic artillery support to a front, see Jeffrey D. McCausland, "Soviet Short-Range Nuclear Forces and Doctrine," *Comparative Strategy*, Vol. 5, No. 3, 1985, p. 312.

6. *Soviet Military Power 1987, op. cit.*, in Note 4, p. 67. An air regiment can have as many as 45 aircraft.

7. For a detailed evaluation of recent Soviet technological advances in aircraft, see John W. R. Taylor, "Fulcrum: A Close Look," *Jane's Defence Weekly*, 2 August 1986, pp. 163–164.

8. *Soviet Military Power 1987, op. cit.*, in Note 4, p. 37.

9. Donald R. Cotter, James H. Hansen, and Kirk McConnell, "The Nuclear 'Balance' in Europe: Status, Trends, Implications," *USSI Report 83-1* (Washington, D.C.: United States Strategic Institute, 1983), pp. 41–45.

10. Stephen M. Meyer, "Soviet Theatre Nuclear Forces, Part II: Capabilities and Implications," *Adelphi Papers*, No. 188 (London: IISS, 1983/84), p. 2.

11. *Ibid.*, p. 56. Midpoint on the uncertainty scale has been selected as the developmental starting point for each new missile.

12. Reference to the KY-3 as a product-improved Scud is made in Steven J. Zaloga, "Soviet Weapons Designations: Part 1," *Jane's Defence Weekly*, 2 May 1987, p. 837. The Scud-C is reported in Isby, *op. cit.* in Note 2, p. 213. Barton Wright, *Soviet Missiles* (Lexington, MA: Lexington Books, 1986) reports various ranges for the Scud-C from 450 to 724 km.

13. Meyer, *op. cit.*, in Note 10, p. 54. Meyer reports accuracies (averaged) of 200, 300, and 400 m for the SS-21, SS-22, and SS-23, respectively.

14. Quoted in William Arkin and Jeffrey T. Sands, "The Soviet

Nuclear Stockpile," *Arms Control Today*, June 1984, p. 5.

15. The official was Undersecretary of Defense for Research Engineering, Richard D. DeLauer, as reported by Walter Andrews, "Allies' Weapons Said to be Inadequate to Threat of New Soviet Missile Power," *Washington Times*, 1 November 1984. An accuracy of 50 yards is reported in "Missile Deployment Strains US-European Alliance, Tass Claims," *Washington Times*, 30 May 1984.

16. A. Starostin, "Tactical Rockets," *Tekhnika i Vooruzheniye*, No. 11, November 1981, pp. 8–9.

17. Frog, Scaleboard, and Scud accuracy estimates (800, 463–927, and 570-900 m, respectively) are derived from Secretary of Defense, *The Effectiveness of United States Military Aid to Israel (ISMILAID)*, Vol. 1, December 1974, declassified; and Department of State, *Memorandum for the Verification Panel Working Group*, 2 October 1972, declassified.

18. I. Vorob'ev, "Modern Weapons and Tactics," *Krasnaya Zvezda*, 15 September 1984, p. 2. It is difficult to imagine ballistic missiles. achieving better than perhaps 5 to 10-m accuracies in the future, given their re-entry velocities. Cruise missiles, on the other hand, hold the promise of achieving accuracies of 1 to 3 m. See *Armed Forces Journal International*, March 1983, p. 80.

19. The term was employed, for example, by Moscow Radio Peace and Progress, 16 May 1984, as translated by the BBC, *USSR International Affairs*, 17 May 1984.

20. Michael Getler, "New Generation of Soviet Arms Near Deployment," *Washington Post*, 11 October 1983.

21. *Soviet Military Power 1987, op. cit.*, in Note 4, p. 66.

22. Deployment figures are derived from *op. cit.* in Note 4, p. 41, and Kerry L. Hines, "Soviet Short-Range Ballistic Missiles," *International Defense Review*, December 1985, p. 1913.

23. *Soviet Military Power 1987, op. cit.* in Note 4, p. 41.

24. Hines, *op. cit.* in Note 22 reports the SS-23's initial operational capability as 1980. For details on the INF treaty's data base and Memorandum of Understanding, see *Arms Control Today*, January/February 1988, p. 28.

25. *Ibid.*

26. See Robert P. Berman and John C. Baker, *Soviet Strategic Forces: Requirements and Responses* (Washington, D.C.: The Brookings Institution, 1982), p. 54.

27. *International Defense Review*, No. 4, 1984, p. 373.

28. According to *Soviet Military Power 1987*, the new Scaleboard's accuracy is sufficient to permit the weapon to be employed with non-nuclear warheads.

29. Caspar W. Weinberger, *Annual Report to Congress, Fiscal Year 1988*, p. 30.

30. *Force Structure Summary – USSR, Eastern Europe, and Mongolia*, Defense Intelligence Agency, DDB-2680-170A-85, November 1985, p. 39.

31. The notion of much-improved accuracy is implied in the description of the new Scaleboard in *Soviet Military Power 1987* (see Note 28). The INF data base disclosure at least indirectly bears out this characterisation.

32. FM-100-2-3, *Soviet Army Troops Organization and Equipment*, Coordinating Draft, August 1982, p. IV-177. Launcher expansion is also reported in *Soviet Military Power 1987, op. cit.* in Note 4, p. 41.

33. For an account of Soviet force expansion, see *Development of the Soviet Forces in Our Sphere of Interest During the Past 20 Years*, Headquarters, Norwegian Defence Command, Norwegian Embassy, Washington, D.C., 8 March 1985.

34. *Soviet Military Power 1984* (Washington, D.C.: USGPO, 1984), p. 53.

35. *Soviet Military Power 1987, op. cit.* in Note 4, p. 42.

36. *Arms Control Today*, in Note 24, Protocol on Procedures Governing the Elimination of the Missile Systems, p. 9 of the special INF supplement.

37. Meyer, for example, employs this explanation for limited or no storage in Eastern Europe in *op. cit.* in Note 10, pp. 31–32.

38. Eltran Bronner, "US Says Soviet Has A-Arms in E. Europe," *International Herald Tribune*, 2 June 1983, p. 1. For an official acknowledgement, see *Soviet Military Power 1984, op. cit.* in Note 34, p. 81.

39. BBC, USSR Annex, Section III, 21 October 1983: "Zamyatin, Chervov Interviewed on Missile Issue," reports on a 20 October 1983 interview of Col Gen Nikolay Chervov, head of the Legal Department of the Soviet General Staff by *Stern* editors. The interview was reported in *Stern*, 20 October 1983, pp. 234–235. Chervov stated that "wherever our divisions are stationed outside the Soviet Union, the missile units of the appropriate divisions have tactical nuclear weapons with a range of about 100 km."

40. Robert Hutchinson, "NATO's Nuclear Stockpile Reductions 'A High Risk'," *Jane's Defence Weekly*, 9 June 1984, p. 903.
41. For a detailed analysis of the targeting implications of improved Soviet missile accuracy, see Dennis M. Gormley, "A New Dimension to Soviet Theater Strategy." *Orbis*, Fall 1985, pp. 537–569.
42. *Arms Control Today, op. cit.* in Note 24, p. 26.
43. Details on the make-up of the Soviet chemical stockpile are taken from *Soviet Military Power 1987, op. cit.* in Note 4, p. 91.
44. *Report of the Secretary of Defense Caspar W. Weinberger to the Congress on the FY 1987 Budget, FY 1988 Authorization Request, and EY 1987-1991 Defense Programs*, 5 February 1986, p. 255.
45. K. P. Kazahov, ed., *Artillery and Missiles* (Moscow: Voyenizdat, 1968), pp. 341–344.
46. *International Defense Review*, No. 4, 1984, p. 373. Official confirmation of this revelation is found in *Soviet Military Power 1985* (Washington, D.C.: USGPO, 1985), p. 38.
47. Hines, *op. cit.* in Note 22.
48. Aleksander Musial, "The Character and the Importance of Air Operations in Modern Warfare," *Polish Air Defence Review*, No. 2, 1982, translated by the Soviet Studies Research Centre, Royal Military Academy, Sandhurst UKTRANS No. 138.
49. Yossef Bodansky, "Soviets Use Afghanistan to Test 'Liquid Fire'," *Jane's Defence Weekly*, 26 May 1984, p. 819.
50. I. Karenin, "Aviation Weapons for Striking Airfields," *Zarubezhnoye Voyernoye Oboyreniye*, No. 12, December 1984, JPRS-UMA-85-031, 7 May 1985, pp. 132–141.
51. Musial, *op. cit.* in Note 48.
52. Hines, *op. cit.* in Note 22, p. 1911.
53. *Soviet Military Power 1987, op. cit.* in Note 4, p. 64.

3

The Soviet approach to theatre force employment

Soviet willingness to eliminate an entire class (operational-strategic) of ballistic missiles through arms control compels assessing the complementary relationship between affected and unaffected classes of weapons. Such an assessment is essential to understanding the impact of arms control on Soviet strategy and related military options. Unaffected classes of weapons – such as front operational-tactical weapons and the High Command's strategic nuclear forces – clearly can, in theory, reconstitute lost target coverage resulting from deep cuts in forces. But compensating measures are more complicated than a simple examination of the range capability of unaffected weapons against the principal targets of interest. Unaffected classes of weapons have important missions to accomplish – in many cases, missions of equal or greater urgency than the ones calling for compensation. Thus, Moscow's efforts to redress the impact of the INF treaty inevitably call for compromises that can only be understood in the context of the Soviet approach to force employment – conventional as well as nuclear – in the theatre.

Emerging Operational Concepts

Soviet military planners view the mass introduction of qualitatively new aircraft and missiles into Warsaw Pact air and ground formations as the means to achieve the decisive effects, previously the exclusive domain of nuclear weapons. Then Chief of the General Staff, Marshal Nikolai Ogarkov, expressed the implications of this "qualitative leap" in conventional weapon effectiveness in a 9 May 1984 interview in the Soviet newspaper *Krasnaya Zvezda*:

> Rapid changes in the development of conventional means of destruction and the emergence in the developed countries of automated search and destroy complexes, long-range high-accuracy terminally guided combat systems, unmanned flying machines and qualitatively new electronic control systems make many types of weapons global and make it possible to sharply increase (by at least one order of magnitude) the destructive potential of conventional weapons, bringing them closer, so to speak, to weapons of mass destruction in terms of effectiveness. The sharply increased range of conventional weapons makes it possible immediately to extend active combat operations ... to the whole country's territory, which was not possible in past wars. This qualitative leap in the development of conventional means of destruction will inevitably entail a change in the nature of the preparation and conduct of operations. This, in turn, predetermines the possibility of conducting military operations using conventional systems in qualitatively new, incomparable, more destructive forms than before. Operations and the role and significance of the initial period of the war and its first operations become incomparably greater.[1]

The Soviet force development process dictates that qualitatively new means deployed in sufficient quantities ought to engender changes in the forms and methods of combat operations. Of special note here is Ogarkov's belief that long-range conventional weapons can immediately – in the first operations of the initial period of war (that is, before the enemy has fully dispersed and mobilized its forces) – achieve levels of effectiveness approaching those of nuclear weapons.

The necessity to exploit the initial period of war is dominated by the requirements of the air operation. No longer can forward-based short-range missiles remain dormant during the early hours of war, as under both the massive-use and escalating contingencies. The modern air operation has become, in effect, an operational surrogate for the initial mass nuclear strike; the success of subsequent ground operations rests on its achieving pre-emptive shock effect on an unprepared NATO. In this regard, an air operation's timing is crucial. In fact, the first shots of a European war today would consist of an air operation's leading edge attacks by conventionally armed short-range missiles. And the overall air operation would precede any contact between first-echelon Warsaw Pact ground units and NATO covering forces by at least a couple of hours.[2] Direction of such a critical operation, involving the co-operative efforts of army- and front-level missiles and aircraft belonging to both fronts and strategic air armies, would have to come from a command entity with broad controlling authority.

Pre-emptive incentives are also manifested in changes in Soviet fire-support concepts. To exploit fully new conventional missiles, especially as they act in concert with improved air- and artillery-delivered conventional firepower, Soviet military planners have introduced a new conventional fire-support concept. Soviet fire-support doctrine traditionally included three phases: "fire preparation of the attack," initiated shortly before Soviet forces engage enemy defences; "fire support of the attack," undertaken as Soviet forces penetrate enemy defences; and "fire accompaniment," conducted to support increasingly deeper exploitation of the enemy's rear areas.[3]

But in view of the potential impact that new long-range conventional weapons can have at the very beginning of war, Soviet planners have adopted a new, preliminary fire-support phase called "fire support of advance from the depths." This new phase calls for conventional strikes supporting Soviet forces immediately as they depart their initial assembly areas deep in the Warsaw Pact rear and move to the front where they can begin to engage enemy defences.[4] Because Soviet planners envision the commitment of up to division-size operational manoeuvre groups either immediately at the outset of an offensive or within the first few hours of combat, short-range missile strikes performing "fire support of advance from the depths" will probably occur on the heels of the air operation's leading-edge missile strikes. As with the air operation, however, missile strikes would be executed before the actual engagement of combat units.

This new conventional fire support phase is strikingly similar to a pre-emptive nuclear strike. Soviet planners see many new conventional weapons drawing closer to nuclear weapons in effectiveness, especially when they are employed simultaneously to achieve pre-emptive shock effect. Indeed, because each side will possess increasingly effective long-range conventional weapons in the near future, Soviet planners see great operational advantages to the side that strikes first.[5] Accordingly, an offensive operation would begin with

> strikes of all types of weapons and the resolute attack of tank and motorised rifle subunits. ... It [a fire strike] is executed on the march or from a position of direct contact with the opponent. If nuclear weapons are used, the first way [that is, immediately after departure from assembly areas] is the basic one. *It is also advantageous when highly accurate conventional weapons are widely used*, since it permits maintaining to a great degree the combat capability of troops until the beginning of the attack.[6] (Emphasis added.)

Thus, the need to achieve operational surprise (thereby pre-empting the enemy's nuclear *and* deep-strike conventional weapons) appears among the primary motivations for recent changes in Soviet fire-support concepts.

Of operational significance to surprise is a recent report that a portion of Soviet nuclear forces in Eastern Europe has been placed on "quick alert" for the first time.[7] The alert rate of Soviet nuclear forces, shorter-range delivery systems in Eastern Europe, in particular, had generally been believed to be quite low.[8] This change in Soviet operational planning may relate to the introduction of new longer-range missiles into Eastern Europe; it would roughly correspond to NATO's quick-reaction alert forces consisting of some number of Pershing missiles and dual-capable aircraft. But at the same time, missiles (nuclear and conventional) on alert status squarely deal with the need to achieve pre-emptive surprise in support of both the air operation and "fire support of advance from the depths."

Command and Control Arrangements

The expanded scope of warfare resulting from the improved range and lethality of new dual-capable theatre forces has enjoined Soviet military planners to focus on comprehensive command, control, and planning. The ability of these weapons to influence the course of war immediately at its outset, deep in NATO's strategic rear areas, has made planning from a front point of view obsolete. This new focus was confirmed in 1981 when Chief of the Soviet General Staff, Marshal Nikolai Ogarkov, wrote that front operations were no longer "the basic form of military operations." As Ogarkov noted, "Today the command authorities of fronts can have at their disposal weapons (missiles, missle-armed aircraft, and aircraft with a considerable combat radius, etc.) ... which substantially exceed the framework of front operations."[9] Thus, the "strategic operation in the theatre of military operations ... should be regarded as the basic operation in a possible future war."[10]

The broader scale of the strategic operation in the TVD emerged from its participants which might include several fronts, strategic nuclear forces, strategic aviation, air defence forces, and naval forces. The initial mass nuclear strike within the TVD could entail integrating strikes by front short-range forces with those of the Strategic Rocket Forces and Strategic Air Armies. In fact, even the conventional air operation is beyond the "pale" of the front; it involves the joint operation of strategic and tactical aviation, short-range missiles, airborne, heliborne, and special-purpose troops and would, by necessity, have to be planned and executed by a higher command authority than a front.

Precisely what form this higher command and control entity would take was foreshadowed in a 1979 historical article on World War II strategic command and control by Col I. Vyrodov.

> The experience of world wars showed that it became practically impossible for a supreme high command to exercise direction of military operations of major groupings of armed forces without an intermediate echelon and that both an overall system of strategic leadership and its echelons must be set up ahead of time, before the beginning of a war, and their structure must correspond strictly to the character and scope of upcoming military operations.[11]

A permanent High Command was created in Soviet Asia toward the end of 1978.[12] The exact peacetime status of High Commands opposing NATO is less certain. Although Marshal Ogarkov occupies the premier command billet for the Western TVD *vis-à-vis* Central Europe, Moscow faces difficult political constraints in openly advertising a permanent High Command of forces encompassing allied as well as Soviet military forces.[13] Implementation of Soviet High Commands in the Warsaw Pact area embodies the loss in peacetime of what little residual control Moscow's eastern bloc retains over their internal military matters. Yet, the emerging capacity of longer-range conventional weapons to achieve decisive results only reinforces the Soviet need to maintain absolute command and control from the very outset of war.[14] Indeed, Soviet military authorities view the ability of the Warsaw Pact to operate cohesively during this period as essential to winning a future war. At the same time, they see internal contradictions, which similarly sap the effectiveness of NATO as a unified political alliance in peacetime, as having the potential to degrade the Western Alliance's military cohesion in wartime.[15]

To avert such consequences for the Warsaw Pact, Soviet military planners cite the need for detailed peacetime preparations for operating as a cohesive alliance in wartime. This goal dictates that clear-cut command relationships be arranged in peacetime to obviate what would certainly be a time-consuming (and politically sensitive) process during crises. The Soviet re-establishment of the intermediate high command concept at least suggests the possibility that non-Soviet Warsaw Pact military forces are currently subordinated to Soviet-led High Commands in the Western and Southwestern TVD, and that command and control procedures attending the transition-to-war period have already been worked out.[16] A unified Warsaw Pact command structure under the singular direction of the Soviet Union would give Soviet military planners greater confidence that allied support would be forthcoming during the initial period of any future war with NATO. Sustained cohesion would then hinge on attaining decisive early success.

Structural reform in theatre command and control has apparently reduced the time required for the Soviet military to prepare for war. Shrinking war preparation time is consistent with Marshal Ogarkov's emphasis on the exigencies of the initial period of war. No less consequential to improved force readiness are the reorganising and resultant streamlining of the Soviet air force, the placing of portions of the short-range missile force in Eastern Europe on "quick alert," the tailoring of conventional fire support doctrine to accommodate pre-emptive-like missile and air strikes before a major ground offensive, and the continuing expansion of deep-penetration forces including airborne, air assault, and OMG formations. Many of these new forces and concepts were demonstrated for the first time in September 1981, in a large Warsaw Pact exercise (Zapad-81) that included testing the High Command in the TVD controlling multiple fronts, rehearsing OMG operations, and generally emphasising rapid force readiness.[17] In 1982, Defence Minister Ustinov finally declared the highest peace-time readiness norm ("combat alert duty") for ground and naval forces "stationed on the forward edge of our motherland and the socialist community."[18] Previously, only the Strategic Rocket Forces and, occasionally, submarines carrying ballistic missiles and the National Air Defence Troops have been singled out to perform "combat alert duty."

The principal motive for reinstituting the High Command in the TVD seems to be more effective control and co-ordination of theatre forces for deep-strike conventional attack; nevertheless, the theatre command would be no less effective if escalation to theatre nuclear warfare were required. Indeed, the Soviet planning process for a strategic offensive in a TVD entails preparing parallel conventional and nuclear fire plans, a major focus of both being the disruption of NATO's nuclear forces. In addition to a nuclear weapon fire plan, commands from division to TVD level prepare an "integrated fire destruction" plan which concentrates the application of conventional missile, air, and artillery fire against precisely the same targets as in the nuclear fire plans.[19] Not surprisingly, the most critical part of the conventional fire plan at the TVD level is the air operation. All in all, the theatre command appears ably suited to integrate short- and longer-range missile and air resources, whether for conventional or nuclear contingencies.

Just what military instruments might be subordinated to a High Command in the TVD is not entirely clear. The Japanese have reported that the Soviet High Command in the Far East controls an unknown number of Backfire bombers and SS-20 missiles.[20] The creation of five Strategic Air Armies, four of which are regionally oriented, would suggest that each regional air army corresponds with, and is perhaps subordinate to, a theatre command. Several SS-12/22 missile brigades, which were moved from the western USSR into East Germany and Czechoslovakia beginning late in 1983, could very well come under the aegis of the High Command in the Western TVD. They, of course, will be eliminated within 18 months of INF treaty ratification.

In wartime, many if not all of the fronts' longer-range missile and air assets would initially support the conventional and nuclear fire plans of the theatre command. Because front commanders have strike plans of their own to support, the High Command would release temporarily usurped missiles and aircraft as quickly as practical. Still, the timing and resource needs of the conventional air operation or the initial mass nuclear strike overshadow all else; without initial success, Soviet planners view subsequent front offensive operations as problematical.

Theatre and front planning authorities would also interact in drawing up plans for the initial mass nuclear strike. As with the conventional air operation, the theatre command probably has approval authority for the fronts' initial nuclear strike plans. Front planning authorities, in turn, would co-ordinate the strike plans of their subordinate armies by stipulating which targets to engage and which assets to allocate to specific targets. The complexity of co-ordinating theatre, front, and army strike assets (called *deconfliction* in planning parlance) will vary according to precisely when nuclear escalation occurs. If it happens at the beginning of or early into a war, co-ordination between front and theatre is relatively straightforward. Missiles and aircraft organic to fronts would concentrate on fixed and dispersed NATO targets within the operational-tactical zone or out to roughly 250 km from the line of contact. Theatre-subordinate missiles and aircraft (SS-20s, Backfires, and Fencers) would strike targets primarily beyond the front zone.

Front and theatre nuclear strike co-ordination will be far more complex if nuclear escalation occurs well into a war (say, several days to weeks). As fronts advance, a number of operational-strategic targets will come within range of front missiles and aircraft. And many NATO targets for operational-tactical strikes will have already been destroyed by conventional means. The condition of front missiles and aircraft may also have changed dramatically by virtue of their involvement in extended conventional operations. To that extent, Soviet planners must rely on survivable, homeland-based nuclear missiles and aircraft for required nuclear support.

In the end, cautious Soviet planners must concern themselves with the targeting requirements in each of the three contingencies outlined in Chapter 1. In the massive-nuclear and conventional-only contingencies, the critical factor will be the nature of the NATO target set at the time strikes occur. If NATO decision-makers prove dilatory in mobilising and dispersing vulnerable military forces, increasingly potent shorter-range forces based in Eastern Europe offer Soviet planners several attractive conventional and nuclear attack options even without the participation of homeland-based strike assets. But the latter, especially the highly survivable SS-20 force, embodies the most critical portion of the Soviet theatre nuclear threat in an escalating contingency involving protracted conventional conflict. Ways of compensating for the loss of this force will be evaluated in Chapter 5.

Planning Considerations in Warsaw Pact Targeting

In assessing Warsaw Pact nuclear and conventional targeting plans against NATO, we find that most of NATO's capacity to defend against air attacks, sustain conventional ground and air operations, and escalate to nuclear warfare is situated within range of an expanding force of dual-capable Warsaw Pact short-range missiles and aircraft. But the nature of the targeting process is vastly more complex than just the drawing of weapon range arcs.

Soviet military planners judge individual targets on their threat to Warsaw Pact operational objectives. Therefore, target criticality changes as time passes; if certain temporarily fixed targets are not attacked decisively early in a war before they multiply through dispersal, they may become less important if only because of the difficulty of locating them. Equally important, Soviet targeteers are known to select and target only the most critical components or nodes from an overall target class. The loss of just one node, (a central command and control site for air defence, for example) might devastate the overall performance of an entire NATO air defence sector.[21]

Another important, indeed pacing, targeting consideration is the fundamentally political dimension of warfare. One Soviet military author notes that "in wartime, military doctrine drops into the background somewhat since, in armed combat, we are guided primarily by military-political and military-strategic considerations."[22] Accordingly, political considerations could influence target selection and relative attack size. Finally, perhaps the greatest difference in the NATO and Warsaw Pact approaches to targeting lies in NATO's purposeful avoidance of targeting the Warsaw Pact's nuclear weapons during conventional operations. Discussions with NATO targeteers suggest that they view conventional strikes on Warsaw Pact nuclear forces during conventional warfare as highly escalatory. In contrast, Warsaw Pact military writers place NATO's nuclear arsenal at the top of their target lists, independent of the nature of conflict.[23] Recall that the conventional air operation, executed at the very start of a war, is designed to replace an initial mass nuclear strike. Its principal aim is to strike at the heart of NATO's ability to threaten and execute nuclear escalation.

In broad outline, Soviet planners employ a two-step procedure in cataloguing targets, whether for conventional or nuclear attack. This process entails creating prioritised target sets.[24] Group I includes NATO nuclear systems capable of striking the Soviet homeland. Group II comprises nuclear delivery systems of shorter ranges. These highest priority groups also include the supporting nuclear infrastructure, such as relevant command, control, and communications (C^3) links, air, ground, and naval bases, and nuclear storage sites. Group III contains NATO general purpose forces and related reinforcement, mobilisation, and logistics infrastructure. Group IV encompasses the NATO air defence system, interceptor airfields, surface-to-air (SAM) missile sites, and related C^3 facilities. Group V consists of military industry, political centres, and key transportation centres. The rank order of the five groups is not immutable. Various circumstances, political ones among them, might compel Soviet decision-makers to modify targeting priorities. Changing target criticality might also prompt alterations in attack plans.

Once prioritisation is complete, the second step divides targets into several regions within a TVD. Although evidence is lacking with respect to exactly how large these regions are, a plausible scheme might consist of dividing the TVD according to the Soviet notion of offensive depths and front objectives (See Table 2.1 in Chapter 2). Broadly conceived, two regions would predominate in planning: the operational-tactical out to 250 to 300 km from the line of contact and the operational-strategic from that point out to the full depth of the TVD. Each region would contain a mix of targets from each group.

Regional grouping of targets would facilitate planning interaction between shorter- and longer-range forces and their respective commands. As a 1966 Soviet military commentary noted,

> [it] is obvious that such attacks on the most distant objectives [targets] of the enemy will be carried out with the use of the long-range forces. . . . one must suppose that within the bounds of their [operational-tactical missiles and frontal aviation] range they will be the most effective means of attack at medium distances.[25]

Despite the impression left in this commentary that short-range forces would handle all targets within the operational-tactical zone while long-range assets would be assigned to operational-strategic targets, the then-existing theatre nuclear force structure simply could not accommodate such a design. Given NATO Europe's lack of strategic depth, the number of critical NATO targets within the operational-tactical zone certainly must have exceeded the existing arsenal of available short-range delivery systems. Moreover, there is strong suspicion that nuclear warheads for frontal missiles and aircraft in the mid-1960s were stored in the USSR, making short-range forces in Eastern Europe uncertain participants in the early stages of the prevailing contingencies. Thus, before the dramatic increase in the short-range inventory (which doubled in size between 1965 and 1975), longer-range theatre nuclear forces (SS-4, SS-5, and TU-22) were expected to perform yeoman's duty. They were to strike not only all prescribed targets in the operational-strategic zone but also uncovered targets in the operational-tactical zone as well.

The magnitude of long-range theatre support to the front commander's needs has diminished since the mid-1960s. The doubling of the operational-tactical inventory by 1975 permitted the Ground Forces to become increasingly capable of meeting the objective implicit in the 1966 Soviet commentary already cited: that of comprehensively covering all targets in the operational-tactical region. A product of short-range force growth was the growing Soviet confidence in new operational contingencies; by the mid-1970s, Soviet planners thought beyond a single-variant nuclear contingency to a war by stages, in which Soviet front forces would attempt to pre-empt NATO's limited nuclear use with strikes by operational-tactical nuclear systems.[26]

But the ability of short-range nuclear forces to deal with the full target set within the operational-tactical region hinged critically on two factors: first, the extent to which NATO responded to warning and thereby multiplied the target set by several orders of magnitude; and second, the length of conventional operations, during which time Soviet fronts would reduce the size of the nuclear target set as much as possible. Moreover, problems still persisted for short-range forces in the mid-1970s, despite a doubling of the operational-tactical inventory between 1965 and 1975, and growing Soviet doctrinal confidence in a war by stages. One recent study of Soviet theatre nuclear forces notes that short-range performance would improve greatly only after the following changes in operational-tactical force posture were made: (1) adding a full complement of nuclear warheads for short-range forces based in Eastern Europe; (2) increasing the number of army and front missile launchers; and (3) deploying SS-12/22 missile launchers in Eastern Europe.[27]

The fact that these postural changes manifested themselves in the early 1980s helps explain the widespread concern about the shorter-range dimension of Soviet theatre nuclear forces. To a large extent, this concern led the USA to propose a freeze or ban on Soviet short-range ballistic missiles with ranges between 500 and 1000 km as part of any ban on Soviet intermediate-range missiles. These postural changes are important, but the most radical transformation in short-range force performance derives from the estimated 25-fold improvement in accuracy for the new generation of short-range missiles when compared with their predecessors. The effectiveness of targeting options implied by new short-range force developments depends, of course, on the number and nature of NATO targets within the Western TVD and, foremost, on what state the targets are in when attacks actually occur.

Targets for Dual-Capable Theatre Forces

Because NATO's Central Region contains the Western Alliance's most capable defences against Warsaw Pact aggression, we focus here primarily on targets within the Central European sector, while giving some attention to the most critical military facilities in the United Kingdom and France.

NATO's Nuclear Weapons (Groups I and II)

Regardless of which contingency might dominate Soviet military planning considerations, NATO's capacity to employ its nuclear weapons forms the highest priority target set. For the NATO Central Region (West Germany, the Netherlands, and Belgium) this target set consists of roughly 50 nuclear storage sites, 10 air bases with dual-capable fighter-bombers and collocated nuclear bombs, and roughly 20 garrisons housing Pershing, Lance, and ground-launched cruise missile (GLCM) systems.[28] But Soviet planners, who are known to select the main kinds of nodes in various target sets for priority attention, may not view each of these 80 installations with equal gravity.[29] For example, they might plausibly single out for special attack consideration the most threatening of the 50 nuclear storage sites (until Pershing and GLCM warheads are removed; surely these have top attack priority) and missiles and aircraft on quick-reaction alert status. These high-priority targets would roughly correspond to Group I or nuclear weapons capable of performing a strategic mission (attacks on Soviet soil). Outside the Central Region, Soviet planners must concern themselves with perhaps five Royal Air Force air bases in the United Kingdom with nuclear-capable aircraft and GLCMs, 18 missiles in the French intermediate-range ballistic missile (IRBM) force, and perhaps five French air bases housing strike aircraft squadrons and collocated nuclear bombs.[30]

A problem of great concern to NATO operational planners is the growing target concentration of NATO's nuclear stockpile. In the nuclear storage area, the last decade has seen a shrinkage in the overall number of storage facilities – the product of site consolidation and concern over peacetime terrorist threats. With the decision at Montebello taking effect, and continuing public tension regarding nuclear issues unabated, this trend is likely to continue.

The vulnerability of NATO's diminishing nuclear stockpile is most sensitive to whether Western decision-makers act in time to disperse nuclear weapons, aircraft, and missiles from their peacetime bases. Dispersal in the Central Region would render Soviet pre-emptive strike calculations dubious at best by multiplying the nuclear target set from 80 fixed installations to well over 300 mobile (and thus more survivable) field units.[31] For this reason, many view rapid nuclear dispersal as the most sensible course for NATO decision-makers; such an act would, at once, produce substantially greater survivability for nuclear forces and lessen pressures for early nuclear use.[32]

Others are not so sanguine. They deem the alert and dispersal of nuclear weapons so provocative as to create uncontrollable incentives for the Warsaw Pact to attack in a crisis.[33] Critics maintain that nuclear dispersal provokes attack because the widespread distribution of nuclear warheads throughout NATO forces is fundamentally no different from a delegation of authority to lower-level military authorities to use such weapons.[34]

A complicating factor is the lengthy time it could take to complete the nuclear dispersal process. Because of the perceived sensitivity of nuclear dispersal, NATO forces are not practised in its execution. Preparing, outloading, and dispatching large numbers of nuclear weapons could take nearly a full day. Most important of all, nuclear force survivability is materially threatened during dispersal, a process that exposes many weapons and places truck convoys, handling equipment, and personnel at risk. Even a few missiles employing area sub-munitions could disrupt outloading and dispersal operations long enough to permit aircraft to deliver a more telling blow.

NATO Strategic Command and Control Facilities (Group I)
Two parallel command structures direct NATO combat operations above corps level. One supports national C^2 needs; in the case of the USA, this would include the US European Command, US Air Force Europe, and US Army Europe. The other – Allied Command Europe – is headed by the Supreme Headquarters, Allied Air Forces Central Europe (AAFCE), the Northern and Central Army Groups and their corresponding allied tactical air forces (two and four ATAF, respectively). In wartime, each of these ten major commands deploys to an alternate, hardened command post, perhaps best illustrated by Irwin Bunker. Located some 60 km north-west of Ramstein air base in West Germany, Irwin Bunker houses both AFCENT and AAFCE.[35]

Mobilisation and Reinforcement (Group III)
Besides denying NATO its ability to threaten any Soviet-led invasion with a nuclear riposte, perhaps the most important

Soviet objective is to sever NATO's reinforcement potential. Both Soviet and Western planners are intimately acquainted with the extent that NATO's conventional defence hinges on early response to strategic warning. Studies of changing NATO-Warsaw Pact force ratios resulting from competitive mobilisation demonstrate that the West's prospects (albeit only a bean count) materially improve with 10 to 30 days of reinforcement.[36]

Unfortunately, NATO's reinforcement process invites attack for reasons quite separate from an attack's inherent operational value. For one, reinforcement facilities are few (perhaps a couple of dozen installations) and soft in constitution (military equipment in warehouses). Pre-positioned equipment for reinforcing US divisions is concentrated in a cluster of facilities in West Germany, consisting of only six POMCUS (pre-positioned overseas materiel configured to unit sets) depots.[37] Moreover, the Central Region's lifeline from the continental USA depends on the freedom to operate efficiently at a handful of vulnerable air and sea points of debarkation on the European continent. The massive airlifting of troops and mating with pre-positioned equipment are complex activities under the best condition, no less in time of crisis or war. Without shelters for aircraft, logistic airfields are especially vulnerable to conventional attack, particularly during the first few days of war when the pace of activity will be so high as to ensure a cacophony of unloading and refuelling activity virtually around the clock.

NATO's Air Defences (Group IV)

Mastery of the air is an essential Soviet objective in a major contingency in Central Europe. The NATO air defence system in the Central Region embodies air defence forces (surface-to-air missiles and interceptors), surveillance capabilities, and the C^3 network. Measured in sheer numbers, the air defence forces dominate the overall target set, but the Achilles' heel lies in the C^3 network.

Roughly 15 C^3 sites form the most vulnerable link the Central Region's air defences. Headquarters, AAFCE, whose static war location is Irwin Bunker, provides overall general direction.[38] The two ATAF commands (Second ATAF supporting the Northern Army Group and Fourth ATAF supporting the Central Army Group) divide regional direction of the Centre's air defence forces and surveillance assets. Perhaps of greatest importance to cohesive air defence operations are three Sector Operations Centres (SOCs) whose loss could be equated with the loss of air traffic control at a major international airport. Finally, nine fixed Control and Reporting Centres (CRCs) link surveillance, warning, and air defence activities into a management scheme consisting of engagement zones within which interceptors and SAMs are allocated. It would appear that CRCs could furnish some back-up support should SOCs come under effective attack.

Older, hardened structures in NATO, such as many air defence command and control bunkers, are becoming increasingly susceptible to conventional attacks; one Allied Tactical Operations Centre in the Central Region is situated in an old bunker with 1 m of concrete and steel, and 2 m of earth cover.[39] Survivability of even newer underground C^2 bunkers with 2 m of concrete and steel and about 4–6 m of earth and rock cover could be challenged within the coming decade by emerging Soviet conventional systems.

A system of fixed and mobile surveillance radars provides vital early warning of enemy air attack. The NATO Air Defence Ground Environment (NADGE) surveillance system consists of at least five 412L fixed radar sites, supported by 16 mobile 407L Control and Reporting Posts (CRPs). A network of mobile radars, operated by the German defence forces, also supplies radar coverage near the inter-German border. Although major portions of the warning and surveillance network are vulnerable (either because their positions are fixed or because active electronic emitters attract attention), NATO's Airborne Warning and Control System (AWACS) will partially offset this shortcoming through its more survivable mode of deployment.

The Central Region's air defence forces include two major components: (1) interceptor aircraft, based at roughly 10 airfields, each of which has some level of air defence support to cope with enemy aircraft attacks; and (2) high- and low-altitude SAMs forming the Nike-Hercules (being replaced by Patriot) and Hawk air defence belts. The Hawk belt has nearly 500 launchers while the Nike-Hercules has some 450.[40] For targeting, however, a Soviet planner might view the entire Hawk belt as 83 battery-sized targets. Applying this same formula to the Nike-Hercules belt would result in 49 battery-sized targets. All targets are not of equal value; the Soviet air operation would attempt to establish three to six penetration corridors, making large-scale suppression of the NATO air defence system unnecessary. NATO faces serious challenges in maintaining the integrity of its ground-based air defences.

No doubt the simplest means for NATO to complicate Soviet air defence suppression attacks (especially by conventionally armed ballistic missiles) lies in moving SAM batteries. Yet, when SAMs move, they are more difficult to co-ordinate. Frequent movement creates lower battery availability rates, gaps in air defence coverage, and airspace management problems. Moreover, the sheer size and limited off-road mobility of a Patriot battery makes it only nominally mobile.[41] Surface-to-air firing sections include heavy wheeled vehicles with limited off-road mobility, numerous missile semi-trailers, generator vans, a radar set, and hundreds of support personnel. And Nike-Hercules and Hawk batteries are even more cumbersome. Not only are these batteries insufficiently mobile to the extent needed for survivability, their radar sets and control vans are extremely susceptible to conventional area munitions. Moreover, as Patriot deployment plans now stand for the 1990s (less than a one-for-one replacement of the existing air defence belts), NATO air defences will be so thin as to compel virtually all units to maintain high duty cycles during extended deep crises and the first day of hostilities. Such high emission levels mean that even those batteries that manage to relocate (at the risk of creating gaps in coverage) are likely to be found by Warsaw Pact pre-attack electronic reconnaissance. And yet, as worrying as these circumstances may appear, they do not represent the worst, while still plausible, case: a short-warning contingency in which NATO's air defence batteries are attacked while they are still at their semi-permanent (but well-known) peacetime locations.

Thus, despite NATO's sizeable investment in upgrading air defences (Patriot and AWACS being only the most notable examples), the Alliance has been barely able to keep pace with major quantitative and qualitative improvements in the Warsaw Pact air threat. Adding Soviet conventionally armed ballistic missiles to the picture makes the future viability of NATO air defences even more questionable.

Airpower Targets (Groups I, II, and IV)
Because of its tremendous firepower and manoeuvre potential, airpower has increasingly become the *sine qua non* for both Warsaw Pact and NATO defence planners in fashioning operational strategy. Pact planners recognise that NATO air superiority would preclude the execution of both decisive (but potentially vulnerable) ground and airborne manoeuvres designed to encircle and defeat unprepared NATO ground forces. Airborne, air assault, and OMG operations are highly vulnerable to NATO airpower. Moreover, Warsaw Pact airpower must impede NATO's operational reserves from coming to the aid of encircled NATO forces.[42] NATO air forces, by contrast, have an equally critical but perhaps more daunting task: not only must they defeat Warsaw Pact air forces and control air space, they must also survive in significant numbers to help defeat successive waves of echeloned Warsaw Pact ground forces.[43]

The manner in which NATO protects its airpower from growing Warsaw Pact short-range attack resources is, therefore, of special importance in deterring and defending against any possible Warsaw Pact aggression. Equally imperative is the need to appreciate how Soviet planners view and intend to exploit NATO's airpower deficiencies. Already mentioned is the potentially disastrous impact of a pre-emptive Pact missile and air attack that compounds airpower's inherent predilection to operate with reduced efficiency in the first few days of war. Soviet planners see even a partially successful pre-emptive attack conveying a distinct advantage to the attacker.[44] The goal of pre-emptive surprise is not to win in one blow, but, as John Erickson has noted, "to adjust the initial phase in terms of relative force levels so that the war can be continued on a sustainable basis ... [with] an ultimate outcome in Soviet favour."[45] Such a favourable adjustment of relative force levels could result from the temporary closure of NATO air bases; such an abrupt abatement in NATO sortie generation could reduce the availability NATO aircraft for decisive air battles and support missions during the critical initial period of war.

As with the nuclear target set, Soviet planners treat NATO airfields in priority fashion.[46] The Central Region has around 50 tactical air bases, some of which are part of the NATO Collocated Operating Base (COB) programme. The COB programme would accommodate the bedding down of USAF reinforcement from the continental USA. But of the 50 or so airfields, roughly 20 (half supporting air defence interceptors, the others, dual-capable fighter-bombers) represent the heart of NATO airpower.

Despite improvements in the sheltering of aircraft, there are disturbing trends that combine to make NATO airpower vulnerable to attack. One is the rising cost and complexity of high-performance aircraft.[47] As a result, fewer numbers of aircraft are procured; moreover, system complexity encourages peacetime concentration of aircraft and their maintenance and repair facilities at a small number of main operating bases (the 20 just mentioned). Given the increasingly brittle nature of aircraft structures and materials, even modest levels of conventional attack could achieve disproportionate damage. Although future conventional weapon improvements could threaten the survivability of even hardened targets, aircraft protected in shelters do not necessarily represent the most tempting target for Soviet conventional missile and air attacks. Sortie generation from an air base requires a supporting infrastructure to prepare, launch, control, recover, re-arm, refuel, and maintain aircraft.

Perhaps the most frequently discussed airfield attack technique since the advent of hardened shelters is the closure of runways to preclude aircraft take-off and landing. Preventing aircraft departure or diverting already departed aircraft to bases without ready support facilities could severely affect NATO's ability to cope with the initial air battle. As few as six to eight SS-23 missiles could, with a probability of 90%, temporarily close a typical NATO runway and parallel taxiway.[48] These calculations are sensitive to the attacker's damage criteria; not knowing these criteria, the general analytical tendency is to make offence-conservative assumptions. In the case of the foregoing SS-23 attack, changing the damage criteria to a 90% probability of making three times the number of runway cuts (to prevent take-off as well as landing) raises the attack requirement by a factor of two to three. It is highly doubtful, however, that a Soviet planner would expend missile resources in this way. Even assuming that only missiles were being counted on to close the runways (which is a dubious proposition in the first place), a Soviet planner would probably allocate the smaller number in view of the advantages of precluding aircraft recovery (by preventing landing, which requires fewer cuts) to their primary means of logistical support. More important, missiles are expected to work in co-operation with aircraft, making the latter far more effective than they would be if used alone.

The above illustration suggests the importance of keeping a Soviet (*vice* Western) perspective in mind in considering attack assessment. For example, the notion of dealing solely with a one-on-one engagement (missiles *vs* runway surfaces) neither captures the overall short-term effects of an intense missile attack on an air base's capacity to perform its mission or the combined-arms nature of the air operation. Soviet planners do not view missiles as a substitute for aircraft delivery of conventional ordnance (as Western planners did in NATO's Counterair-90 study); rather, by virtue of their surprise shock effect and assured penetration, missiles can temporarily disrupt operations for a matter of minutes, pending the arrival of aircraft.[49] Missiles thereby give leverage to the effectiveness of aircraft.

Such a notion of disruption via missile-delivered submunitions must consider a multitude of coincidental effects that could delay runway use for short time periods (15 to 60 minutes). For example, Soviet submunitions could include a combination of runway penetrators and mines (anti-personnel and/or anti-vehicular); the latter could complicate runway inspection and repair operations by requiring delicate runway sweeping procedures.[50] Moreover, personnel and equipment essential to inspection and runway repair operations could very well be subjected to collateral effects or even direct attack. Indeed, perhaps the most important virtue of Soviet integrated fire destruction planning is its emphasis on meticulous pre-planning (or pre-targeting). In this regard, the unique vulner-abilities of each air base (restricted access runway aprons that create bottlenecks between shelters and main runways; the location of runway repair and mine clearing equipment; and other brittle air-base components) can be identified in advance to influence the preparation of specific air-base aim-points and tailored weapon allocations.[51]

Finally, there are the adverse consequences that flow from the friction of war – in this case, the chaos that inevitably accompanies the reality of being struck by an intense missile attack. Soviet planners have a category of target damage for this effect called harassment, the purpose of which is to lower enemy morale and combat effectiveness.[52] In the few cases where the USA has tested air-base response to attack under quasi-wartime conditions, damage assessment and repair times have been significantly higher than anticipated.[53]

There are solutions to NATO's air-base vulnerabilities. The US Air Force in Europe can operate several "bare bases" by pre-positioning modular support components at dispersed operating fields.[54] But the number of additional bases seems severely inadequate in view of the growing threat; moreover, their effective use rests on the political will to respond to what will inevitably be ambiguous attack signals. NATO is simply not suitably configured to operate from austere air facilities, given the need of modern aircraft for specialised maintenance, readily available fuels, appropriate munitions, and reliable command, control, and communications. Perhaps the best longer-term solution is for NATO to procure simpler aircraft that make less use of vulnerable support services and, thus, are more capable of operating from a large number of dispersal strips. There is, however, little evidence of interest in any redirection in aircraft procurement.

Political, Industrial, and Transportation Centres (Group V)
This target set encompasses the political capitals and major regional administrative centres of NATO's member states, significant military industries, and important civilian air and sea transportation facilities. Soviet planners are sensitive to the strategic implications of attacks against Group V targets; they admit the decision to strike targets in this category is influenced by "political considerations which complicate the strategic situation."[55]

Notes

1. N.V. Ogarkov, *Krasnaya Zvezda*, 9 May 1984, trans. BBC Monitoring Service, SU/7639/C/10, 9 May 1984.
2. Phillip A. Petersen and John G. Hines, "The Conventional Offensive in Soviet Theater Strategy," *Orbis*, Fall 1983, p. 709.
3. *Ibid.*, pp. 711–714.
4. *Ibid.*, p. 712.
5. I. Vorob'ev, "Modern Weapons and Tactics," *Krasnaya Zvezda*, 15 September 1984, p. 2.
6. P. Konoplis and A. Mal'shev, "Modern Offensive Battle," *Military Herald*, February 1984, in *Strategic Review*, Spring 1984, p. 96.
7. Jay Mallin, Sr., "Russia at High Level of Battle Readiness," *Washington Times*, 26 July 1984.
8. Stephen M. Meyer, "Soviet Theatre Nuclear Forces, Part II: Capabilities and Implications," *Adelphi Papers*, No. 188 (London: IISS, 1983/84), p. 31.
9. N. V. Ogarkov, *Always in Readiness to Defend the Homeland* (Moscow: Voyenizdat, 1982) FBIS, JPRS L/10412, 25 March 1982, p. 24.
10. N. V. Ogarkov, "On Guard Over Peaceful Labor," *Kommunist*, No. 10, 1981.
11. I. Vyrodov, "Strategic and Operational Art: On the Leadership of Military Operations of Strategic Troop Groupings in World War

II," *Voyenno-istoricheskiy Zhurnal,* April 1979, trans. JPRS 73677, 13 June 1979, p. 24.

12. Gregory C. Baird, "The Soviet Theater Command: An Update," *Naval War College Review,* November/December 1981, pp. 90–93.

13. *Soviet Military Power 1987* (Washington, D.C.: USGPO, 1987), p. 21.

14. See, for example, Konoplis and Mal'shev, *op. cit.* in Note 6.

15. See, for example, A.I. Gribkov, "On the Command and Control of Coalition Troop Groupings," *Voyenno-istoricheskiy Zhurnal,* March 1984, No. 3, p. 8.

16. Such a subordination is argued well in John J. Yurechko, "Command and Control for Coalitional Warfare: The Soviet Approach," *Signal,* December 1985, reprinted in *Current News,* Special Edition no. 1427, 16 April 1986, pp. 8–16.

17. Jeffrey Simon, "Evaluation and Integration of Non-Soviet Warsaw Pact Forces into the Combined Arms Forces," *Signal,* December 1985, reprinted in *Current News, op. cit.* in Note 16, pp. 23–24.

18. D. F. Ustinov, *We Serve the Motherland and the Cause of Communism* (Moscow, 1982), p. 82, cited by James M. McConnell, *The Soviet Shift in Emphasis from Nuclear to Conventional* (Alexandria, VA, Center for Naval Analyses, June 1983), pp. 27–28.

19. LTC Kerry Hines and MAJ John Hines, *Soviet Front Fire Support,* Defense Intelligence Agency, DDB-1130-8-82, September 1982, especially pp. 69–76.

20. Baird, *op. cit.* in Note 12, p. 92.

21. See the discussion related to radioelectronic warfare as an example of critical node targeting in Phillip A. Petersen and John R. Clark, "Soviet Air and Antiair Operations," *Air University Review,* March–April 1985, reprinted in *Current News,* Special Edition, No. 1327, 31 July 1985, pp. 8–9.

22. S. N. Kozlov, ed., *The Officer's Handbook (A Soviet View),* trans. by the DGIS Multilingual Section, Translation Bureau, Secretary of State Department, Ottawa, Canada (Washington, D.C.: USGPO, 1977), p. 65.

23. See, for example, Aleksander Musial, "The Character and the Importance of Air Operations in Modern Warfare," *Polish Air Defence Review,* No. 2, 1982, translated by the Soviet Studies Research Centre, Royal Military Academy, Sandhurst, ULTRANS No. 138, p. 3.

24. The notion of group prioritisation is employed by Kh.

Dzhelaukhov, "The Infliction of Deep Strikes," *Voyennaya Mysl'*, No. 2, February 1966, trans. FBIS FPD 0763/67, 8 August 1967, pp. 14–15.

25. *Ibid.*
26. Cited in Notra Trulock III, "Weapons of Mass Destruction in Soviet Military Strategy," an unpublished paper presented at the Joint Conference on Soviet Military Strategy in Europe, sponsored by the Boston Foreign Affairs Group and the Royal United Services Institute for Defence Studies on 24–25 September 1984, Oxford, England, pp. 77–78.
27. Meyer, *op. cit.* in Note 8, p. 39.
28. Various sources, including Meyer, *op. cit.* in Note 8, p. 24; map entitled "Nuclear Arms in West Germany," in *Washington Post*, 1 November 1981; and *The Military Balance* (London: IISS, 1983–1984), pp. 9–10 and 25–42.
29. W. T. Lee, "Trends in Soviet Strategic Ballistic Missile Forces," paper presented at a conference sponsored by the USAF Assistant Chief of Staff for Intelligence, "The Soviet Union: What Lies Ahead? Military-Political Affairs in the 1980's," 25–27 September, 1980, p. 13.
30. *The Military Balance* (London: IISS, 1984–85), pp. 32–34, 39, and 132; and Jeffrey McCausland, "The SS-20: Military and Political Threat?" *The Fletcher Forum*, Vol. 6, No. 1, Winter 1982, p. 18.
31. The proliferation of NATO nuclear units results from the distribution of nuclear weapons from 50 storage sites to numerous firing units, such as individual firing batteries of dual-capable artillery battalions.
32. See, for example, Walter Slocombe, review of *Command and Control of Nuclear Forces* (New Haven and London: Yale University Press, 1983), by Paul Bracken, *Survival*, September/October 1984, p. 240.
33. *Lab News*, Sandia National Laboratories, Vol. 37, no. 8, April 26, 1985, p. 9.
34. Bracken, *op. cit.* in Note 32, pp. 129–178.
35. Dan Boyle, "C³ – The Essential Ingredient to Air Defense," *International Defense Review*, No. 6, 1978, pp. 860–864.
36. For more details see Pat Hillier and Nora Slatkin, 'US Ground Forces: Design and Cost Alternatives for NATO and Non-NATO Contingencies," Congressional Budget Office, 1980, especially Figure 24.
37. For details on POMCUS, see *Department of Defense Appro-*

priations for FY 85, Hearings before a Subcommittee of the Committee on Appropriations, House of Representatives, 98th Cong., 2d sess. (USGPO, 1984), pp. 119–140.

38. The discussion of NATO air defences is based largely on Boyle, *op. cit.* in Note 35.

39. *Ibid.*, pp. 862–863.

40. *The Military Balance, op. cit.* in Note 28, pp. 9 and 26–38. The counting rule formula for Hawk is 6 launchers per battery × 3 battalions or 18 launchers per battalion. Nike-Hercules is nine launchers per battery × four batteries per battalion.

41. Richard D. DeLauer, "Emerging Technologies and Their Impact on the Conventional Deterrent," in Andrew J. Pierre, ed., *The Conventional Defense of Europe: New Technologies and New Strategies* (New York: Council on Foreign Relations, 1986), p. 54.

42. For a Soviet account of these concerns, see P. Lashchenko, "Perfection of Methods of Encirclement and Destruction of Large Enemy Groupings Based on the Experience of the Great Patriotic War," *Voyenno-istoricheskiy Zhurnal*, No. 2, February 1985. An excellent Western analysis of Soviet encirclement operations can be found in John G. Hines, "Soviet Front Operations in Europe – Planning for Encirclement," a paper (No. A-74) published by the Soviet Studies Research Centre, Royal Military Academy Sandhurst, April 1985.

43. James A. Thomson, "Strategic Choices: Their Roles in NATO's Defence Planning and Force Modernisation: Part I," in "Power and Policy: Doctrine, The Alliance and Arms Control," *Adelphi Papers* No. 205 (London: IISS, 1986), pp. 32–33.

44. A. I. Eiseev, "On Certain Trends in Changes in the Content and Nature of the Initial Period of War," *Voyenno-istoricheskiy Zhurnal*, November 1985, p. 15.

45. John Erickson, "Soviet Military Potential for Surprise Attack: Surprise, Superiority and Time,' a paper prepared for the SIPRI workshop on Measures to Reduce the Fear of Surprise Attack in Europe, Stockholm, Sweden, 1–3 December 1983, p. 45.

46. For an interesting Soviet historical commentary on attacking airfields with relevance to contemporary Central Europe, see P. S. Kutakhov, "Experience in Fighting for Strategic Air Supremacy During the Years of World Warr II and Its Importance in the Contemporary Situation," *Voyenno-istoricheskiy Zhurnal*, No. 12, December 1984, pp. 19–29. Kutakhov notes

that only the most important airfields were subjected to surprise attacks.

47. See Carl H. Builder, "The Prospects and Implications of Non-
nuclear Means for Strategic Conflict," *Adelphi Papers*, No. 200
(London: IISS, 1985), pp. 7–8. For a provocative indictment of
the military's increasing complexity, see David Evans, "We Still
Don't Have the Arms and Tactics for a Major War," *Washington
Post*, 3 August 1986.

48. Based on discussions with Rand Corporation analysts. The
lower figure is based on a missile reliability of 0.9 and the higher
is based on one of 0.75.

49. Here it is important to note the Soviet approach to target
damage. Three categories are used: destruction, suppression,
and harassment. Destruction means that the target has completely lost its effectiveness and requires major reconstitution.
Mathematically, a point target is destroyed when there is a 90%
probability of serious damage. An area target requires a 90%
probability that no less than 50% of the target's sub-elements
have undergone serious damage. Suppression means the target
has *temporarily* lost its combat effectiveness or been restricted
in its ability to manoeuvre or furnish command and control.
Suppression is met when there is a 90% probability that no less
than 25 to 30% of the target's sub-elements have suffered serious
damage. Harassment's purpose is to lower enemy troop moral
through periodic fires and thereby reduce combat performance.
See note 19, p. 4.

50. Also of concern are the effects of near misses, secondary fires,
and foreign object damage to aircraft forced to take off under
adverse conditions. The notion of judging success on the basis
of temporarily delaying aircraft departure (*vice* a specific level
of damage to runways, for example) is discussed by I. Karenin,
"Aviation Weapons for Striking Airfields," *Zarubezhnoye Voyernoye Obogreniye*, No. 12, December 1984, JPRS-UMA-85-031, 7
May 1985, p. 134.

51. For a provocative treatment of the subject of preplanning for air-
field attack, see B. L. Bluestone and J. P. Peak, *Air Superiority and
Airfield Attacks: Lessons from History*, DNA-TR-84-161 (The BDM
Corporation, McLean, VA, 15 May 1984).

52. Hines and Hines, *op. cit.* in Note 19, p. 4.

53. The Salty Demo series of exercises illustrates the excessive
optimism associated with air-base response to attack. According

to a former senior military official with NATO experience, even a simulated chemical attack with just a few missiles (using smokes) would have a paralytic effect on air-base response times.

54. D.J. Alberts, "Deterrence in the 1980s, Part II: The Role of Conventional Air Power," *Adelphi Papers*, No. 193 (London: IISS, 1984), p. 23.

55. Dzhelaukhov, *op. cit.* in Note 24, reflects this concern. See Trulock, *op. cit.* in Note 26, for a detailed account of this concern.

4

The role of Soviet theatre forces in multiple contingencies

The debate over the merits of eliminating intermediate- and shorter-range nuclear weapons has focused almost exclusively on the INF treaty's effect on Western security interests – a topic we shall turn to in Chapter 6. But any balanced assessment of the treaty's value depends just as much on how the agreement's provisions affect the Soviet military calculus. If the West is to generate a broad consensus on the nature of the threat, we must examine how the loss of intermediate- and shorter-range missiles affects the Soviet military's ability to carry out their responsibilities as they have traditionally come to see them. Indeed, even Soviet political commentators have begun to question why, for example, so many SS-20 missiles were deployed in the first place if, today, the Soviet military can accept their elimination.[1]

How the Soviet military has traditionally come to see their mission responsibilities was the subject of Chapter 1. There we saw a sustained force development process that, from about the mid-1960s to the early 1980s, led Soviet military authorities to plan for dealing with three primary military contingencies against the West. Here we turn to how the products of that sustained military build-up would support these three contingencies. As such, this chapter serves as a baseline (pre-INF) examination of the importance Soviet planners attach to theatre forces in meeting the needs of both nuclear and conventional conflict against NATO. Although emphasis in this chapter focuses on the role of dual-capable theatre forces, longer-range INF systems (SS-20) and other strategic and regional nuclear forces are also scrutinised to identify linkages that may help explain Soviet arms control motivations.

Background Assumptions

Because this chapter investigates the *intended* role of Soviet intermediate- and shorter-range forces, we assume the continued deployment of SS-12/22, SS-23, and SS-20 in accord with the projected estimates made in Chapter 2 (Chapter 5 furnishes a "damage assessment" of the impact of the INF treaty on the Soviet military's ability to meet its contingency requirements). In the following examination, the critical variable in each contingency is the extent to which NATO successfully responds to warning and thereby disperses its primary target set (especially the time-urgent nuclear component) so as to complicate Soviet targeting calculations. Implicit in official Western concern that Soviet short-range ballistic missiles could render the elimination of SS-20s vulnerable to circumvention (which led to the US insistence that Moscow accede to the second double zero) is the assumption of a fixed, non-dynamic target array. It is clearly wrong to assume that the target set against which SS-20s are aimed will retain its characteristic features (fixed, few, and extremely vulnerable), even in the context of an escalating contingency where NATO has had sufficient time to (partially or wholly) disperse and mobilise its forces.[2] As noted in Chapter 3, nuclear dispersal in NATO's Central Region (excluding British and French forces) would transform the fixed nuclear target array from 50 nuclear storage sites and around 20 missile garrisons, to well over 300 individual firing units and special ammunition supply points.

Indeed, Soviet planners estimate that over 70% of the primary target set might be "lost" due to successful NATO dispersal.[3] To recover lost targets, the Warsaw Pact would conduct a massive air reconnaissance and electronic surveillance effort; they would also rely on reporting from in-place agents and Spetsnaz teams. The only thing that can be safely said about such a reconnaissance effort is that it promises unpredictable results – a disquieting condition for Soviet planners. Such unpredictability reinforces Soviet incentives to pre-emptively destroy the primary target set *before* dispersal. Soviet preemptive incentives, however, are quite scenario-dependent; they inevitably are the product of initial war aims, the politico-military situation in Eastern Europe, and a variety of other circumstances. They simply cannot be predicted in advance. The important point is that in peacetime Soviet planners are forced to plan conservatively, in this case, not just on the basis of attacking fixed targets, but a dispersed target set as well.

Massive Nuclear Use Contingency

The paramount objective in Soviet military strategy at the origin of the massive nuclear attack option was the necessity to attack priority targets (as enumerated in Chapter 3) to the stratetic rear of the TVD. Aside from changes in notions of escalation, the deep-attack theme remains a principal feature of contemporary Soviet strategy. Of the mix of delivery means – aircraft, missiles, and artillery – missiles would play the most important role in the massive-use contingency.

Given their stress on achieving predictable damage effects, Soviet planners favour the assured penetrability of ballistic missiles. Just as important, missiles have brief launch-to-target engagement times, making them the primary means of striking time-sensitive targets. The timeliness and assured penetrability of ballistic missiles are also exploited for strikes against air defences timed to occur minutes before Soviet aircraft begin their attacks.[4] Finally, the mobility of missile transporter-erector-launchers and launch support equipment, unlike aircraft that must operate from fixed locations, furnishes mobile ballistic missiles (especially those based in the Soviet homeland) an important survivability advantage over aircraft.

Substantial Soviet investment in operational-strategic (SS-20) and now tactical and operational-tactical (SS-21, SS-12/22, and SS-23) systems provides a surfeit of ballistic missiles from which to choose. Nonetheless, short-range ballistic missiles based in Eastern Europe have engendered substantial concern for several reasons. Increased numbers of missile launchers and improvements in missile coverage augur a budding Soviet capacity to attack a major portion of the high-priority Group I and II targets. The latest increase of launchers to army and front missile brigades (from 12 to 18 launchers) means that these units have tripled their initial delivery capability over the past 25 years. Such augmentation probably stems largely from a Soviet desire to furnish conventional fire support to the air operation; however, additional missile launchers would, in theory, enable Soviet planners to cover time-urgent targets during crises and at the very outset of hostilities.

Furnishing such time-urgent attack capability with short-range missiles at the outset of hostilities implies significant improvements in force readiness. New Soviet short-range missiles offer up to a 50% cut in reaction time (set-up time after arrival at a launch site) compared to the time required of their predecessors.[5] Missile reload times also appear to have been halved.[6] But the foremost requirement to ensure rapid use of short-range missiles at the outset of conflict is the ready availability of nuclear warheads deployed with or near delivery units in Eastern Europe. As discussed in Chapter 2, it seems prudent to assume that a sufficient number of nuclear warheads are indeed now present in Eastern Europe.

An accommodating command and control framework is yet another requirement if short-range ballistic missiles are to play a predominant role in a massive-use contingency. Just such a framework is apparent in the High Command in the TVD. This new command and control entity rationalises the fact that Soviet fronts have shorter-range missiles and aircraft with ranges that substantially exceed a front's traditional area of interest.

A final factor that could influence a decision to employ short-range ballistic missiles is the dramatic improvement in missile accuracy for the new generation of missiles now being deployed in Eastern Europe. One of the principal benefits of the SS-20 force compared with its predecessors (SS-4/5) is the striking reduction in undesired collateral damage which would result from the use of substantially lower nuclear warhead yields due to improved missile accuracy. Such improvements make at least the notion of reconstructing post-war Western Europe's industrial infrastructure more probable; they also promise a major reduction in lethal radioactive contamination, which could adversely affect the Warsaw Pact ground campaign.

Significantly lower collateral damage would also result if the Soviets used appropriate nuclear yields matched to highly accurate short-range missiles. Missile warheads could be fused for low airburst which would greatly reduce the adverse effects of fallout. Finally, highly accurate missiles offer multifold reductions in expenditure rates, as illustrated in Figure 2.1.

Under circumstances in which the Soviet Union decides to initiate war with massive use of nuclear weapons against the primary NATO target set, Soviet planners need not deal with the dual-capability dilemma – that is, determining what percentage of short-range missiles should be loaded up with conventional, chemical, or nuclear munitions. Rather, in this case we assume that the initial allocation is exclusively nuclear and earmarked to strike as many of the primary targets as possible. Naturally, such a decision reflects conscious premeditation; because it would involve loading virtually all available short-range launchers with nuclear warheads, it would leave little or no room for executing a co-ordinated conventional missile attack, should that choice seem more appropriate in the waning moments before the planned start of conflict?

At a minimum, such an attack would have to deal with the critical NATO installations in the Central Region associated with the Warsaw Pact's fundamental attack objectives. These objectives include neutralising NATO's nuclear option, its airpower capability, its command and control means, and its potential to reinforce. As noted in Table 4.1, most targets (139 out of 159) are located beyond 100 km of the inter-German border and thus are candidates for attack by SS-23 or SS-12/22 missiles. Beyond the 159 targets noted in the table, a Soviet target planner would probably also employ ballistic missiles against NATO's SAM belts to ensure the creation of penetration corridors for air attacks. But such an expenditure might be unnecessary if missile attacks against sector operation centres succeed in denying NATO the means of controlling complex air defence operations. If we assume that air defence belts consist of 132 batteries, suppressing half (or 66) of these targets

Table 4.1. Critical NATO installations in the Central Region.

Target categories	Number	Distance from inter-German border (km) 0–100	Distance from inter-German border (km) 100+
Theatre nuclear weapons (Group II)	80		65
Storage sites		15	
Dual-capable airfields			
Missile garrisons			
Air defences (Group IV)	45		40
Major C^3 headquarters			
Sector operations centres		5	
Interceptor airfields			
Warning/surveillance			
Major C^3 headquarters (Group I)	9		9
Reinforcement (Group III)	25		25
POMCUS depots			
Air and sea points of debarkation			

Sources: A map entitled "Nuclear Arms in West Germany," *Washington Post*, 1 November 1981; Stephen M. Meyer, "Soviet Theatre Nuclear Forces, Part II: Capabilities and Implications," *Adelphi Papers*, No. 188 (London: IISS, 1983–1984), p. 24; *The Military Balance* (London: IISS, 1983–1984), pp. 9–10 and 25–42; and Dan Boyle, "C^3 – The Essential Ingredient to Air Defense," *International Defense Review*, No. 6 (1978), pp. 860–864.

would materially aid establishment of perhaps five penetration corridors.

Overall, then, some 225 targets constitute the maximum target set. When we use projected Soviet missile launchers noted in Table 2.7, 62 targets are within range of 96 SS-21 launchers, and 163 are within range of 234 SS-23 and SS-12/22 launchers. If the Soviet goal is to depend exclusively on short-range missiles in Eastern Europe, SS-12/22 launchers in East Germany and Czechoslovakia (totalling 54) are critically important to attacking Group I and II targets outside of West Germany. Such a nuclear attack, limited in weapon numbers and yields, would not be without immense escalatory risks; noticeably uncovered are French and British independent nuclear forces, and US submarine-based warheads assigned for SACEUR's use. Fixed targets in this latter group would have to be attacked by Soviet homeland-based SS-20s.

If we assume that NATO responded to warning of attack by dispersing its nuclear weapons, Soviet planners would have to rely heavily on strike aircraft and nuclear artillery. Aircraft would be allocated largely against high-priority mobile targets, such as missile launchers and ground formations containing nuclear-capable artillery. Soviet nuclear artillery units would conduct counter-battery operations against NATO nuclear-capable artillery and tactical missile units, and line-of-contact strikes to support breakthrough operations.[8] Operational-strategic launchers (SS-20s) would probably also be called upon to accomplish the requisite volume of strikes against a wholly unpredictable (dispersed) target set.

Conventional-Only and Escalating Contingencies

Linkages between Short- and Long-Range Nuclear Forces
In contrast to the massive-nuclear contingency, where Soviet planners intend from war's outset to deal exclusively in nuclear terms, the conventional-only and escalating contingencies would find Soviet planners assigning all, or nearly all, dual-capable systems to the conventional campaign. Both contingencies share the same objective: to win at the lowest level of conflict. In an escalating contingency, however, Soviet planners expect escalation within a matter of days (if not sooner) after hostilities begin; they would be likely to withhold perhaps a third of available short-range missiles and aircraft so as to place them in an advanced state of readiness for pre-emptive

nuclear use. A conventional contingency features a greater expectation of strategic success without nuclear escalation. Still, Soviet planners must squarely confront the transition dilemma. Even though they believe the chances are strong to win conventionally, Soviet planners recognise that they must continue to convey the threat of pre-emptive theatre-wide nuclear use should NATO be seen fit to employ what remains of its nuclear arsenal after conventional operations.

In a conventional contingency, it is far more likely that Soviet planners would allocate all, or nearly all, available dual-capable missiles and aircraft initially to support the air operation and, subsequently, to support the fire plans of divisions, armies, and fronts. Since contemporary Soviet planning for conventional conflict envisages the distinct possibility of protracted wars of at least 30 days and beyond, it is doubtful that planners would have confidence that sufficient numbers of short-range launchers would remain after prolonged conventional war to fulfil the wholly uncertain needs of nuclear pre-emption. Even in the escalating contingency, the range of plausible targeting conditions that might beset the Warsaw Pact is enormous. The size of the target set rests on whether NATO effectively responds to warning of attack and the relative effectiveness of the Warsaw Pact's conventional air operation. One third of the available launchers and aircraft withheld for nuclear use – should they and their command and control survive the conventional phase – could very likely be insufficient to deal even with operational-tactical pre-emption, no less the targeting chores of the SS-20. It is in this regard that the SS-20 force plays its most important role: to survive a *protracted* conventional or uncertain escalating contingency to threaten theatre-wide nuclear attacks against an unpredictable target set.

The Role of Dual-Capable Forces in Non-nuclear Contingencies
The emerging capabilities of short-range ballistic missiles show their greatest contribution in improving the prospects for success of the Soviet conventional air operation. The goals of the air operation stem from two major problems confronting

Soviet planners in conducting a theatre strategic operation. On the one hand, NATO airpower could potentially neutralise the Warsaw Pact's superiority in ground forces.[9] On the other, NATO's theatre nuclear forces threaten escalatory strikes on the Soviet homeland. Conventionally armed aircraft alone are incapable of furnishing the shock and damage effectiveness of nuclear weapons; thus, the air operation involves jointly employing missiles, airpower, radioelectric combat (jamming, chaff, etc.), airborne and heliborne assaults, and special-purpose (Spetsnaz) forces.

According to Warsaw Pact military literature, the principal goals of the air operation are (1) seizing the initiative through surprise by striking simultaneously on several fronts against airfields according to a unified plan, and (2) taking prior measures to neutralise enemy air defences and to seal off and mine enemy airfields to prevent aircraft from taking off.[10] One Warsaw Pact military analyst specifies several component parts to the air operation, including operations by air armies of operational-strategic and strategic air forces; frontal air operations to destroy enemy air forces on airfields; and attack by missile troops employing cluster munitions against air-fields, anti-aircraft defences, and command and control. The most important targets are airfields, nuclear delivery systems and storage sites, air defences, command and control systems, and logistical support facilities. Critical to airfield attack is disrupting operations through blockading and mining.[11]

Recently declassified lecture materials from the Voroshilov General Staff Academy in Moscow confirm the general description of the air operation found in the open Soviet and Pact literature. For example: "Success in air operations is ensured by delivering surprise mass initial strikes on enemy airfields where the main body of enemy aircraft is concentrated, with first priority on enemy nuclear-armed aircraft." The lectures further state that the weight of the initial blow can "create favourable conditions for effective actions of friendly air forces, ensure better results of actions against enemy air-fields, contain the deployment or redeployment of the enemy air forces, neutralise its activity, and deprive it of the initiative and the capability to support ground forces."[12]

Warsaw Pact authors indicate various quantitative measures of success to express what is meant by "decisive losses to the air and nuclear rocket forces of the enemy."[13] One specifies that 60% of NATO aircraft must be destroyed in the air operation.[14] A figure of 50–60% of NATO's major fire-support weapons (probably representing dual-capable aircraft and nuclear missiles) appears elsewhere in the literature.[15] Soviet planners also emphasise an equally important quantitative dimension: lengthening the time needed for the enemy to reconstitute its capacity to retaliate. For example, the Voroshilov lectures stress that "subsequent massed strikes must be brought to bear on the enemy after the shortest of intervals following the initial mass strikes, so the enemy is denied the chance of restoring his airfields and regrouping his air forces."[16] Where nuclear weapons promise simultaneous results, conventional success depends on sequential application of force, but delivered with only brief intervals so as to approximate (as best as possible) the effects of nuclear weapons.

Mass waves of attacking aircraft clearly play a featured role in the air operation. Over a decade and a half ago Soviet Marshal of Aviation P. S. Kutakhov described the air operation's primary task as neutralisation of the main force of enemy aviation on the first day of hostilities.[17] Two to three mass strikes can be expected on the first day of war, with one to two for a few days thereafter. The initial mass strike is the largest;[18] it is designed to achieve the decisive results previously discussed, no doubt aided in part by the inherent tendency of NATO airpower to operate with reduced efficiency in the opening stages of war.[19]

Soviet experience in air operations during World War II bears out their contemporary expectation of achieving the highest level of effectiveness in the initial mass strike. That experience shows that more than 40% of enemy aircraft losses occurred during the initial mass strike, 30% during the second, and 20% during the third.[20] In this regard, suppressing the adversary hinges on the intensity of fire, or, as one Soviet analyst succinctly puts it, "on the density of fire and the rate of destruction . . . in a unit of time on a unit of area."[21] Compared to the Soviet war experience, modern high-performance aircraft and conventionally armed ballistic missiles today permit the delivery of a significantly increased density of fire within a dramatically reduced time window. The three mass attacks of World War II would today be compressed into the first day with each mass strike consisting of two to three waves of closely timed air strikes, preceded by a precursor missile attack. In addition, the other components of the air operation – radio-electronic combat, air assault, and special-purpose forces – in some cases supplement, and in others exploit, the effects of multiple-wave mass strikes.

Perhaps the most important employment interaction is that between missiles and aircraft, especially with respect to timing sensitivities.[22] A brief example will help illustrate the benefits of missile and air interaction.

Before the advent of highly accurate conventional ballistic missiles, Soviet planners were compelled to allocate a majority of their first-wave aircraft to air defence suppression. Soviet military writers note that roughly two-thirds of the typical World War II air-strike force had to neutralise enemy air defences, leaving only a third to attack primary targets.[23] In a contemporary setting, Warsaw Pact aircraft would be expected to open three to six penetration corridors in the Central Region about 40 to 50 km wide, and 150 to 200 km deep.[24] Aided by the massive use of stand-off jammers and chaff, first-wave aircraft would disrupt an organised NATO air defence through attacks against warning and surveillance radars, air defence batteries, and interceptor airfields.

Although such an allocation strategy was conceived out of necessity (and substantially reinforced by the growing sophistication of NATO air defences), it suffered from several important drawbacks. To begin with, it risked the loss of tactical surprise. Even under circumstances where Soviet decision-makers chose to attack without reinforcing Eastern European air bases with aircraft from the Soviet Union, NATO could still track Warsaw Pact aircraft from take-off. Successful tracking and quick response permit at least some NATO interceptors to fill potential air corridors and thereby increase Pact aircraft attrition rates during the initial mass strike. Moreover, by not being assured that NATO's ground-based air defences were effectively suppressed, Warsaw Pact pilots would fly less-preferred, low-altitude penetration routes, but only at the risk of suffering losses from traditional, yet effective, low-altitude anti-aircraft guns and missiles.[25] Most important of all, however, the need to suppress enemy air defences with aircraft dissipates the weight of the initial blow on the primary target set: NATO nuclear weapon sites and airfields.

A precursor missile attack, executed minutes before the first-wave air strike, could mitigate the drawbacks just enumerated. The chances of achieving tactical surprise – thereby catching NATO aircraft on the ground – are materially improved by employing missiles first; their flight times range from 30 seconds to 5 minutes, the latter being roughly half the flight time of aircraft. By taking over primary responsibility for the suppression of NATO air defences, missiles provide a form of sequential leveraging for subsequent aircraft strikes. The product of leveraging is a predictable enhancement in aircraft performance. Indeed, as one Soviet writer puts it, "the use of a missile can replace a number of aircraft sorties which are expensive and which stand a chance of being destroyed by the enemy's air defence means."[26] What many view as the cost-ineffective use of expensive missiles to deliver conventional payloads, Soviet planners see as just the opposite: missiles do not simply replace aircraft for certain missions, but enable more expensive and re-useable manned platforms, each of which can deliver on the average of seven times the payload of a missile, to achieve decisive results in the critical opening hours of conflict.[27]

Missiles give leverage to the effectiveness of aircraft in several ways. Because missiles have a greater assurance of penetrating to suppress air defence targets, aircraft released from such missions can then fly to the primary target set using higher and deeper routes with heavier payloads. Moreover, if missiles succeed in pinning down the main body of aircraft at NATO airfields, fewer allied interceptors will enter penetration corridors to meet the first-wave air strike. Soviet interceptors stand a better chance of success against those NATO aircraft that are successfully launched because of more favourable force ratios than would otherwise be the case without a precursor missile strike.

Another example of leveraging lies in the number of aircraft freed from air defence suppression to concentrate on NATO airpower and nuclear targets. One rough measure of just how many aircraft might be freed up can be determined by comparing an aircraft attack of a Hawk air defence fire battery to a missile attack. In the former case, two flights of four fighter-bombers or eight aircraft are required. And the attack manoeuvre is by no means simple. Two aircraft armed with anti-radiation missiles (ARMs) conduct low-altitude penetration runs, pop up, and fire their missiles. As discussed above, Soviet pilots foresee considerable risks in low-altitude tactics. The ARM engagement is designed to force the Hawk battery to disengage or be destroyed. The remaining six aircraft then pop up, roll in, and deliver bombs on single passes of two aircraft from three different directions.[28] In contrast, two conventionally armed missiles are sufficient to meet the Soviet damage criterion (suppression or neutralisation); three missiles would permanently incapacitate the targets.[29] Attacking just 20 of the air defence batteries in the Central Region with missiles instead of fighter-bombers would free four and a half air regiments (of 36 aircraft each); each regiment is suitably configured to attack a major NATO air base.

Allocating first-wave aircraft to the primary target set also has a leveraging effect on subsequent waves of aircraft in the first mass strike. Assuming an unreinforced attack, the first mass strike today could conservatively entail around 1300 aircraft from forward-based Frontal Aviation and the Legnica and Smolensk Air Armies (Table 2.5). Fighters and bombers from Frontal Aviation units in East Germany, Czechoslovakia, and Poland would form the first wave. Within minutes of the precursor missile and first-wave air strikes, a major strike force comprising primarily bombers from the Legnica and Smolensk Air Armies would deliver the main blow of the first mass strike. Configured into squadrons of seven to eight bombers each, this wave (or waves) could attack around 45 major airfields or nuclear targets. Its effectiveness would be materially aided by virtue of the air defence suppression and pin-down attacks by missiles and the first wave's shock effect against primary air-fields and nuclear weapon targets. In effect, the preceding elements of the first mass strike are becoming increasingly capable of rendering the primary target set more vulnerable to decisive attrition by the main body of the first strike.

Air reconnaissance would help determine the course of sub-sequent mass strikes which must be brought to bear as soon as possible after the first in order to prevent NATO from recovery. As many as three mass strikes could be planned for the first day. The primary strike force for the first and third strike would likely be the Soviet High Command's long-range aviation, while the main blow for the second strike would come from Frontal Aviation's fighter-bombers.

At least two to four hours (at a minimum) would be needed for recovery and reconstitution between mass strikes. One to two such strikes could be planned for each successive day for Warsaw Pact aircraft recovery and reconstitution. Refire times for new Soviet short-range missiles are such that launch units could readily support a second and third mass strike on the first day, spaced two to four hours apart.[30] For example, were NATO decision-makers to delay dispersal of nuclear weapons until the onset of the war, by the second wave (let's say H plus 4 hours), a substantial portion of NATO's nuclear stockpile sites and missile garrisons would still be in the early stages of outload activity. During dispersal these targets are especially vulnerable to disruption. To that end, a part of the second-wave missile attack might, therefore, be allocated to "pinning down" or disrupting dispersal long enough for aircraft to attack exposed equipment and vehicles. After the first day's operations, however, important decisions would have to be made by the theatre command regarding continuing missile support to the air operation versus organic missile support to front, army, and division integrated fire destruction plans (that is, offensive ground operations).

Exemplary Attack Options
Given the above operational considerations and NATO target vulnerabilities discussed in Chapter 3, it is possible to sketch

out several pre-planned missile strike options in support of the air operation. The difference between each option reflects the status of the intended target set (fixed or in some state of movement) at the time of attack and changes in damage objectives. A 1990 projected missile force (derived from Table 2.7), consisting of 96 SS-21 launchers, 180 SS-23 launchers, and 54 SS-12/22 launchers from Soviet units in East Germany and Czechoslovakia, is assumed. (East German and Czech missile units could be allocated conventional missions if Soviet planners felt compelled to set aside a small percentage of launchers as a nuclear withhold.)

Option 1 represents a short-warning contingency in which NATO has failed to exercise its alert options and is tactically surprised. Nuclear weapon and aircraft dispersal have not taken place and air defence batteries are still in their semi-permanent peacetime locations. Under such favourable Warsaw Pact circumstances, Soviet planners might choose to suppress perhaps one-third (or 33 firing batteries) of the NATO air defence belts in the Central Region by employing two missiles per battery to achieve the Soviet damage criterion "suppression" (25–30% area coverage). The precursor missile attack for Option 1 might also include suppression attacks against the Central Region's 20 main operating bases for interceptor and dual-capable aircraft. Six missiles per airfield would be assigned to temporarily disrupt (15 to 30 minutes) damage assessment and repair operations long enough to permit direct and stand-off attacks by the first wave of aircraft. Soviet planners might also want to expend a portion of the precursor missile attack on high-priority nuclear storage sites, missile garrisons, and quick-reaction alert sites supporting Pershing II and GLCMs (two missiles each against perhaps 25 targets). The purpose here would be to disrupt an already cumbersome dispersal process which depends on the ready availability of extremely vulnerable handling and transport equipment. Subsequent waves (most important of which is the wave consisting of Fencers and Backfires from Strategic Air Armies) would follow within the hour to exploit the disruptive effects of the precursor missile and first-wave attacks. Two additional mass strikes might follow within the first 24 hours of battle.

Option 1 would require allocating 20 of the 96 tactical missile launchers (assuming 10 of the 33 air defence batteries are within range of these missiles), and 200 of the 234 operational-tactical missile launchers. Such an allocation leaves more than enough Soviet launchers for a nuclear withhold. Other Warsaw Pact launchers could also supplement Option 1's allocation, if necessary.

Option 2 increases the weight of the precursor missile attack on NATO airfields to increase the probability of pinning down NATO aircraft (or alternatively preventing recovery and forcing them to land at austere airfields) until the arrival of the second and third waves of the initial mass strike of aircraft. Twelve missiles per airfield are allocated, which requires all of the Soviet operational-tactical launchers. A combination of tactical missile launchers and aircraft would stand on nuclear alert. Option 2 assumes that NATO air defence batteries have departed semi-permanent peacetime locations. Some can possibly be re-acquired before the attack by Warsaw Pact signals units; close-in batteries could be targeted by tactical missile launchers. For the most part, however, Option 2 would concentrate roughly two-thirds of first-wave aircraft on air defence suppression. By virtue of missiles compelling air defence batteries to move more frequently, a degree of virtual attrition is achieved. Frequent movement creates lower battery availability rates, gaps in coverage, and complex command and control problems. The effectiveness of first-wave aircraft is thereby leveraged.

Several variations on the above options would likely flow from detailed planning, which is precisely the Soviet approach. Unique target vulnerabilities would be identified so as to achieve economy of force in weapon allocations.

Observations on an Escalating Contingency
Because of the inherent difficulty of anticipating the size, nature, and approximate location of potential targets during an escalating contingency, illustrating possible attack options for short-range theatre forces is fraught with difficulty. On the one

hand, if the Warsaw Pact succeeded in catching NATO forces inadequately prepared, and destroyed or disrupted the majority of NATO's most valuable military assets during the air operation, yet NATO still managed to threaten a co-ordinated escalatory response, the size of the attack would probably, of necessity, be quite small. If, on the other hand, a Western-preferred scenario arose in which Warsaw Pact and NATO forces are alerted, dispersed, and deployed before the start of conflict, then the ultimate size of any operational-tactical nuclear strike rests primarily on the extent to which Warsaw Pact forces locate and destroy NATO Group I and II targets during conventional operations.

Soviet planners are not at all confident of dealing with a scenario in which they fail to exploit the initial period of war in a decisive manner. Targets become more difficult to locate after dispersal. With enough time, POMCUS divisions from the continental USA could mate with pre-positioned heavy equipment. Some limited dispersal of NATO aircraft could occur under less than frantic combat conditions. Faced with the consequences of failing to exploit NATO's vulnerabilities, Soviet decision-makers might opt to manipulate the crisis to arrange a more favourable set of initial conditions. Failing that, and confronted with war, Warsaw Pact planners would commence the air operation by disrupting located NATO air defences with short-range conventionally armed missile attacks. Although such missile attacks might permit Warsaw Pact aircraft to operate with relative impunity in NATO's rear, the problem of lost targets (the foremost being nuclear ones) remains. To that end, the conventional period affords Pact planners the opportunity to conduct a massive air and ground reconnaissance campaign to locate and target NATO's capacity to escalate. Aircraft are the preferred means of attack against mobile nuclear and conventional targets.

Of course, Warsaw Pact dual-capable theatre forces are not immune from attack during the conventional phase of war, as are (relatively speaking) Soviet longer-range forces like SS-20s husbanded in the homeland sanctuary. Because of the comparatively vulnerable circumstances facing dual-capable missiles and aircraft, conservative Soviet planners are forced to size their theatre nuclear force posture on the presumption that dual-capable forces may not be available for substantial use after extended conventional operations. Needing to pre-empt NATO's intended use of nuclear weapons and finding their force structure depleted of operational-tactical delivery means of the required number and range, Soviet planners could call upon an intact SS-20 force for a variety of nuclear targeting demands.

It should be noted that the first-echelon front's missiles (formed from the GSFG's five armies) by no means represent the full short-range missile capacity of the Western TVD. Second-echelon fronts, formed from ground forces in the USSR's western military districts, would replenish the Warsaw Pact combined-arms campaign with fresh organic missile support. And because the overall Pact ground campaign may have advanced hundreds of kilometres into NATO territory, fresh short-range missiles could cover remaining targets to the full depth of the theatre upon arriving in the forward area. Nonetheless, the uncertainties of effective command and control and interdiction-free transit from the USSR to the battle front would probably combine to diminish Soviet confidence in the performance of short-range theatre forces to meet time-sensitive nuclear pre-emption requirements.

Soviet interest in non-nuclear contingencies conducted under the constant threat of nuclear escalation offers an explanatory framework for considering the role of dual-capable artillery. First, the expectation of extended conventional operations characterised by deep manoeuvre penetrations suggests a thorough intermingling of attacking and defending forces. Under such circumstances, self-propelled nuclear-capable artillery offers an attractive option to a Soviet commander needing nuclear support. Second, and equally important, the smaller yields of artillery-fired atomic projectiles mitigate troop safety problems endemic to close-in targeting by higher-yield tactical nuclear missiles. Third, by dispersing their nuclear capability throughout the force structure, Soviet planners improve nuclear force survivability, especially in contrast to deploying nuclear artillery rounds exclusively in heavy artillery brigades. Lastly, we should not dismiss the political dimension of matching and then exceeding NATO's perennial lead over the Warsaw Pact in nuclear-capable artillery. Soviet military strategists are quite sensitive to the perceived political value of escalation dominance.[31]

There is, finally, an intermediate escalatory option between conventional and nuclear war that is worth remembering. Soviet planners could employ missile-delivered chemical warheads against nuclear weapon storage sites, airfields, and C^2 installations lacking chemical protection. More precise delivery systems enhance the selective employment of chemical weapons in co-ordination with the movement of Warsaw Pact ground forces. But improved delivery accuracies will not compensate for unpredictable meterological conditions. Nonetheless, precise missile-delivered chemical attacks on just a few rear-area targets in NATO would produce devastating military effects. The consequences for NATO air operations are well known. Less familiar are the effects of chemical attacks on NATO reinforcement. According to recent US Congressional testimony, chemical attacks on POMCUS sites alone would create delays in reinforcement of at least several days and require most of Europe's decontamination units. Moreover, the rapid supply of incoming units to Europe would undergo serious disruption because POMCUS sites depend heavily on local civilians "who may not have enough equipment and be well trained for operations in chemical conditions."[32]

Notes

1. An unusual questioning of the wisdom of deploying the SS-20 was made in a *Moscow News* article, to which a Soviet general officer responded defensively. See the Supplementary Notes to Jeremy Azrael, *The Soviet Civilian Leadership and the Military High Command, 1976–1986* (Santa Monica, CA: RAND R-3521-AF, June 1987), furnished at a conference on Soviet military policy sponsored by the Wilson Center, Washington, D.C., on 21–23 September 1987.
2. The analytic tendency is to calculate expected levels of destruc-

tion against the primary target array after having assumed an indeterminate conventional phase followed by a transition to nuclear use. One must assume that by the nuclear phase, NATO's primary target array will look substantially different than at the outset of war. Depending on the initial conditions (NATO either succeeds or fails to respond to warning of attack) and the relative amount of success of conventional strikes, the primary target set could range from nearly completely destroyed to virtually fully intact, dispersed, and expanded in number. But surely it will not include fixed nuclear storage sites (unless, of course, handling and transportation resources are destroyed and are not reconstituted) and ground force garrisons after several days or weeks of combat.

3. Joseph D. Douglass Jr., "The Theater Nuclear Threat," *Parameters*, Vol. XII, No. 4, 1982, p. 77.

4. F. Shesterin, "The Experience of the Battle for Air Superiority in World War II and its Significance under Modern Conditions," *Voyennaya Mysl'*, No. 2 (1969), trans. FBIS, FPD 0060/69 (18 June 1969), p. 74.

5. Kerry L. Hines, "Soviet Short-Range Ballistic Missiles," *International Defense Review*, December 1985, p. 1913.

6. Stephen M. Meyer, "Soviet Theatre Nuclear Forces, Part II: Capabilities and Implications," *Adelphi Papers*, No. 188 (London: IISS, 1983/84), p. 23 notes that the SS-23 reload time is expected to be about 30 minutes or roughly half that of the Scud missile.

7. Of course, Soviet decision-makers could choose to delay the start of an attack to allow for changes in warhead loadings but only at the expense of a possible loss of tactical surprise.

8. G. Peredel'sky, "Soviet Artillery Main Assault Force in War," *Voyenno-istoricheskiy Zhurnal*, 4 April 1975, p. 66.

9. The Soviets believe that half of NATO's overall firepower is vested in its air forces. See M. M. Zaitsev, *Voenny Vestnik*, February 1979, pp. 23ff.

10. N. N. Ostroumov, "Employment of Air Forces in Strategic Operations," *Voyennaya Mysl'*, September 1975, as cited in Phillip A. Petersen and John R. Clark, "Soviet Air and Antiair Operations," *Air University Review*, March–April 1985, reprinted in *Current News*, Special Edition, No. 1327, 31 July 1985, p. 5.

11. Aleksander Musial, "The Character and the Importance of Air Operations in Modern Warfare," *Polish Air Defence Review*, No. 2, 1982, translated by the Soviet Studies Research Centre, Royal

Military Academy, Sandhurst, UKTRANS No. 138, pp. 3–4.

12. "Air Operations to Destroy Enemy Groupings," lecture materials from the Voroshilov General Staff Academy, quoted in Petersen and Clark, *op. cit.* in Note 10, p. 12.

13. Jan Blumenstein, "Frontal Aviation in an Air Operation," *Vojenska Mysl'*, August 1975, cited in Petersen and Clark, *op. cit.* in Note 10, p. 7.

14. *Ibid.*

15. *The Soviet Conventional Offensive in Europe*, Defense Intelligence Agency, Washington, D.C., 1982, pp. 41–43.

16. Quoted in Petersen and Clark, *op. cit.* in Note 10, p. 10.

17. P. S. Kutahkov, "The Conduct of Independent Air Operations," *Voyenno-istoricheskiy Zhurnal*. No. 6, 1972, pp. 20–28, as cited in John Erickson, Lynn Hansen, and William Schneider, *Soviet Ground Forces: An Operational Assessment* (Boulder: Westview Press, 1986), p. 203.

18. Blumenstein, cited in Petersen and Clark, *op. cit.* in Note 10, p. 5.

19. For a recent expression of concern about air power survival on the first day of a future war, see Rick Atkinson and Fred Hiatt, "The Changing Blue Yonder," *Washington Post*, 7 June 1986, p. 1.

20. Erickson, Hansen, and Schneider, *op. cit.* in Note 17.

21. A. A. Sidorenko, *The Offensive* (Moscow: Voyenizdat, 1970), trans. and published by the US Air Force (Washington, D.C.: USGPO, 1974), p. 22.

22. There are certainly additional employment interactions that bear on the ultimate role missiles and aircraft will play as damage mechanisms. For example, radioelectronic combat (jamming) can be employed in combination with missile or air attacks. And missile strikes can be co-ordinated with the insertion of air assault or Spetsnaz forces.

23. Erickson, Hansen, and Schneider, *op. cit.* in Note 17.

24. Petersen and Clark, *op. cit.* in Note 10, pp. 6–7.

25. Col E. Tomilin, "What to Take from Combat Experience," No. 12, *Report: Military Affairs*, No. 1567, JPRS 77371, 11 February 1981, p. 33.

26. B. T. Surikov, *Combat Employment of Ground Forces' Missiles* (Moscow: Voyenizdat, 1979), pp. 160–161.

27. There are also considerable sunk costs stemming from the fact that the Soviet Union and its allies have had tactical and

operational-tactical missiles for the ground forces since the late-1950s. NATO, by contrast, would be forced to add costly new force structure were the Alliance to decide upon adding a significant conventional missile capability.

28. Petersen and Clark, *op. cit.* in Note 10, p. 9.
29. For a detailed discussion, see Dennis M. Gormley, "A New Dimension to Soviet Theater Strategy," *Orbis*, Fall 1985, pp. 537–569.
30. See Note 6. It should not go without mention that a substantial defensive component (known as the "anti-air operation") exists in Soviet theatre strategy. If the Pact's pre-emptive air operation succeeds, the aim of the anti-air operation would be to blunt NATO's surviving retaliatory responses. Thick, overlapping air defences together with an emerging Soviet anti-tactical ballistic missile capability (the SA-12B, which operates much like the dual-mode Patriot system), furnish the wherewithal. If, however, the Pact fails to take the initiative in the air, the anti-air operation would consist of both offensive and defensive components in order to wrest the initiative away from NATO.
31. Soviet appreciation of escalation dominance is reflected throughout Notra Trulock's "Soviet Perspectives on Limited Nuclear War," in Fred Hoffman, Albert Wohlstetter, and David Yost, eds., *Swords and Shields: NATO, the USSR, and New Choices for Long-Range Offense and Defense* (Lexington, MA: Lexington Books, 1987), pp. 53–85.
32. Department of Defense Appropriations for FY 85, hearings before a Subcommittee of the Committee on Appropriations, House of Representatives, 98th Cong., 2d sess. (Washington, D.C.: USGPO, 1984), p. 129.

5

Arms control and Soviet military strategy

Many in the West were completely surprised by the Soviet Union's willingness to accept President Reagan's so-called "zero option," which will eliminate the two countries' medium- and intermediate-range ballistic missiles. And they were equally astonished when Mikhail Gorbachev – with apparent selflessness – removed the last obstacle to an INF treaty by proposing to eliminate all ballistic missiles between 500 and 1000 km range – the so-called "double zero" proposal. To many, this dramatic change in Soviet arms control negotiating strategy signalled a fundamental break with the past; no longer did Moscow appear to insist on an extra margin of security to compensate for her long borders and three other nuclear-armed adversaries. What is more, not only did Moscow agree to equality of forces with her principal adversary (that is, zero on both sides), but the agreement means that the Soviet Union will have to eliminate more than twice as many missiles (1836) as will the USA (859). In effect, Moscow's willingness to accept asymmetric force reductions seems to augur well for other arms control initiatives where the East holds clear advantages over the West.

The preceding chapters offer an explanatory framework that attempts to rationalise the Soviet Union's enormous defence expenditures since the mid-1960s for the provision of short- to intermediate-range nuclear and dual-capable theatre forces. The delivery means purchased since that time have permitted conservatively oriented Soviet military strategists to plan for supporting the diverse needs of multiple contingencies. But now a portion of these military tools will be eliminated, sug-

gesting perhaps an important change in Soviet military doctrine, or at least in the fundamental planning assumptions
underlying the military-technical dimension of doctrine.

From the Soviet perspective, there are surely important
politico-military benefits associated with eliminating NATO's
Pershing II and ground-launched cruise missiles. Any agreement that creates even the perception of denuclearisation with
an alliance so dependent as NATO is on the threat of escalation
seems inherently attractive. And the INF agreement generally
seems to play to Soviet strengths in the conventional area.
Nevertheless, these are surface reactions; important as they are
as public perceptions, they furnish little insight into what, at
heart, may be motivating Soviet arms control positions. Nor do
they shed light on the impact (positive and negative) of Soviet
positions on the ability of the Soviet military to carry out their
responsibilities as they have traditionally seen them.

This chapter attempts to provide insight into these issues by
examining how not only the Soviet military establishment but
also the current political leadership might view the military
implications of the INF treaty. Clearly, the analytic view here is
that the Soviet Union is not a unitary strategic rational actor[1] in
the way it makes decisions either on defence procurement or on
arms control. General Secretary Gorbachev's recent shake-up
of the senior military leadership is only the most glaring
manifestation of underlying differences between the Soviet
political and military leadership over key national security
matters. Even though it is possible to identify the broad
outlines of these differences as they relate to such matters as
resource allocation and threat definition, the particular nature
of internal debates remains shrouded in secrecy. Focusing on
the impact of Soviet arms control positions on the Soviet
military's ability to do its job may, therefore, yield useful insight
into the nature of the internal debates and the future course of
Soviet military and arms control developments.

A corollary subject also deserving scrutiny here is the matter
of INF's second "zero option" covering missiles between the
ranges of 500 and 1000 km. Since the Washington Summit and
the INF treaty signing in December 1987, the issue of how to

deal with missiles below the INF treaty's 500-km threshold has become the centrepiece of NATO deliberations on the future of both Alliance military and arms control strategy. Many European observers now argue that West Germany, Britain, and France never, in the first place, wanted the INF agreement to include all shorter-range missiles encompassed in the "double zero" solution.[2] Just what precipitated the US desire to insist upon limits to shorter-range missiles as a collateral component of any INF agreement? Was this insistence in NATO's security interests? And just how selfless a gesture was Mikhail Gorbachev's willingness to propose the total elimination of shorter-range missiles, as now embodied in the "double zero" solution? The analytic backdrop to these questions will be examined here while its implications for future Western arms control strategy are assessed in Chapter 6.

The Effect of the INF Treaty on Soviet Contingency Planning

The elimination of all ground-based ballistic and cruise missiles with a range of 500 to 5500 km would have both positive and negative effects as seen from the perspective of a Soviet military planner. The following assessment considers the implications of such an agreement for each of the three theatre warfare contingencies as presented and analysed in Chapter 4.

Massive Nuclear Use

Recalling that the paramount objective of the massive-use contingency is the need to attack priority targets to the full depth of the TVD, and that missiles would represent the weapons of choice because of their assured penetrability and timeliness, it seems clear that the INF agreement will compel serious readjustments in planning for the massive-use contingency. Even were NATO caught largely unawares, leaving Soviet planners with a relatively small and fixed target set to deal with, constraining readjustments are still in order.

For example, the attack option outlined in Chapter 4 strives to achieve most of its objectives using short-range ballistic missiles stationed in East Germany and Czechoslovakia. The Soviet force of SS-20s would have only been called upon to attack the few targets beyond the range of operational-tactical missiles. Under an INF agreement, however, the "double zero solution" eliminates SS-12/22 and SS-23 missiles. While the Scud-C or a 450 km-range Scud follow-on missile (permitted under the treaty) might compensate for the loss of the SS-23, replacing the target coverage of the SS 12/22, which is critically important to attacking Group I and II targets outside of West Germany, is far more cumbersome. By virtue of the SS-20's elimination, operational-strategic missiles would not be available to compensate for such a loss. In the end, Soviet planners would be forced to rely upon intercontinental-range ballistic missiles or perhaps submarine-launched ballistic missiles to perform a regional strike role. Such a decision would not be unprecedented; Soviet military planners adapted 300 SS-11 ICBMs in the late 1960s to serve in a regional strike role. And a portion of Soviet Yankee-class submarines were probably also earmarked for a regional strike role during the 1970s.

Matters only get worse if we assume that NATO has responded to warning of attack by dispersing its nuclear weapons. Even though strike aircraft would be allocated largely against dispersed nuclear targets, the volume of support that would have been expected from the SS-20 force would grow in an unpredictable way. Under such circumstances, Soviet planners would have to count even more heavily on ICBMs to play a theatre strike role. It is also important to bear in mind that these highly escalatory circumstances represent a decision period during which Soviet planners must make hard choices about intercontinental strike requirements as well.

Beyond gross target coverage for the massive-use contingency, there is another qualitative Soviet targeting dimension that is circumscribed by the INF agreement. In terms of matching an appropriate nuclear yield to target characteristics, relying on ICBMs instead of shorter-range or even intermediate-range missiles represents a non-ideal condition. As pointed out in Chapter 2, highly accurate short-range missiiles can, in theory, effectively attack around 70% of the target set with yields of much less than a kiloton. The remainder of the targets require no higher than 10-KT yields. Although the escalatory risks and potential damage of this "discriminate" nuclear attack would doubtless be enormous, the outcome of depending more heavily on higher yield ICBMs is incalculable. Thus, one consequence (albeit limited in this observer's view) of the agreement is to deny Moscow the theoretical potential of a discriminate surgical strike capability with nuclear missiles based outside the Soviet homeland.

The Effect of Eliminating Shorter-Range Missiles on Conventional-Only and Escalating Contingencies
Despite the theoretically appealing features of a discriminate nuclear attack capability, the preponderance of Soviet military writings and force developments supports a distinct preference for non-nuclear contingencies. Only a matter of expectations about the prospects for escalation stands as the difference between the conventional-only and escalating contingencies; each would focus on achieving success with conventional means. On the surface, at least, it would appear that foresaking the right to deploy conventionally armed ballistic missiles with ranges between 500 and 1000 km would seriously impair the effectiveness of the conventional air operation. The opening missile salvo would strive to disrupt NATO air operations long enough to permit mass waves of aircraft to deliver a more crippling blow. Without success in the air, Soviet military strategists predict stalemate on the ground, tank asymmetries notwithstanding. But upon closer examination, the "double zero solution" would only marginally affect Soviet planning for non-nuclear contingencies.

Several reasons account for the marginal impact of eliminating the SS-12/22 and the SS-23 missiles. The first is that most (over 80%) of the critical targets associated with the air operation (air defence batteries, interceptor and dual-capable airfields, and nuclear storage sites) are located within 300 to 350 km of the inter-German border – that is, within the Federal

Republic of Germany. As discussed in Chapter 2, the Soviets may already have an interim solution for the ageing Scud-B problem: a product-improved Scud-C with a range of 400 km and the capability to incorporate an advanced guidance system that would permit the effective delivery of improved conventional munitions. And a new SS-23 follow-on missile, with a range just under the treaty's 500-km threshold, could become operational by 1994, if not sooner.

The second reason for concluding that "double zero" will have only marginal impact on non-nuclear contingencies is that the treaty does virtually nothing to control quantitative growth in short-range missile launchers in the tactical and operational-tactical missile classes. As Soviet planners so frequently stress in their military writings, conventional effectiveness hinges on the volume of fire delivered within a narrow timeframe. Only by placing a cap on further launcher growth for missiles below the INF treaty's lower threshold of 500 km could the West limit the Warsaw Pact's capacity to support the demanding volume requirements of the air operation discussed in Chapter 4.

The INF treaty affects only launchers supporting missiles with a range of between 500 and 1000 km – that is, less than 200 of the roughly 1900 launchers in the entire Soviet and non-Soviet Warsaw Pact inventory of short-range ballistic missiles.[3] It leaves intact – with a potential for further growth – the two most important classes (tactical and operational-tactical) of short-range ballistic missiles (see Table 2.8 for projected 1990–1995 launcher numbers facing the NATO Central Region). Indeed, there is nothing in the treaty to preclude the Soviet Union from filling evacuated SS-12/22 and SS-23 garrisons with treaty-permitted systems like the Scud-B or, more likely, the longer-range Scud-C. In effect, the only category of short-range ballistic missile capability forfeited by the Soviets under the INF treaty is the anomalous "enhanced range operational-tactical" one, consisting of the 900 km-range Scaleboard, which has never had much institutional support and, consequently, has experienced little growth in launcher force structure. It is, clearly, an exaggeration to claim – as have both US and Soviet officials and the news media alike – that a "double zero" INF agreement eliminates two "entire classes" of missiles.[4] The truth is that the so-called shorter-range class of missiles eliminated under the treaty is not a class at all (in the nature of the "operational-strategic" class of SS-20 missiles or the "operational-tactical" class of Scud missiles), but simply the artifact of the peculiar US negotiating stance (about which more will be said later) that led up to the "double zero" solution.

Besides having only a marginal impact on non-nuclear contingencies in general, one particularly important military consequence of the INF agreement for Soviet planners stems from the removal of Pershing II and GLCMs. As noted in Chapter 4, the goal of the air operation is to destroy around half of those major NATO weapon systems that either directly threaten the Soviet homeland, or can materially disrupt the Warsaw Pact ground campaign. This necessarily includes NATO's ground-based nuclear forces and its airpower. For several reasons, Pershings and GLCMs are the most worrisome targets for Soviet planners. Because they can reach Soviet territory, medium-range missiles present Soviet decision-makers with the awesome prospect of nuclear strikes on their homeland in immediate retaliation – as part of a selective employment plan – for a massive Warsaw Pact conventional attack. And Pershings and GLCMs embody the most survivable component of NATO's ground-based nuclear forces; not only do missiles become mobile upon alert, but all of NATO's GLCM deployment (or over 80% of the planned 572 INF missiles) was slated to be housed in shelters hardened against conventional attack and distributed amongst five allied nations.

Furthermore, eliminating the most survivable and highest priority NATO targets frees Soviet conventionally armed short-range missiles and strike aircraft to concentrate on NATO's vulnerable airpower infrastructure. For example, if we recall attack option 1 of the conventional-only contingency outlined in Chapter 4, 50 missiles were expended to temporarily delay (long enough for follow-on aircraft strikes) the departure of Pershing and cruise missiles from their garrisons. Beyond this missile expenditure, Soviet planners would have been forced to devote considerable aircraft resources to find and attack any Pershings and GLCMs that had successfully managed to disperse. Absent this requirement altogether, NATO airpower is certain to become the overwhelming focus of Warsaw Pact targeting attention. And for the few Central Region targets outside of West Germany that might be freed from a precursor missile strike by conventionally armed SS-12/22s, Soviet planners will be able to assign aircraft which otherwise would have been earmarked for attack against dispersed Pershing and cruise missiles. Very few observers ever doubted that the Soviet leadership sees great political value flowing from the elimination of Pershing and GLCMs. Less obvious to all but the military planner are the improved military consequences of eliminating Pershing and GLCMs for Soviet non-nuclear contingency planning.

The Impact of SS-20 Elimination on Non-nuclear Contingencies
Granted that the INF treaty will have only a marginal impact on Soviet contingency planning for conventional warfare, the elimination of over 400 SS-20 launchers and more than 1200 warheads will impose unwanted constraints on Soviet planning for the escalating contingency. The problem with planning for SS-20 use after prolonged conventional war (and perhaps even some tactical nuclear use) lies in the inherent difficulty of predicting how many missiles might be needed to deal with an uncertain target set. From the military-technical perspective of the Soviet General Staff, worst-case, yet plausible, contingencies are conceivable in which hundreds of NATO nuclear systems and well-dispersed aircraft survive a protracted conventional campaign. NATO has already begun the process of seeking ways to compensate for the elimination of Pershing and cruise missiles. And French and British independent nuclear forces are growing in both numbers and sophistication. France, alone, is in the midst of a five-year build-up of its stockpile of nuclear warheads from 285 to 930.[5] Not unexpectedly, Marshal Akhromeyev, Chief of the Soviet

General Staff, has already indicated that US compensatory measures have aroused deep suspicion in the Soviet military.[6]

Facing such an uncertain array of nuclear forces and the prospects of escalation, conservative Soviet military planners could no longer count on having a force with the SS-20's combination of features: terminal effectiveness, survivability, penetrability, targeting flexibility, and quick reaction time. Even though Soviet planners view nuclear-armed aircraft as better suited for attacking mobile targets, a sufficient number of long-range bombers might not be available, having been exhausted in several waves of an intense conventional air operation. Moreover, the need for a timely pre-emptive nuclear strike could supercede any preference for aircraft.[7] To the extent that short-range ballistic missiles are involved in extended conventional operations, they would be uncertain participants in theatre-wide nuclear escalation. The only forces that could reliably compensate for the SS-20's elimination are ICBMs and SLBMs retargeted to perform regional strike roles.

INF's provisions will also adversely affect Soviet nuclear planning in Asia. Generally speaking, the manner in which Soviet forces are organised and the strategy that guides their use in wartime apply equally to Asian as European contingencies. For example, the air forces in Soviet Asia have been reorganised to emphasise deep operations just as in the west. That said, there are important differences that distinguish Asian from European contingencies. These differences are largely the product of geography.

In contrast to Central Europe, where virtually all critical targets are within reach of shorter-range ballistic missiles, comparatively few critical targets are threatened in Asia. Important targets in South Korea and Japan are, for the most part, outside the range of all Soviet short-range missiles save the SS-12/22, which will be eliminated under the treaty. China's greatest protection lies in its great strategic depth and relative target survivability, especially against conventional attack. Whereas most dual-capable Warsaw Pact ballistic missiles facing Europe would most likely be fitted with conventional warheads, a nuclear mission would probably prevail in the case of Soviet short-range missile launchers in Asia – especially against China's hard and diffuse target set. But given the nature of Asian targets together with the great strategic depth of Moscow's Asian adversaries, the loss of the SS-20's deep targeting capability has to be viewed dimly by Soviet military planners.

To be sure, the most straightforward way of compensating for the elimination of the SS-20 force lies in greater reliance on ICBMs. But such an approach is not without its potential constraints, the foremost being the distinct possibility of a START agreement that cuts US and Soviet strategic nuclear arsenals by 50%. Without such an agreement and with SALT II restrictions explicitly abandoned by the USA, the Soviets would have strong incentives to discard SALT restrictions as the principal means of making up for INF reductions.[8] This would lead them to deploy additional SS-25 mobile ICBMs, which is probably the three-stage ICBM counterpart to a follow-on two-stage intermediate-range ballistic missile that would likely have replaced the ageing SS-20 within the next decade. In any event, the SS-25 shares the same concept of operation, logistics, training, and manning as the SS-20. Because the SS-25 delivers only a single warhead compared to the triple-warhead SS-20, the Soviets would have to test and deploy the SS-25 (or an SS-20 follow-on with a third stage) with three multiple, independently targetable re-entry vehicles (MIRVs) to compensate fully for the SS-20's elimination, or else accept the expense of proliferating single-warhead SS-25s.

Ironically, however, if the Soviets were to choose this path but nevertheless ended up accepting a START agreement entailing a 50% warhead reduction, the Soviet military would find itself faced with roughly the same circumstances (*circa* 1972) that once helped to justify the Soviet Union's heavy investment in the SS-20 force: being forced to count several hundred ICBMs and perhaps some SLBMs slated for regional strike missions against a strategic nuclear force ceiling. Moreover, even though the US targets (ICBMs in particular) against which a future Soviet ICBM force will, in part, be aimed will naturally shrink with a 50% START reduction, there may still be growing requirements for ICBM warheads to saturate expected mobile ICBM deployment areas so as to compensate for target uncertainty. In short, to a Soviet strategic planner worried about perceptions as well as practical targeting matters, such a condition affects the nature of parity at the intercontinental force level.[9] In many respects, senior Soviet military planners must be feeling a distinct sense of *déjà vu* in the aftermath of the INF treaty.

The new political leadership of the Soviet Union may view matters differently. Since the mid-1960s, the Party had provided the Soviet military with massive resources to support both nuclear and conventional contingencies. By the early-1980s, senior Soviet military planners were sufficiently confident in the results of that investment that Soviet military doctrine was reformulated to include the likelihood that a future war could remain conventional throughout its duration.[10] Preference for the conventional-only contingency is built upon greater expectation of strategic success without nuclear escalation. In this regard, the SS-20's role is to survive a protracted conventional war in order to threaten massive theatre-wide nuclear escalation against a wholly unpredictable but presumably small target set. Or at least the political leadership might conclude that it would be small in view of the military's confidence in new conventional capabilities. Nuclear forces to substitute for the SS-20 (ICBMs, for example) would certainly be available to deal with such an outcome. Given these assumptions, together with Moscow's longstanding goal of undoing NATO's hard-fought Pershing II and cruise missile deployments, the political leadership's definition of the threat and related military needs appears to have prevailed.

Such matters as described above are rarely as black and white as painted here. No doubt, "forward-looking" elements in the Soviet military establishment recognise that in order to cope with the revolutionary changes occurring in military technology, the military must co-operate with Gorbachev's economic restructuring and arms control initiatives, even if it means temporary reductions in resources allocated to the military. Otherwise, the Soviet Union may fall dangerously behind the USA to such an extent that quantity will no longer compensate for the Soviets' traditional qualitative disadvantages *vis-à-vis* the West. Arms control, in effect, offers a way of imposing predictability in US-Soviet relations. With a less assertive adversary, Moscow may see herself better positioned to control the technological competition in a way more favourable to long-term Soviet interests. While the assumption of such a farsighted position by at least a portion of the senior military leadership represents an uncertain bargain, they appear to have little choice but to adopt this stance, given the awkward economic and technological circumstances facing the Soviet Union today.

Narrowing the Soviet Military's Planning Framework

On balance, the INF treaty narrows the broad planning framework of the Soviet military – the primary legacy of the Brezhnev years. That framework permitted the Soviet military to plan and procure forces to deal with three primary theatre contingencies. The only contingency left relatively unscathed and, in some ways, aided by the provisions of the INF treaty is the most preferred one: a conventional-only war. That INF benefits only one of three contingencies inevitably suggests comparison with Khrushchev's single variant notion (albeit a nuclear one) of warfare. But the Soviet Union has accumulated enormous military potential since Khrushchev's demise. Notwithstanding the INF treaty's effects on Soviet planning for nuclear contingencies, the Soviet military is left with a wide – though less flexible – array of capabilities suitable to meet the needs of multiple contingencies. It has become increasingly clear, however, that the current Soviet political leadership judges the issue of need with considerably less clinical detail than does a conservative military leadership, accustomed as it had become under Brezhnev to receiving "everything necessary" to do its broadly defined job.[11]

With raw military power playing a less noticeable role as a guarantee of fundamental Soviet national security and foreign policy interests, it will become important for the Gorbachev-led leadership to demonstrate the effectiveness of political means in adequately safeguarding the nation's security and promoting its interests abroad. There is already one important success in that regard: Mikhail Gorbachev's sophisticated handling of the "double zero solution" to the INF treaty.

Assessing US Motivations for Limiting Soviet Shorter-Range Missiles

In general, the analysis thus far suggests that the elimination of intermediate-range missiles (especially the SS-20 force) will impose unwanted constraints on several important aspects of Soviet planning for nuclear contingencies. By contrast, however, the elimination of shorter-range missiles will cost the Soviets little, particularly with respect to the preferred conventional-only contingency. The same cannot be said about the consequences of eliminating shorter-range missiles for NATO. Where Soviet planners depend on short-range missiles primarily for conventional fire missions, their NATO counterparts rely on a significantly smaller arsenal of shorter-range missiles exclusively for nuclear missions. NATO simply banks far more on nuclear options for deterrence than does the Warsaw Pact.

Given NATO's lack of strategic depth on the continent, a more sensible constraint on Soviet short-range ballistic missiles would have been limitations – or even a cap – on future launcher growth for missiles with ranges between 150 and 1000 km. Unlike the "double zero" solution, such an approach would have placed constraints on the "operational-tactical" missile category which furnishes most of the conventional firepower associated with support to the critical air operation. Instead, "double zero" merely postponed modernisation of the Scud missile family by eliminating its intended replacement (the SS-23), but not the Soviet right to produce virtually the same missile system as long as it is not test flown to 500 km.

In effect, the only shorter-range missile loss for the Soviets, as suggested by this chapter's contingency analysis, is 115 deployed SS-12/22 Scaleboard launchers – a marginal loss at best. For this, the USA forfeits the right to deploy 108 single-stage Pershing IBs as replacements for the longer-range Pershing II, while the West Germans will unilaterally dismantle 72 Pershing IAs at the conclusion of the three-year period. And what little remains in NATO's tactical missile stockpile (88 100 km-range Lance launchers compared with over 1600 Soviet and Warsaw Pact ones) is being subjected to virtual arms control. Feeling singularly threatened by Moscow's huge asymmetric advantage in remaining short-range missiles, Bonn has suggested that it may modify its 1983 support for modernising Lance by endorsing a less than one-for-one replacement of Lance's 88 launchers.[12] All in all, Mikhail Gorbachev's willingness to accept a "double zero" solution may not have been the selfless gesture it appeared at the time.

If NATO loses more than the Warsaw Pact as a consequence of "double zero," why in the first place did the USA pressure Moscow for limits on shorter-range weapons? The reasons behind the US position on shorter-range systems reflect a dangerously myopic view of the role of these weapons in Soviet strategy – certainly a poor basis upon which to fashion an arms control negotiating strategy. At the heart of US concern over so-called Soviet short-range INF (SRINF) lay the issue of treaty circumvention. According to Assistant Secretary of Defense Richard Perle, the SS-12/22 could attack "some 85% of the NATO targets assigned to the SS-20," while the SS-23 could target "as much as 50% of European NATO." Perle further argued that barring a limitation on shorter-range missiles, any agreement on SS-20 reductions would be "hopelessly vulnerable to circumvention."[13]

Yet, analysis presented in the preceding chapters suggests that the circumvention issue is far more complex than just substituting operational-tactical for operational-strategic missiles on a one-for-one basis. Such an assumption implies that Soviet military planners attach little or no importance to operational-tactical missions for these missiles. On the contrary, however, Soviet planners now view shorter-range forces as essential to two critical missions: first, as an intermediate escalatory option between conventional and theatre-strategic conflict and, second (and most importantly), as the linchpin of the conventional air operation.

Western planners need to weigh not only the opportunities, but also the constraints Soviet planners face in coping with a broader range of planning contingencies than what is suggested by the circumvention scenario described above. Generally speaking, the Soviet military will have a wide range of choices in trying to compensate for the elimination of intermediate-range nuclear missiles: ICBMs for peripheral strikes; submarine-launched ballistic and cruise missiles; strategic and theatre bombers; and operational-tactical ballistic missiles organic to Warsaw Pact ground formations in Eastern Europe. None of these choices, however, possesses the SS-20's combination of terminal effectiveness, survivability, penetrability, targeting flexibility, and reaction time. Moreover, future strategic arms control agreements may constrain the use of ICBMs, SLBMs, and SLCMs. In the end, the predominant influence on Soviet choices is likely to be how well particular systems can (1) reconstitute the SS-20's most important wartime mission – attack against high-value, time-critical targets; and (2) compensate for the loss of the SS-20's qualitative features, the foremost being its survivability and sustainability.

To analyse Soviet circumvention options properly, we must consider more than just the need to replicate the SS-20's expected damage to its primary target set. Indeed, the SS-20's predecessors (SS-4s, SS-5s, and peripherally targeted SS-11s) quite handily met Soviet-imposed damage criteria for the several hundred targets Soviet planners have worried most about.[14] Relying on large, cumbersome, unstorable liquid-fuel missiles, which took eight hours to prepare for firing and could be held in that state for only five hours,[15] the SS-4/5 missile force was not sufficiently survivable and sustainable to meet the needs of any contingency, save for massive theatre-wide use at the outset of hostilities. Planning interest in the escalating contingency during the mid–1960s must surely have led the Soviets to select the more costly mobile-basing mode over silo basing of the SS-20; more recent interest in conventional-only contingencies merely reinforces the need for a secure and enduring theatre-strategic nuclear reserve. Therefore, any Soviet circumvention attempt would at the very least strive to reconstitute both minimum essential target coverage and adequate nuclear force flexibility to support the three prevailing planning contingencies.

In examining the three theatre contingencies of greatest concern to Soviet planners, we find that only in a premeditated surprise nuclear attack against an undispersed NATO can shorter-range missiles substantially reconstitute the SS-20 force's fixed-target coverage. Such an attack is not without enormous escalatory risk; British and French nuclear forces are left uncovered, not to speak of US strategic nuclear forces earmarked for SACEUR's use. It is not the purpose here to suggest that such an emerging attack capability is not worrisome; rather, it is to argue that Soviet planners would not base circumvention choices on just one planning contingency – especially the least preferred one.

In conflicts fought either without recourse to nuclear weapons or with an indeterminate phase of conventional operations preceding nuclear escalation, three major constraints would inescapably complicate Soviet reliance on shorter-range missiles to reconstitute SS-20 target coverage. The first arises from complications surrounding what on the surface appears a virtue: the dual-capability of shorter-range missiles. To the extent it is the Soviet goal to succeed without nuclear escalation, Soviet planners will allocate available shorter-range missile launchers to non-nuclear uses, leaving a smaller percentage available for nuclear target coverage. The only solution to this dilemma lies in adding more launchers to existing units in Eastern Europe, which is precisely what has happened. But there is not a surfeit of launchers available to Pact first-echelon units in Eastern Europe. Even projected launcher growth for the 1990s (Table 2.7) leaves Pact planners little margin for error.

The second and third constraints arise from a common feature: the very unpredictability of the war planning process. On the one hand, it is virtually impossible for Soviet planners to predetermine the target array (principally, the number of targets and their location), given an indeterminate period of conventional warfare. On the other hand, it is nearly as difficult to predict just how many shorter-range launchers will survive NATO attacks and the rigours of prolonged conventional operations to be available for pre-emptive nuclear strikes. In fact, the more shorter-range missile launchers are engaged in conventional fire missions, the greater is their vulnerability to detection and NATO counterfire, simply by virtue of furnishing a tell-tale firing signature to Western intelligence units.

On balance, Soviet short-range ballistic missiles cannot simultaneously sharpen the effectiveness of the Warsaw Pact's conventional threat to NATO and offer a way for Soviet planners to circumvent a zero-option agreement. In view of the fundamental roles played by the SS-20 force, short-range ballistic missiles would seem to offer little capacity to reconstitute SS-20 target coverage lost through the INF treaty. Specifically, short-range missiles standing alert in Eastern Europe could pick up a portion of SS-20 coverage to meet the needs of a surprise massive nuclear contingency. Beyond this marginal contribution, short-range missiles furnish little in the way of reconstituting the SS-20's more critical mission: that of surviving a protracted conventional and possibly limited nuclear conflict to threaten massive theatre-wide nuclear escalation. Indeed, the better shorter-range missiles perform in their primary missions of conventional pre-emption and operational-tactical nuclear escalation, the less the chance they could in any way replace lost SS-20 coverage. It is far more likely that Soviet planners will call upon more secure forces (a combination of mobile ICBMs, SLBMs, and SLCMs) to reconstitute the SS-20's theatre nuclear reserve mission.

A reinforcing factor underlying the West's perceived need to constrain Soviet shorter-range ballistic missiles probably related to growing recognition within NATO of the conventional delivery potential of these missiles and the corresponding consideration of anti-tactical ballistic missile defences. If, in fact, any such a consideration was operative, then US negotiators failed to achieve anything of great substance in view of "double zero's" marginal impact on the Soviet-preferred conventional-only contingency. In sum, perhaps what propelled the USA in the end to extend missile elimination downward to 500 km was the general notion that without some constraints on Soviet shorter-range missiles, NATO would face an enormous asymmetric Soviet advantage in that category after the elimination of INF weapons. But, as evidenced by the prominence of the current debate within NATO about the "short-range issue," the INF treaty did little to alleviate Western fears; if anything, these fears have been aggravated.

Demonstrating the Effectiveness of Moscow's New Political Strategy

Mikhail Gorbachev's series of INF-related offers surrounding US Secretary of State Shultz's visit to Moscow in April 1987 demonstrated that Moscow's new political strategy is far more sophisticated than most Westerners had anticipated. It also suggests an underlying vulnerability in Western negotiating strategy – specifically, in the care with which Western negotiating positions are formulated. Gorbachev's willingness to eliminate short-range missiles with ranges between 500 and 1000 km provides a pointed illustration, especially in view of the peculiar set of US motivations for limiting Soviet shorter-range missiles.

The original US draft treaty tabled in December 1981 disingenuously proposed collateral measures to limit Soviet SRINF missiles with ranges the same as or between those of the SS-23 (500 km) and SS-12/22 (1000 km) to the number deployed as of 1 January 1982.[16] Given that the Soviets had yet to deploy the SS-23 at that time, the treaty would have effectively prevented the deployment of the SS-23 while freezing in place the SS-12/22 force. No reciprocal measures affecting NATO shorter-range missiles were proposed or discussed. Not surprisingly, the Soviets showed no interest. To get discussions moving, the USA offered, in June 1983, to apply limits on US Pershing I.

All during the original (pre-Soviet walkout) INF talks, Soviet negotiators shed little light on how they viewed limits on shorter-range missiles. At first they argued that limits on these missiles with a range less than 1000 km were unnecessary, but later agreed in principle to quantitative limits on missiles with ranges between 500 to 1000 km. No concrete provisions were introduced, however. Indeed, outside of the negotiations, a senior Soviet General Staff officer, Col Gen Nikolay Chervov, who is now a prominent Soviet arms control figure, aptly reflected official Soviet disinterest by flatly declaring that the "SS-22 and SS-23 missiles do not exist at all; they exist only in the American's imagination."[17]

The short-range missile issue remained an obstacle right up to Secretary of State Shultz's April 1987 visit to Moscow. Gorbachev's position until then had been that the short-range question be taken up in negotiations to commence after a "zero option" INF agreement. By holding his position until the April meetings, Gorbachev could then appear to offer a selfless concession on the issue by proposing not only to eliminate missiles with ranges between 500 and 1000 km, but also those below 500 km.[18] American officials immediately backed off the proposal to ban all missiles, claiming it was impossible to verify. But, after considerable wrangling within NATO over the merits of accepting a proposal that would prevent the USA from the right to change longer-range Pershing IIs into shorter-range Pershing IBs, the Alliance finally agreed to eliminate both categories of missiles. The Soviets shortly thereafter added the West German Pershing IAs to the "double zero" list, precipitating another Alliance mini-crisis that was eventually settled in favour of the Soviet position. What started out in late 1981 as an disingenuous effort by the USA to place unilateral limits on Soviet shorter-range nuclear missiles had suddenly been turned around to Soviet advantage six years later by a shrewd new Soviet leader. It is bitter irony indeed that the set of assumptions (relating to concerns about Soviet circumvention) underlying the original US initiative were so fundamentally flawed.

Finally, in creating the appearance of making an undesired concession (particularly one that the Soviet military ostensibly would not favour) on shorter-range missiles, Gorbachev's negotiating strategy also has had an important secondary benefit. Besides spawning the perception, if not the reality, of denuclearisation within the Alliance, Gorbachev's "concession" has drawn attention away from concern about the need for an anti-tactical ballistic system.[19] But the "double zero" solution only marginally affects the planning contingency NATO worries about most: a Warsaw Pact short-warning conventional attack in which conventionally armed missiles are currently assured of penetrating to their targets. Perhaps this provides an object lesson for the Soviet military on how effective diplomacy and arms control initiatives can be in achieving positive national security results.

Notes

1. The strategic rational actor model of decision-making views a nation as a rational, unitary decision-maker that employs coherent policies and programs to achieve discernable aims.
2. See, for example, Robert Mauthner, "NATO Policy is Ripe for Review," *Financial Times*, 19 January 1988, p. 23.
3. Launcher numbers are derived from *The Military Balance* (London: IISS, 1986-87).
4. See, for example, Robert McCartney, "Soviet Missile Offer Wins Bonn's Accord," *Washington Post*, 2 June 1987, p. 1.
5. James M. Markham, "Paris and Bonn Start to Think of a Special Alliance," *New York Times*, 24 June 1987, p. A3.
6. Bill Keller, "Soviet Marshal Sees 'Star Wars' Giving U.S. Edge," *New York Times*, 30 October 1987, p. 1.
7. V. Ye. Savkin, *The Basic Principles of Operational Art and Tactics* (Moscow: 1972), trans. by USAF (Washington, D.C.: USGPO, 1976), pp. 147-148.
8. See Bruce D. Berkowitz, "An INF Treaty Discredits Arms Control and Promotes Conflict," *Orbis*, Winter 1988, pp. 119-126.
9. For a detailed account of how the Soviets dealt with this problem in the early 1970s, see Raymond L. Garthoff, *Détente and Confrontation: American-Soviet Relations from Nixton to Reagan* (Washington, D.C. The Brookings Institution, 1985), pp. 870-886.
10. M.M. Kir'yan, ed., *Military-Technological Progress and the USSR Armed Forces* (Moscow: Voyenizdat, 1982), pp. 312-313.
11. The standard formulation of CPSU support to the military under-

went a change in preparations for the 27th Party Congress in February 1986. Rather than employing the standard formulation that the Party will do "everything necessary," Gorbachev's new formulation indicated that "The CPSU will make every effort to ensure that the Armed Forces of the USSR are on a level which excludes the achievement of strategic superiority by the forces of imperialism." For an insightful interpretation of this reformulation, see Notra Trulock III, *Soviet Military Thought in Transition: Implications for the Long-Term Military Competition*, Pacific-Sierra Research Corporation, PSR Interim Report, 22 May 1987.

12. James M. Markham, "Kohl Would Keep Tactical Missiles," *New York Times*, 7 February 1988, p. 9.

13. Cited in Jed C. Snyder, "European Security, East–West Policy, and the INF Debate," *Orbis*, Winter 1984, p. 968; see also William Durch and Peter Almquist, "East–West Military Balance," in Barry M. Blechman and Edward N. Luttwak, eds., *International Security Yearbook 1984/85* (Boulder: Westview Press, 1985), p. 69.

14. Stephen M. Meyer, "Soviet Theatre Nuclear Forces, Part I: Development of Doctrine and Objectives," *Adelphi Papers*, No. 187 (London: IISS, 1983/84), p. 26.

15. Robert P. Berman and John C. Baker, *Soviet Strategic Forces: Requirements and Responses* (Washington, D.C.: The Brookings Institution, 1982), p. 15.

16. INF deliberations are discussed in *Summary of Special Consultative Group Progress Report to Ministers*, 8 December 1983.

17. Nikolay Chervov, head of the Legal Department of the Soviet General Staff, was quoted in an interview in *Stern*, 20 October 1983, pp. 234–235.

18. David K. Shipler, "Gorbachev Offers to Render Europe Clear of Missiles," *New York Times*, 15 April 1987, p. 1.

19. See, for example, Jurgen Altmann, Benoit Morel, Theodore Postol, and Thomas Risse-Kappen (ed.), *Anti-Tactical Missile Defenses and West European Security* (Frankfurt am Main: Hessische Stiftung Friedens-und Konfliktforschung, 1987), where the authors open their report with the following statement: "At first sight, it might seem anachronistic to concern oneself with the question of a tactical missile defence system in fall 1987. After all, President Reagan and General Secretary Gorbachev will sign a treaty before the year is out, freeing Europe and the world of all land-based inter-

mediate (*sic*) missiles with ranges from 500 to 5500 km. Where is the sense in developing defences against the SS-20 and the SS-23 when these very missiles are to be scrapped under the double-zero soltuion anyway?" The authors of this monograph focus only on what has been eliminated by the INF treaty at the expense of examining Soviet options which remain unaffected by the treaty's provisions.

6

Implications for Western security and arms control policy

The Soviet Union's current internal predicaments pose both opportunities and dilemmas for the West. Certainly, Moscow and Washington broadly share an interest in managing the nuclear competition. Beyond the INF treaty, the basis apparently exists for significant reductions in strategic nuclear forces and at least some arrangement on SDI research and deployment. Yet, what some view as hope, others see as a dilemma. They see a Soviet Union grappling with systemic decline and desperately in need of restructuring a long-term political strategy of negotiations and *détente* with the West. In that way, arms control offers the Soviet Union a means of broadly controlling the technological competition with the West while they continue to challenge any Western notion of extended deterrence. To make the Soviet military rest easier, Soviet political strategists are challenged to box the West into its own single variant strategy: one that eschews credible nuclear options and increasingly relies on conventional defence alone.

Mikhail Gorbachev's newly emboldened political strategy, working in combination with the Soviet military's enduring advantages in the conventional warfare area (now being politically recast in a new "defensive" military doctrine), poses serious challenges for the Western Alliance. Never before has there been such a compelling need for the Atlantic Alliance to build a coherent framework that rationalises military strategy, force modernisation, and arms control. Clearly, the absence of a coherent planning framework led to the disadvantageous inclusion of a "second zero option" in the INF treaty.

Coherent defence planning depends on understanding the

156

adversary's major strengths and weaknesses. At the heart of the Soviet search for new military flexibility, begun in the mid-1960s, lies the desire to dominate the escalatory process – preferably with conventional weapons alone – and especially to avoid escalation to the Soviet homeland. But not until the modernisation programmes of the 1970s started to bear fruit did Soviet confidence increase to the point that they could conduct decisive missions with conventional means, although always under the threat of nuclear escalation. By 1982, the Soviet military could claim that their armed forces had perfected appropriate methods and a force structure capable of conducting warfare "both with the use of nuclear weapons and with the use only of conventional means."[1]

Granted that there was a basis to make such a confident prediction, it is not standard fare in Soviet military assessments. In fact, despite major strides in force development, the Soviet military has expressed uncertainty about several critical features of dealing with Western strategy and forces. It should be the goal of Western defence planning to identify and exaggerate these areas of Soviet uncertainty about war with NATO.

For example, the very notion of escalation introduces complex uncertainties into the Soviet force planning process. Given an indeterminate phase of conventional operations, followed perhaps by front nuclear strikes, how should forces be sized and employed? What percentage of dual-capable forces should be withheld from conventional operations (with attendant adverse consequences for conventional success) to prepare the way for a smooth transition to nuclear warfare? Especially difficult is predicting precisely when NATO might choose to escalate. Soviet planners place highest priority on destroying NATO's in-theatre nuclear capability by conventional means before escalation. But success in this endeavour is highly uncertain, especially if NATO manages to employ various survivability measures, not the least of which is effective dispersal. And finding lost targets is quite problematic. Even if useful targeting information could be obtained, the notion of combining it with highly ready strike forces and achieving predictable success does not induce even a modest degree of confidence.

A far more important area of uncertainty relates to the adverse consequences of even a relatively confined level of nuclear use within the theatre. It is typical of most Western accounts of Soviet theatre nuclear use to predict enormous Warsaw Pact success by virtue of ground-force exploitation of nuclear strikes.[2] But recently declassified lecture materials from the Voroshilov General Staff Academy tell a different story.[3] By the mid-1970s, Soviet planners had concluded that nuclear use would not necessarily improve the average rate of advance over the course of an offensive, but might even constrain it. For planning purposes, the expected rates of advance in nuclear and non-nuclear environments were identical. A mutual nuclear exchange in the theatre – the dominant scenario – was expected to disrupt command and control significantly, creating the need to reconstitute forces and re-establish control. As long as Soviet decision-makers worry as deeply as they now do about the adverse operational and strategic consequences of a NATO nuclear riposte, survivably based and credibly planned nuclear weapon options should remain a central feature of NATO strategy.

Recognition of these effects and uncertainties has encouraged the Soviets steadily to improve their ability to defeat NATO conventionally (substituting mass conventional firepower for nuclear use at the outset), especially to destroy pre-emptively as much as possible of NATO's in-theatre nuclear capability, airpower, and reinforcements. Surprise (at least tactical if not operational) is such an important feature of Soviet theatre strategy because it exaggerates a longstanding NATO weakness: building up and sustaining sufficient conventional staying power long enough to plausibly threaten nuclear escalation. A war that could not be won quickly has enormous implications for Soviet planners. Foremost, prolongation of conventional conflict increases the prospects of a coherent nuclear response by NATO. Moreover, the Soviets must fragment Western cohesion before the seeds of disarray similarly affect their own even more vulnerable alliance system.

Not surprisingly, most of the Soviet concepts and improved conventional capabilities discussed in this book are designed to exploit NATO in the initial campaign of a future war. Soviet military strategists fully appreciate the contemporary consequences of Helmuth von Moltke's admonition, "No plan of operations can look with any certainty beyond the first meeting with major forces of the enemy."[4] The goal is not to win in one blow but to adjust the initial conditions so as to predetermine a favourable outcome.

Unfortunately, NATO is conspicuously vulnerable during the so-called initial period of war. Most analyses of the NATO-Warsaw Pact conventional balance see the West's most egregious vulnerabilities occurring within the first ten days of a war. Should the Alliance fail to respond to what history suggests will inevitably be ambiguous signals (compounded by a natural reluctance to take even prudent defensive measures for fear of provoking unintended reactions), the first ten days of conflict would be conducted with very unfavourable force ratios. Generally, a Warsaw Pact-to-NATO force ratio of not more than 1.2 to 1 is viewed as the minimum acceptable to hold a continuous defence line theatre-wide. But the US Congressional Budget Office has estimated (Figure 6.1) that the Warsaw Pact could achieve nearly a 2 to 1 force ratio during the ten days following the onset of Western mobilisation. Only the arrival of US reinforcement divisions would begin to restore the situation on the ground. Although the Warsaw Pact's longer-term mobilisation potential would return the advantage to them after about 35 days, crisis or war prolongation risks all of the previously discussed vulnerabilities, which the Soviets would like to avoid through decisive success.

Changing force ratios on the ground are surely reason for concern. But they have drawn so much analytic and emotional attention in the West as to overshadow an equally or perhaps even more important feature (in the Soviet view) of the initial period: that of the air war.[5] Put simply, Soviet military planners calculate that success on the ground – tank asymmetries notwithstanding – cannot happen without decisive success first in the air. Soviet ground force operational doctrine is inherently

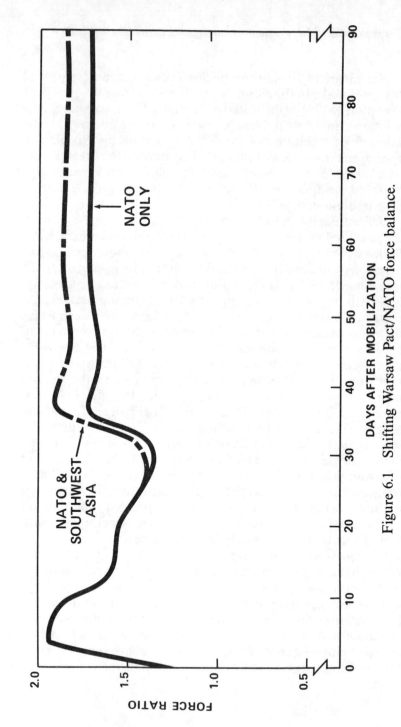

Figure 6.1 Shifting Warsaw Pact/NATO force balance.

Source: As adapted from US Congressional Budget Office, *Rapid Deployment Forces: Policy and Budgetary Implications* (Washington, D.C.: USGPO, 1983) p. 23.

risky; it calls for concentrating (and thereby exposing) armour, mechanised infantry, air assault, and airborne forces against narrow sectors along the front so as to penetrate, envelop, and paralyse thinly deployed NATO forces. Its Achilles' heel is vulnerability to airpower. And in that regard, Soviet planners have enormous respect for NATO airpower; they see over 50% of NATO's firepower represented in the form of strike aircraft. They also see that NATO's airpower resources have become increasingly concentrated at a few main operating bases in the Central Region. No more apt a description of this growing problem can be found than in Paul Kennedy's recent book, *The Rise and Fall of the Great Powers*:

> The fact that the Reagan administration in its first term spent over 75 percent more on new aircraft than the Carter regime but acquired only 9 percent more planes points to *the* appalling military-procurement problem of the late twentieth century: given the technologically driven tendency toward spending more and more money upon fewer and fewer weapon systems, would the United States and its allies really have enough sophisticated and highly expensive aircraft and tanks in reserve after the early stages of a ferociously fought conventional war? (Emphasis in original.)[6]

Making certain that NATO does not is the *sine qua non* of Soviet theatre warfare strategy.

This brief overview of major Soviet uncertainties and weaknesses suggests that, in the aftermath of the INF accord, the Western Alliance should devote itself to two comparatively modest goals (in both financial and political terms).[7] The first entails recognising the continuing importance of survivably based and credibly planned nuclear options. In this regard, various compensatory measures are essential as a consequence of the removal of Pershing II and cruise missiles. The second is a corollary of the first. To bolster the credibility of nuclear deterrence, NATO must demonstrate an improved capacity to survive the weight of the Warsaw Pact's initial conventional blow. This is nowhere more pressing than in the area of airpower survivability, given the respect Soviet planners have for this component of NATO's deterrent forces. The remainder of this chapter turns to the specific requirements and choices associated with these goals, including the contribution of arms control measures.

Refurbishing Nuclear Deterrence in NATO

The very notion of tinkering with the nuclear component of NATO's Flexible Response strategy must be handled with great caution. Europeans and Americans hold broadly differing perspectives on the role of nuclear weapons in NATO strategy.[8] American security planners have tended to focus on the clinical details of nuclear weapon roles, missions, target analysis, survivability, and the like, while their European counterparts see nuclear weapons largely through a political prism. Perhaps the most important features of the political dimension of theatre nuclear weapons have been the persistent efforts by the USA to allay European concerns over the credibility of the US nuclear guarantee and what role the European allies might play in the nuclear consultation/decision-making process. Yet, despite European questioning of the US guarantee, the USA's allies paradoxically swing between doubt and anxiety, the latter induced by the fear that the USA might introduce nuclear weapons too hastily – as opposed to not at all. Thus, the US nuclear role and presence in Europe is, as Michael Howard describes it, double-edged: not just simply to deter Soviet aggression but to reassure West Europeans.[9]

Even though nuclear weapons have served largely as political instruments, there are important military roles which serve to enhance the credibility of nuclear deterrence *vis-à-vis* the Soviet Union. Depending on the way these military roles and options are formulated, they can also contribute to enhancing the political credibility of the US nuclear guarantee. Indeed, the more NATO can convey – rather than brandish – credible escalatory attack options which are survivably based and which focus on exaggerating the uncertainties associated with Soviet-led conventional warfare options, the better off the Alliance will be in meeting the fundamental requirements of nuclear deterrence in NATO.

The simplest, yet perhaps the most operationally useful,

military function of nuclear weapons is that they compel the aggressor to disperse his forces, thus making it riskier to concentrate for breakthrough operations – even local ones. Elaborate plans for nuclear use have been formulated based on detailed target and weapon-effect analyses. Nuclear plans inevitably interact with conventional warfare ones; battlefield nuclear and conventional weapons deal with the same targets and have much the same operational goals. There is even more overlap between US strategic nuclear planning and NATO planning for deep use of nuclear weapons. This overlap helps explain why there has been a split reaction in the USA to the loss of Pershing II and cruise missiles. In view of the fact that INF's targets in the Soviet Union were always covered by US strategic nuclear forces, the tacticians of nuclear targeting never felt that INF weapons made any serious military contribution. But this narrow technical view overlooks the doubt of many Europeans and Americans (and perhaps Russians, as well) that a US president would promptly authorise the limited use of strategic nuclear forces to forestall Soviet conventional aggression in Europe. Equally important, many Europeans have felt all along that they would have a share in the decision to escalate only if the weapons were deployed on their own soil rather than on US territory alone.

Because INF weapons have played an important role in NATO selective employment planning (SEP) for nuclear use, the SEP process is perhaps the most useful framework within which to consider ways the Alliance might compensate for the elimination of INF missiles.[10] The SEP process allows for the discriminate and mindful use of nuclear weapons to achieve specified political and military objectives. The political aim is to terminate conflict by causing the aggressor to reconsider his original war aims. Militarily, selective employment entails employing force against specific military targets in a way that achieves enough damage to the target without excessive civilian damage. The objective here is to convince the aggressor to terminate the conflict before further undesired collateral damage occurs.

Two planning factors dominate the SEP process. The first is

timing. A natural tension exists between the desire not to forego conventional operations too soon and the need to avoid exercising nuclear use too late. Despite the concern about "use them or lose them" pressures, premature use is highly doubtful given the length of time needed for political consultation and military authorisation for first use of nuclear weapons.[11] More probable is tardy use and the prospect of friendly forces being destroyed or overrun; in such disarray it is highly doubtful that NATO's forward-based forces would be capable of employing nuclear weapons in any coherent way. This prospect only underscores the need to bolster NATO's capability to withstand the weight of the Warsaw Pact's first blow.

The second critical factor in SEP planning is the location of enemy targets selected for the first use of nuclear weapons. Since initial use is supposed to convey an important political as well as military message, attacks against the aggressor's homeland are thought to carry the most deterrent weight. Thus, Pershing II and cruise missiles presented Soviet decision-makers with the awesome prospect of immediate nuclear escalation to their homeland. Although such a threat may convey an unambiguous political message, it is not at all clear that such deep strikes would carry equally unambiguous military effect. By the time NATO decides to release nuclear weapons for first use, the Soviets may already have introduced more than enough forces into Eastern Europe to make NATO's deep strikes militarily superfluous. Close-in use of nuclear weapons might make more military, if not political, sense in such a case. But regardless of the detailed military circumstances, one thing ought to be perfectly obvious: NATO cannot credibly threaten an escalatory response – close-in or deep – without (1) enough conventional staying power and, thus, time to plausibly threaten a coherent response, and (2) a survivable means of command and control and survivably based theatre nuclear forces from which to configure a nuclear response.

Choices in Compensating for INF Missile Elimination
In considering how to go about compensating for the removal of Pershing II and cruise missile deployments, it is important to

keep the requirements of the SEP process in mind. Nuclear weapons assigned to replace INF missiles need to be effective against a broad class of military targets. At the same time, they should not be so indiscriminate that they would be seen to cause unnecessary collateral damage. In addition, both the weapons and supporting command and control must be sufficiently survivable to maintain their integrity through more than just a few days of conventional warfare. Finally, no matter what systems are assigned to replace INF missiles, NATO's general military posture must be seen as capable of exploiting the effects of nuclear use.

One approach would be to allocate a certain percentage of the Strategic Air Command's (SAC) air or missile capabilities to SACEUR. As already noted, US strategic nuclear forces can already cover most, if not all, of the targets that current INF weapons now cover. Perhaps the best way to accomplish this mission lies in assigning 10 or 15 B-52 air-launched cruise missile carriers to a NATO mission. Such an allocation would contribute 200 to 300 warheads,[12] which together with SACEUR's allocation of 400 submarine-launched ballistic missiles, would more than compensate for INF missile reduction in purely warhead terms.

Technically, configuring such a compensatory force is rather straightforward. There would probably be a need for some command, control, and communications patching, but the expense would pale in comparison with the need to create an entirely new C^3 system associated with a dedicated force of INF systems.

Politically, matters are not so simple. The major area of concern would inevitably be over the extent of "coupling" of such a force to the US nuclear guarantee. Moreover, the simple existence of INF weapons deployed in five allied countries gave America's European allies a visible stake in nuclear decision-making. One possible solution to this dilemma would be to create mixed American and allied crews on ALCM carriers assigned to SACEUR.

A variation to the above approach would consist of allocating to SACEUR a portion of SAC's 60 or so FB-111s based in the north-eastern USA. The FB-111 is a two-seat, medium-range strategic bomber version of the F-111 tactical fighter. It can carry up to six nuclear bombs or six short-range attack missiles (SRAMs) armed with nuclear warheads. The FB-111 force's location in the north-eastern USA means that these aircraft could support NATO's Northern and Central Regions. As far as timing of support is concerned, aircraft could be launched from comparatively secure air bases in the USA (compared at least to the uncertain security of bases in central Europe), refuelled *en route*, and capable of striking targets within roughly two hours of launch. These aircraft could recover at their home bases or perhaps in the United Kingdom at air bases supporting F-111s. To reinforce the notion of NATO assignment, these aircraft should probably be reassigned to the US Air Force Europe; they could also be included in NATO exercises and periodically inspected by NATO tactical evaluation teams to underscore their commitment to NATO.

Using submarine-launched cruise missiles as a means of compensating for INF systems has received more attention than the preceding option. Despite the attractiveness of using SLCMs, many problems stand in the way. Perhaps the most serious one relates to the competing roles and missions of SLCMs. Submarines are not dedicated just to delivering SLCMs. As long as these boats remain multi-mission oriented, there will remain questions about the ready availability of SLCMs to respond to SACEUR. Of course, the European members of NATO could share in the costs of creating a dedicated force of SLCM boats. Here, a number of issues would have to be studied closely, including those of manning, command and control, choice of surface or subsurface vessel, and whether or not the force should be dual-capable.

Putting aside this critical problem for the moment, the SLCM does offer great potential as a substitute for INF systems. It has sufficient range (assuming boats are deployed in ocean areas from which they can be responsive to SACEUR needs) and accuracy not only to perform the INF mission but conventional delivery as well. An advanced follow-on cruise missile in the 1990s offers an even more significant conventional capability than is currently the case with today's SLCMs. According to US Department of Defense testimony to Congress, the USA plans a force of 2643 conventionally armed cruise missiles for use at sea and aimed at targets on land.[13] In this regard, the primary deep targets covered by INF weapons are probably Soviet and East European airfields, but unless they are struck relatively early in a conflict these targets may no longer be appropriate by the time nuclear use occurs. Having the capability to employ highly accurate conventionally armed cruise missiles – as well as nuclear-armed ones – thus represents a potent deterrent force.

In sum, each of the potential compensatory measures has its strengths and weaknesses. Certainly the greatest strength of these measures lies in the area of survivability. The greatest challenge is in the area of coupling. Although Pershing and cruise missiles were more vulnerable than the options discussed above, the reason for their vulnerability (basing in the heart of Europe) coincidentally furnished substantial coupling, in that the USA's allies had a substantial stake in the consultation process for using these weapons. This would not hold true to the same extent, but there are ways, as previously mentioned, to increase coupling. Perhaps the best solution of all would be to rely on a combination of measures so as to permit strengths to offset weaknesses. For example, the current SSBN boats earmarked for SACEUR support can carry 100 to 200 warheads per boat. It would be foolish to risk the loss of a boat by launching only a handful of warheads, as might be the case in initial use. By contrast, B-52 ALCM aircraft are packaged to carry 20 cruise missiles each, and could be launched one at a time; however, they are not the most responsive of the alternatives discussed above, especially if aircraft are not already on station off the coast of Europe. SLCM boats have other missions; consequently, perhaps only a few boats of the total afloat would be within range of targets at any one time. Given these overall pluses and minuses, SLCMs would appear appropriate for small initial attacks, while ALCMs seem suitably configured for medium-sized attacks, and SLBMs for a general nuclear response.

NATO Nuclear Force Modernisation

Despite the agreement to eliminate INF missiles, the course taken by NATO at Montebello in late 1983 makes both military and political sense. Though the Montebello decision will reduce the US-NATO stockpile to its lowest level (4600) in 25 years, its size will still remain larger than the Soviet Union's reported stockpile of 4000 nuclear warheads in Eastern Europe.[14] Of much greater consequence than its overall size are its make-up and enduring survivability.

Many analysts have called for the complete elimination of nuclear artillery shells, which, at present, account for a little over one-third of the European-based stockpile. Certainly in view of Soviet nuclear artillery deployments, the presence of large numbers of nuclear artillery shells no longer furnishes NATO with the edge it once possessed. Moreover, the fixed storage sites for these shells are extremely vulnerable; reportedly, 13 of these storage sites are within 62 miles of the East German border.[15] Such placement raises fears of quick overrun, which some believe could cause SACEUR, with presidential approval, to prematurely delegate release authority to artillery commanders. This prospect, it is claimed, increases the chances of Soviet pre-emption.[16]

Instead of a large nuclear artillery deployment, some have called for greater dependence on a missile with a range of 300 to 400 km,[17] which might solve many of the dilemmas forward-deployed nuclear artillery reputedly face. But before we completely dismiss the military use of nuclear artillery, we must look more closely at the purpose of these weapons in the context of contemporary Soviet strategy and military capabilities.

Because of the dramatic improvements in Soviet deep-strike conventional attack capabilities discussed in the preceding chapters, it is not clear that a rearward storage of nuclear warheads for a new longer-range missile would offer much greater survivability than closer-in storage sites. Moreover, while rearward placement would lessen the likelihood of overrun by conventional ground forces, such sites would still be susceptible to special-purpose forces (Spetsnaz), airborne, and air assault attacks. And, in contrast to the relatively large number (roughly 20) of small storage sites for nuclear artillery, deploying rear-area missiles would probably entail placing warheads in a much smaller number of larger storage sites. Concentrating missiles and their warheads this way would at once reduce the number of fixed targets confronting Soviet targeteers and increase the gravest period of vulnerability by considerably lengthening dispersal time.[18]

It is also not evident that any of the alternatives to nuclear artillery can at once furnish the same degree of credible first use and seriously complicate Warsaw Pact offensive operations and counternuclear targeting. Given the purposeful ambiguity of NATO's flexible-response strategy, nuclear artillery is a double-edged sword: one dimension fosters fear of premature delegation; the other promotes credible use against a determined adversary. As for complicating Warsaw Pact offensive operations, Soviet planners freely admit to the extreme difficulty of acquiring and targeting NATO dual-capable artillery because of the large number of nuclear-certified artillery units. Such a targeting complication, in effect, increases the raid size of any Soviet pre-emptive strike with tactical nuclear weapons, thereby magnifying the escalatory burden for Soviet decision-makers.

Finally, completely eliminating NATO's nuclear artillery threat would diminish Warsaw Pact fears of concentrating their ground formations for local breakthroughs. Longer-range nuclear fires from rearward-based nuclear delivery systems are not nearly as effective in responding rapidly to local battlefield conditions as are dual-capable artillery units.

Having noted the military use of nuclear artillery, we can ask if the size of NATO's deployment (roughly over one-third of the total stockpile) makes sense. Unfortunately, NATO's flexible-response strategy does not offer a standard by which to calculate the Alliance's needs with any precision.[19] Suffice it to say, however, that too heavy an emphasis is currently placed on nuclear artillery within NATO's overall nuclear deterrent posture. A drawdown from the roughly 1700 warheads in today's stockpile to no more than 700 over the next decade would not only retain most of the military advantages of these weapons but would also be consistent with the growing political opposition to nuclear warfighting on friendly soil. New air-to-ground nuclear-armed missiles with a range of around 250 km could replace withdrawn artillery rounds so as not to allow the overall stockpile size to diminish. They would materially improve the prospects of reaching Warsaw Pact targets and greatly improve the survivability of NATO fighter-bombers by virtue of their stand-off capability.

A stockpile of 700 modernised nuclear artillery shells,[20] featuring longer ranges and improved safety and security devices, would complicate Soviet target acquisition and compel local Warsaw Pact dispersion without auguring a prolonged nuclear warfighting capability at the lower end of the theatre nuclear force spectrum. Most important, such a stockpile would credibly convey NATO's capability and intent to execute, if necessary, a rapid escalation to longer-range strikes on Soviet soil furnished by a more survivably based force of intermediate-range systems.

Reducing the shorter-range end of NATO's nuclear stockpile, while emphasising the threat of escalatory strikes on Soviet soil, makes compelling political sense for another reason. Consider the asymmetrical NATO–Warsaw Pact stockpile trends as Eastern Europeans must view them. NATO's planned stockpile adjustments primarily reduce battlefield nuclear weapons, which threaten destruction of Eastern Europe, not the Soviet Union. And while NATO decreases the nuclear threat to Eastern Europe, compensatory measures for dealing with Pershing II and cruise missile elimination increase the risk of attacks on Soviet territory. By contrast, Moscow's new short-range ballistic missile deployments in Eastern Europe – even though they are primarily there to deliver conventional munitions – together with the re-emergence of nuclear artillery appear to transfer the nuclear risk from Russian to Eastern European soil.

This trend in the Warsaw Pact's tactical nuclear stockpile could exacerbate a longstanding but muted disagreement within the Warsaw Pact over nuclear deployments in Eastern Europe, limited nuclear war, and Soviet security guarantees.[21] As discussed in Chapter 1, Soviet planners envisaged in the early 1970s a decoupling of the theatre from the intercontinental level of warfare. In fact, Henry Kissinger has reported that during US–Soviet negotiations in 1972, the Soviets described certain acceptable conditions for nuclear weapon use as including confinement to the territory of allies.[22] Although the principal purpose of this blatant Soviet initiative was to drive a wedge between the USA and its European allies, its implications cut both ways for Eastern and Western Europeans alike. Thus, as the Western Alliance draws down the battlefield portion of its nuclear stockpile, the political costs of Moscow's growing short-range arsenal in Eastern Europe may loom larger.

Improving the Survivability of Nuclear Weapons

The credibility of NATO's nuclear deterrent depends on more than just the inherent plausibility of employing a particular number of nuclear weapons against certain adversary targets; it fundamentally rests on the ability to sustain a viable defence and thus to protect the ability to escalate through an intense initial period of war. This would not be the first time that the survivability issue was raised. The USA and its European allies have witnessed far too many failed attempts at trying to upgrade the survivability of NATO's nuclear stockpile. The Alliance does not lack for technical solutions but, rather, the political will to carry them out. Vulnerability may not be seen as a serious problem in peacetime because the mere existence of nuclear weapons is enough to deter any rational adversary. But it is during deep crises when deterrence is put to its most stressful test. The manner in which NATO has postured its nuclear stockpile ought to be a stable feature of Alliance strategy; instead it represents a potentially dangerous instability that could provoke the very action it seeks to deter.

As discussed in Chapter 4, it is difficult to pinpoint how much of NATO's nuclear capability must be disrupted – in Soviet eyes – to disintegrate NATO's will to escalate. Perhaps the closest figure of merit lies in the goal of the air operation: 50–60% of the primary NATO target set, of which the prime component is nuclear. Essential to effective deterrence – and raising the nuclear threshold – is configuring NATO's nuclear force posture so that it can survive the Warsaw Pact's initial conventional blow.

Perhaps the most sensitive and critical area of nuclear survivability is effecting dispersal, or the rapid movement of land-based nuclear forces (delivery vehicles as well as nuclear warheads, which frequently are separately stored) from peacetime storage locations to safer havens. Effective dispersal would upset Soviet pre-emptive calculations by multiplying the nuclear target set from roughly 80 known locations to 300 to 400 mobile field-deployed units. Moreover, dispersal clearly signals NATO's resolve to increase the risks of any Warsaw Pact aggression.

But enormous risks are associated with any decision to disperse nuclear weapons. Given the goals of the Warsaw Pact air operation, together with the enormous advantage afforded by striking during the pre-mobilisation period, Soviet decision-makers would be beset in a deep crisis with intense pressures to substitute military for diplomatic action before NATO's vulnerabilities dissipated through dispersal. Covert, early dispersal of a portion of the arsenal – achieved through deceptive techniques – represents a possible solution, but even the ambiguity created by such an endeavour could produce precisely the opposite of what is desired. The difficulty lies in not knowing whether Soviet actions are founded on desperation or premeditation.

US nuclear modernisation programmes do offer improvements which could alleviate problems that inhibit frequent peacetime dispersal exercises. Insertable components would permit the special nuclear material to be held securely and separately away from the bulk of the warhead. In that way, warheads – without their nuclear cores – could be handled in the same manner as conventional warheads. In this less constrained environment, responsible NATO units would certainly become more proficient in executing rapid dispersal operations. But it is not completely clear that such an improvement would ever entirely reduce the natural tension between military response and provocation in a delicate crisis. Even though special nuclear materials are separated from the remaining components, the warhead dispersal process signals the first act in a chain of events that could very well be misperceived as signalling hostile intent and, therefore, the "last best chance" to pre-empt.

As for hardening, nuclear weapons stored at roughly 50 storage sites in the Central Region are already protected against direct conventional attack in hardened bunkers or igloos. But that does not ensure their survivability from conventional attack. The process of dispersing nuclear weapons is both time consuming and susceptible to disruption; it depends on the ready availability of trucks, handling equipment, and support personnel, all of which may be exposed to conventional strikes for lengthy periods (probably upwards of 24 hours for large storage facilities). A few well-placed missile strikes (with fuel air explosives, for example) on the motor pool and equipment storage areas could disrupt dispersal operations until subsequent aircraft strikes deliver a more substantial blow. Although different in detail, nuclear delivery units deployed in their garrisons are also susceptible to disruptive conventional attacks. Providing hardened shelters for critical support equipment and weapon-handling areas throughout the Central Region would require an extensive construction programme, the costs of which are unknown. Surely, however, the costs of hardening would compare favourably with that of extensive active defence. But how such a massive hardening effort would fare politically is uncertain.

Hardening nuclear bomb storage at NATO air bases makes good sense. NATO's current plans to collocate the storage of nuclear weapons (in weapon storage vaults) and dual-capable aircraft would permanently distribute a main air base's nuclear weapons to several relatively hard aimpoints.[23] Unfortunately, Warsaw Pact targeteers could still seriously disrupt sortie generation capability at the few dual-capable airfields through intense missile and air attacks against runways and airfield infrastructure targets. Primarily because of burdensome security requirements, NATO has no plans for dispersal of dual-capable aircraft and nuclear bombs to alternate airfields. Therefore, without substantial improvement in air-base survivability (a matter discussed later on), NATO's air-delivered nuclear capability could find itself "pinned down" during a time when they are most needed.

NATO should also work on ways to complicate Warsaw Pact targeting of Western nuclear forces once they have dispersed. A combination of efforts to reduce signatures (reducing or eliminating visual, acoustic, electronic, and radiation signatures unique to nuclear units) and proliferate decoys could inhibit Warsaw Pact capabilities to acquire and attack NATO's mobile nuclear forces. Finally, efforts should be supported to multiply the number of targets facing Warsaw Pact planners. For example, if NATO were to decrease its stockpile of nuclear artillery shells to 700, the number of certified nuclear-capable units spread amongst the allies should remain unchanged.

Counters to Soviet Short-Range Ballistic Missiles

For economic reasons alone, NATO faces hard choices over whether active, passive, or a combination of defensive counters would best contend with new Soviet short-range ballistic missiles. As we have seen, the INF treaty does not eliminate the ballistic missile threat quantitatively or qualitatively under the treaty's 500-km lower threshold. Nor does it eliminate the threat of long-range ballistic missiles such as ICBMs or SLBMs that have been retargeted for theatre missions. Most important, however, Western planners have yet to comprehend the operational pay-offs that short-range ballistic missiles furnish Soviet military planners, how these pay-offs are derived and, consequently, what the most effective and affordable means are for NATO to blunt them.

A first-order issue entails asking what is new about the challenge short-range missiles pose for Alliance strategy. Without any form of ballistic missile defence, NATO has deterred war over nearly four decades despite dramatic improvements in the Soviet nuclear missile threat to Europe. The most recent manifestation of these improvements lies in advances in range, accuracy, and terminal effectiveness for short-range ballistic missiles. Although these missiles offer the Warsaw Pact qualitatively new nuclear and chemical attack options, such attacks would, nonetheless, entail immense escalatory risks for Soviet decision-makers. Of gravest concern is the potential inherent in these new missiles – operating principally in tandem with aircraft – to exploit longstanding NATO vulnerabilities decisively below the nuclear threshold.

Aside from any notion of premediated Soviet exploitation of this capability, even the widespread perception of vulnerability that such an attack option might engender could dangerously aggravate European crisis stability. Counters to this emerging potential should, therefore, be viewed as minimum essential defence capabilities worthy of priority attention.

Analytical Prerequisites

Any balanced appraisal of counters to the changing Soviet theatre warfare threat rests on making correct assumptions about weapon roles and capabilities and setting an appropriate Soviet (*vice* Western) analytic context. As for assumptions about weapon roles and capabilities, many Western analysts have exaggerated the near-term capacity of Soviet conventional ballistic missiles to substitute for nuclear weapons. Several assessments have characterised new Soviet conventional missiles as independently capable of destroying such complex targets as NATO airfields.[24] This development should come as no great surprise; Western analysts and policy-makers continue to debate the potential of NATO's advanced conventional munitions to substitute directly for low-yield nuclear weapons. Warsaw Pact specialists, by contrast, seem far less sanguine about directly substituting conventional for nuclear weapons. They do see emerging conventional weapons approaching nuclear weapons in effectiveness and are far more likely to view the effects of conventional weapons in a true combined-arms context. As discussed in detail in Chapter 4, missiles provide a form of sequential leveraging for subsequent aircraft strikes by taking over primary responsibility for suppressing NATO air defences and by disrupting air-base and nuclear dispersal operations for short intervals. Soviet planners find this feature especially attractive, for its product is a predictable enhancement in aircraft performance in the initial campaign with NATO, which is the only engagement that can be planned with any certainty.

An exaggerated view of new Soviet short-range missiles can lead to oversimplifying the assessment of counters to this emerging threat – a simplification that eschews the multifaceted complexities of a combined-arms (conventional) air operation for the relative ease of something akin to strategic counterforce targeting. Certainly the latter approach is useful for analysing SDI architectures, but it has little use in a theatre-conventional context where missiles are rarely the exclusive damage mechanism.

The full implications of the emerging Soviet threat and the best means to cope with it can be derived only from considering the role of missiles in the proper context. The essential analytic *milieu* is the Soviet notion of a theatre-strategic operation in a theatre of military operations. As analysed in Chapter 4, the inner workings of the conventional air operation (a principal component of a theatre-strategic operation), including its targets, force employment interactions, and timing sensitivities, must be fully weighed in evaluating counters to Soviet short-range ballistic missiles.

Especially critical is the Soviet recognition that conventional effectiveness rests on volume of fire delivered within a narrow time window. The analysis in Chapter 4 shows that projected force sizes for Warsaw Pact short-range missile units (the important figure of merit being launchers with the first operational echelons in Eastern Europe) leave little margin for error when we consider their use against only high-priority NATO targets in support of the air operation. At the same time, however, we must recall the incremental growth that has occurred in Warsaw Pact tactical and (especially) operational-tactical missile units. The utility of these systems as an important means of delivering conventional firepower will furnish a strong incentive for the Soviets to continue expanding missile force structure.

Passive Measures

Chapter 3 points out that NATO airfields, nuclear storage sites, and air defence facilities are likely to be the principal focus of attention for the precursor ballistic missile salvo in the Warsaw Pact conventional air operation. There are four general categories of passive defence measures of relevance against this threat: hardening, proliferation, reconstitution, and dispersal. The individual measures in each category are of foremost value to airfield survivability. Several offer important advantages independently or in combination with active defence. Importantly, passive measures are also of value against the dominant aircraft threat.

Stimulated primarily by dramatic Israeli successes against unprotected Egyptian aircraft in the 1967 Middle East War, both NATO and the Warsaw Pact initiated extensive hardened shelter programmes for aircraft in central Europe in the late 1960s. Sheltering makes conventional attack against protected aircraft questionable; aircraft kills require a direct hit on the shelter together with sophisticated fusing designs. This fact does not suggest that the advent of hardened shelters forever obviates such an attack option; plausible future improvements in missile accuracy and tailored munition effects promise such a capacity.[25] Rather, the effect of aircraft sheltering has been to shift the focus of attention to runway surfaces.[26]

In the critical initial days of the Warsaw Pact air operation, effective attacks on airfield runway surfaces (main runway and taxiway) can create virtually the same adverse effect on aircraft sortie generation as successful direct attacks on unsheltered aircraft. Because the sortie-generation infrastructure for NATO high-performance aircraft has become so concentrated and brittle, even aircraft that manage to launch before runways are attacked may end up "operationally ready" at a recovery air-field, but not "mission capable."[27]

Building More Runways

The most cost-effective way to combat attacks against run-ways lies in proliferating the number of alternate launch and recovery strips (ALRS) at existing NATO airfields. Six to eight missiles armed with kinetic-energy penetrating submunitions are required to close the main runway and its parallel taxiway. Building an additional 75×5000 ft limited-use runway at each of 20 main operating bases in the Central Region would double the attack requirement from 120 to 240 missiles. If Soviet plan-ners concentrated the precursor attack against these high-priority airfields (as in Option 2 of the illustrative options discussed in Chapter 4), they could still substantially disrupt airfield operations, but only at the expense of sparing other high-priority NATO targets (air defences and theatre nuclear forces) from the initial attack. ALRS proliferation could, thus, serve to limit the flexibility of Soviet attack planning.

The costs of ALRS proliferation also make this approach attractive. Assuming that any additional ALRS are constructed within the confines of existing airfields, each additional run-way would cost in the neighbourhood of $5 million.[28] But what makes this appealing approach politically problematic is the absence of enough space within a goodly number of NATO's main operating bases and the consequent necessity for additional real estate. The notion of buying up precious real estate in the centre of Europe for the purpose of absorbing con-ventional fire in wartime is seen by most (especially German) political observers as simply too unattractive a solution.[29] Finally, even though proliferating ALRS makes good sense in general, it is virtually impossible to assess whether or not ALRS alone could confidently deny the Soviets the leveraging effect of the precursor missile attack. As Chapter 4 describes in detail, the combined shock and damage effects of that attack are meant to disrupt and delay airfield operations just long enough to permit waves of aircraft to deliver more lasting airfield damage. Damage assessment alone, after the precursor missile attack (no less orchestrating the launching of large numbers of high-performance aircraft from insufficiently but nonetheless partially damaged runways strewn with foreign objects), is likely to take longer than the time needed for Warsaw Pact aircraft to reach these bases. Still, however, ALRS proliferation – like other passive measures – would help cope with damage caused by aircraft and missiles alike. It is a sound and essential investment.

Better Runway Repair
Complementary to furnishing additional ALRS is a more effective means of reconstituting damaged runways – known as rapid runway repair (R^3). R^3 capabilities within NATO are in need of great improvement, but even with significant upgrading they alone will be insufficient to cope with the expected levels of damage. This is especially true in view of the emerging capacity of short-range ballistic missiles to deliver precursor strikes against NATO airfields.

To appreciate the difficulty that even very effective R^3 will have in coping with successive attack waves, we must briefly examine how R^3 works.[30] The basic objective of R^3 is to repair runway surfaces fast enough to launch aircraft before another wave of attackers revisits the airfield. In late 1979, the U.S. Air Force (supported by the Army Corps of Engineers) established a requirement to repair three large craters in four hours. As one might imagine, the R^3 function depends on the rapid availability of skilled engineer support personnel and unique equipment. At US airfields in Europe, R^3 teams consist of around 100 support personnel and 50 heavy vehicles. Crater repair first entails a damage assessment phase to locate where damage has occurred and to evaluate how best to allocate men and equipment in view of the specific damage. Broken pavement and debris are next removed (or backfilled in the case of large craters); in this regard it is important to note that the small but numerous craters created by modern runway-busting sub-munitions are more difficult to repair than large bomb craters. The remainder of the runway must then be cleared of any extraneous debris before large aluminium matting is secured over the compacted crater holes.

Several tests of R^3 performance have demonstrated the chimerical nature of repair time expectations. Repair times repeatedly have exceeded established goals. Aside from the difficulty of ever simulating the psychological and physical effects of actual combat conditions, these tests underscore the complex nature of the R^3 mission. As the threat to airfields worsens, the Air Force solution is to lower the required repair time (14 craters in 1 hour) and to acquire more and improved engineering equipment and better trained (and dedicated *vice* mobilised) personnel.

It is highly doubtful that a one-hour goal could ever be met. Moreover, even could it be met, it would still represent a necessary but insufficient counter to combined missile and aircraft attacks. The one-hour remedy is dubious because it fails to consider the adverse collateral effects of harassment attacks on the R^3 teams. Soviet planners discuss attack techniques to disrupt or limit the manoeuvre capacity of a target.[31] Put differently, ballistic missile and aircraft-delivered payloads could consist of both runway penetrator submunitions and delay-fused, anti-personnel and anti-vehicle mines. The seeding of runways, taxiways, and approach aprons with such mines would at once delay assessment and repair and possibly even destroy mission-critical heavy equipment. Moreover, the one-hour goal assumes that personnel and equipment are free of damage that might result from stray munitions meant for the runway. Although these collateral effects are impossible to quantify, it seems prudent to assume that such a complex operation as a R^3 is highly likely to be adversely affected by the shock and weight of the initial attack.

Even more important, the one-hour R^3 goal, in and of itself, appears insufficient to cope with the closely timed waves of attack that are the trademark of the Warsaw Pact air operation. The Voroshilov General Staff Academy lectures state bluntly that "subsequent mass strikes must be brought to bear . . . after the shortest of intervals" to deny NATO the chance to reconstitute its airfields.[32] The time between the precursor ballistic missile attack and the first wave of aircraft is measured in a few minutes or, clearly, within one hour. In addition to the precursor missile attack, the first mass strike would probably entail two to three waves of aircraft, each wave arriving within the R^3 goal of one hour. From two to four hours of Warsaw Pact recovery and reconstitution time would separate the first and second and second and third mass strikes (each of which repeats the multiple waves of attack). There is certainly room to argue whether the Pact could meet these goals, but passive rideout and reconstitution seem inadequate as the exclusive means of countering the Warsaw Pact air operation.

Aircraft Dispersal

Effective aircraft dispersal depends on a combination of time, capability, and political will. Unfortunately, NATO faces problems in each area. As for time, launching interceptors on tactical warning (that is, after detecting missile launches) seems infeasible given the short times of flight of Pact missiles based in East Germany and Czechoslovakia.

Capability for aircraft dispersal is also questionable. NATO's Central Region simply has too few airfields to accommodate both in-place and US reinforcement aircraft. The latter are being accommodated through NATO's Collocated Operating Base programme. But in-place aircraft – those that must cope with the initial weight of the air operation – have few alternatives for widespread dispersal. Given the time to respond, the US Air Force in Europe can operate 12 "bare bases" by pre-positioning modular support components at civil airfields.[33] But the number of additional bases seems severely inadequate in view of growing Warsaw Pact attack options.[34] Otherwise, high-performance aircraft, which are pinned out from their primary base of support due to runway closure or damage to supporting infrastructure, will be compelled to operate with substantially reduced efficiency from austere airfields.

Finally, there is the dubious nature of the political will to respond to warning. History suggests that political decision-makers will be reluctant to act on what will surely be ambiguous signals for fear of provoking attack. In light of the tension between prudent military response and provocation, NATO should avoid depending primarily on dispersal to shore up its aircraft and nuclear storage vulnerabilities. Active defence and passive hardening measures, which are designed to protect targets during crises and long enough after war starts to permit them to disperse to safer havens, are far better suited to the needs of conventional deterrence and crisis stability than is counting on dispersal to shore up vulnerabilities.

Active Measures

Growing concern about the modernisation and expansion of Soviet short-range ballistic missiles has stimulated an increasingly controversial debate on the merits of anti-tactical ballistic missiles (ATBMs) and European participation in the US Strategic Defence Initiative (SDI). The purpose here is not to disentangle the complex political motives underlying notions of "extending" air defence, on the one hand, to SDI-sponsored Theatre Defence Architectures, on the other.[35] It should only be noted in passing that the SDI program has had a profound (adverse) effect on evaluating the need for active measures against short-range ballistic missiles. SDI proponents, on the one hand, have tended to promote ATBM defences of a more exotic character without analysing in detail the role missiles play in the air operation. Nor have they given much thought to more cost-effective approaches. SDI opponents, on the other hand, have serious difficulty divorcing ATBM from the SDI program. They see ATBM as a "stalking horse" for SDI; their analytic tendency is to downgrade the threat generally by assigning to ballistic missiles alone the job of closing an airfield for one to three days. Under these artificial circumstances, missiles always fail to achieve their objective and passive measures alone are suitable counters to such a threat.

Instead, the purpose here is to help comprehend emerging Soviet attack capabilities in the proper operational context so as to evaluate the role of different kinds of active defences. Comprehending the nature of the threat (conventional only? chemical? nuclear? short- and/or long-range missiles? what timing and force employment interactions? etc.) is certainly central to the ATBM question, but it is by no means the only analytical component. Also essential to any evaluation of ATBMs are several other considerations: what is to be defended (critical military targets? populations?); for what duration (until critical military units disperse? until threat launchers have fired all reloads?); at what minimum level of performance (i.e., how many missiles can NATO afford to have leak through its defences?). ATBM system objectives range from, on the modest end, denying the Warsaw Pact a "free ride" in its precursor missile attack to, on the grandiose – and thus expensive – end, eliminating the use of theatre ballistic missiles altogether. Modest solutions, which extend the existing capability of air defences, would raise the Warsaw Pact's price of success (i.e., they must increase launchers to leak through or saturate ATBM defences) and complicate the co-ordination of combined missile and air attacks. Such solutions have inherent military value separate from other NATO defence programmes. Grandiose schemes, akin to what can be expected from the SDI Theatre Defence Architecture studies, would furnish significant population protection; however, their value would depend critically on substantial NATO investment in other areas (such as much improved air defences). The cost differences between these alternative approaches are enormous; roughly calculated, the modest side represents a ten-year investment of between $3 and $10 billion, while the grandiose is likely to cost in the hundreds of billions range.[36]

Components of ATBM Defence
The necessary elements to defend against tactical ballistic missiles include (1) radars capable of acquiring and tracking incoming warheads; (2) signal processing that rapidly fires

ground-based interceptor missiles within seconds of threat detection; (3) high-acceleration missiles; and (4) missile terminal homing sufficient to defeat incoming warheads. In large measure, the re-entry speed and size (or shape of the re-entering object, which produces a radar cross-section) determine the required sophistication of these system components. Shorter-range tactical ballistic missiles, such as the SS-21, SS-23, and SS-12/22, have shorter boost phases and flight distances and larger radar cross-sections than ICBMs, SLBMs, and longer-range theatre missiles (SS-20s); consequently, although the short flight times and boost phases of shorter-range missiles heavily burden radar warning systems, these missiles' slower re-entry speed and relatively large sizes make them susceptible to terminal interception.

Defence against conventionally armed tactical ballistic missiles is also considerably less demanding than against missiles with nuclear and chemical warheads. Blunting the effectiveness of a Soviet conventional missile attack requires altering the course (and thus, the accuracy) of the warhead to cause it to hit outside of the conventional submunitions' damage radius. Against nuclear warheads, however, interception must occur at a sufficiently high altitude and range to preclude direct damage to the target, as well as collateral damage. This requires early attack warning and a very high-acceleration missile which, in any event, might be negated if Soviet nuclear warheads were "salvage-fused." Such back-up fusing causes the incoming warhead to detonate upon impact.

Interception of chemical warheads also presents difficult technical demands. Unless the warhead is intercepted at a very high altitude, chemicals will be disseminated either over the target or nearby, depending on weather conditions. In both the nuclear and chemical warhead cases, therefore, an airborne or spaceborne sensor and high-acceleration interceptors may be needed to furnish the required early acquisition and high-altitude interception capabilities. Yet, one should not dismiss the value of modest point defences in deterring limited nuclear and chemical attacks by raising the attacker's entry price.

Imperfect defences raise the attacker's entry price when the nature of coping with such defences is compared to a "free ride" environment. A free ride would allow the Soviets to optimise nuclear warhead yield and height of burst in accord with target vulnerability, thereby maximising terminal effectiveness while minimising unwanted collateral damage. Imperfect defenses like the dual-mode (capable of sequentially intercepting both aircraft and missiles) Patriot are criticised because the intercept altitude against a nuclear-warhead missile that is salvage-fused (designed to achieve a full-yield detonation upon intercept) would not be high enough to preclude collateral and perhaps even some target damage. Moreover, Patriot's accuracy and warhead may not be sufficient to destroy the attacking warhead but only to divert its course, which is adequate for dealing with conventionally armed missiles but not for nuclear ones (where the Soviets could simply use higher yields). Chemical warhead interception must also be very high to prevent high-altitude dissemination over the target.

But in each of these cases, the Soviets would pay an entry cost in that non-ideal conditions would confront them. Increasing nuclear yields, employing salvage fusing, and subjecting dispersed chemicals to uncertain meteorological conditions increase attack complexity and thereby affect the decision to use such limited attack options.

ATBM Programmes

Both the more modest and the grandiose ends of the ATBM spectrum could potentially be fused into a single theatre ballistic missile defence programme, standing apart (programmatically) from the Strategic Defence Initiative.[37] Two panels within the US Department of Defense have discussed creating a new programme that encompasses upgraded versions of the Patriot and Hawk air defence systems as well as the architecture studies that explore new sensors, tracking, weapons, and battle management. As momentum builds for some kind of active solution to the Soviet short-range missile threat, it is important to keep the nature of that threat in mind, especially with respect to those aspects of it that present new challenges to NATO strategy.

The nearest term and cheapest active solution involves improvements to the Patriot and Hawk air defence systems to permit defence against ballistic and cruise missiles, respectively, without loss of their capability against aircraft. The initial improvement programme consists of software changes to Patriot's surveillance radar to permit high angle-of-attack tracking of ballistic missiles. Also a part of Patriot's upgrading is a warhead modification programme, involving a conventional warhead with larger fragments and higher fragment velocities. Hawk's improvements were initially thought only to permit it to cope more effectively with non-ballistic or cruise missiles. But the Raytheon Corporation, the Army's prime contractor for both Patriot and Hawk, is advocating a greatly enhanced version of Hawk that comes much closer than Patriot to furnishing broad-area protection.[38] Such "enhancement" to Hawk implies a much higher acceleration missile and an augmented radar system, making it virtually a new system (with all the attendant costs). Upgrading Patriot, by contrast, entails less than half a billion dollars in research and development (software changes and design and testing of the dual-mode feature) and around $100 million for warhead procurement.[39] Acquistion of additional missiles and radars over that required for the air defence mission could add several billion dollars to the dual-mode tab over a ten-year period, but operations and maintenance costs would not be materially different given the sunk investment in Patriot.

Soviet Counters to Active Measures
Given the evident Soviet preference for a conventional-only contingency, any evaluation of how the Warsaw Pact might react to NATO ATBM decisions ought to consider possible ATBM counters primarily within the context of the air operation.

A first-order counter consists of employing alternatives to compensate for losses in missile effectiveness. They include cruise missiles and a greater dependence on aircraft and on special operations forces; but none is wholly satisfactory in meeting the time-urgent requirements associated with the air operation and deep penetrations into NATO's rear areas. Each fails to replicate the more predictable leveraging effect of co-ordinated missile and air operations, while imposing serious timing constraints of sufficient consequence to foster hesitancy and caution in an already conservatively oriented Soviet planning process. Indeed, it may serve NATO well to steer the Soviet Union in the direction of slower reacting threats, given the Warsaw Pact's emphasis on a strategy that so strongly relies on speed of execution, pacing, and timing. European crisis stability could only benefit from such developments.

Certain technical and operational counters ought to be mentioned briefly. It is unlikely that the Soviets would modify the re-entry payloads of short-range missiles to overstress ATBM defences. Such modifications could include using multiple independently targetable re-entry vehicles (MIRVs) and decoys. But MIRVs and decoys take weight from the payload, which is critical for conventional attack effectiveness. Furthermore, such technical counters are expensive, require extensive testing, and hardly "buy back" the free-ride environment that exists now.

Soviet planners might wish to consider a shift in operational tactics as a counter. One would stress the capacity of an upgraded Patriot to switch rapidly between its air defence and ATBM radar modes by having missiles and aircraft arrive simultaneously rather than sequentially, as is the preferred tactic. But such an operational countermeasure has severe drawbacks. Besides losing the advantage of freeing aircraft for other critical missions, such a modified tactic would also eliminate the element of surprise by forcing Soviet planners to marshal aircraft before (rather than after, as would be the case in the preferred sequential tactic) short-range ballistic missiles are launched. This is required to permit slower reacting aircraft to arrive on target simultaneously with short-time-of-flight missiles. If NATO detected the Pact's marshalling of aircraft before missile launch (which is likely), it would permit NATO interceptors to surge into the air to meet the first-wave air attack as well as to avoid the pin-down effects of a precursor missile attack. In short, such a tactic would eliminate the surprise effect of ballistic missile use.

Perhaps more consistent with the Soviet style of warfare are brute-force counters that overwhelm ATBM defences. Sheer firepower to exhaust ATBM interceptors and saturation attacks designed to overstress ATBM traffic handling are obvious choices. In the first case, it is probably safe to assume that the Warsaw Pact's stockpile of on-line and refire missiles will exceed NATO ATBM interceptors, especially in view of the large reserve of second-echelon launchers and missiles in the Soviet homeland. (Rather than building up interceptor inventories to cope with a large reserve of missiles, NATO would perhaps benefit more by counting on offensive counter-air to attack the Warsaw Pact's prolonged refire capability.) That ATBM exhaustion could eventually occur is likely, but this prospect is immaterial from the Soviet standpoint of decisively exploiting the initial blow in the first few days of the war. What is more, although its inventory of short-range missiles is clearly large, the Warsaw Pact's capacity to sustain the complex command, control, communications, and intelligence network needed to support prolonged missile use is highly dubious – that is, unless the Pact succeeds initially.

Saturation, on the other hand, is a theoretically viable counter, particularly against more modest defences such as a dual-mode Patriot system. The idea is to employ several missiles against a fire battery simultaneously so as to saturate its radar's traffic-handling capability. This tactic allows the necessary number of missiles to "leak through" and destroy the target. Because this tactic could be used in the precursor missile attack of the air operation, it has special relevance as an ATBM counter.

But imposing a need to saturate an ATBM system on top of non-ATBM attack requirements would clearly stretch Soviet attack resources. For example, Soviet planners might assign two missiles against each Patriot air defence battery if Patriot lacked an ATBM capability, but they might have to allocate more than double that number to defeat a dual-mode Patriot.[40]

The requirements of saturation would draw a first-salvo missile population away from its primary job and deny the leveraging effect that flows from close missile and aircraft interaction.

Viewed in terms of cost and its adverse impact on the Soviet operational style of warfare, furnishing Patriot a self-defence capability has substantial merit, especially if it were combined with various passive measures such as ALRS and R³ at NATO air bases. By furnishing Patriot with a self-protection capability against conventionally armed ballistic missiles, and perhaps even clustering such dual-mode Patriot batteries around NATO's highest-priority air bases, NATO could substantially raise the Soviet entry cost for a precursor missile attack and thereby deny Soviet planners the leveraging effect of combined missile and aircraft interaction. If the ballistic missile threat matures beyond what is projected here – especially in the context of the air-breathing threat – consideration should be given to formulating requirements to cope with these improvements as part of a Hawk follow-on programme.

Offensive Solutions

Clearly the most active measure to combat the emerging capabilities of Soviet short-range ballistic missiles lies in employing counterfire against Warsaw Pact missile launchers. Counterfire solutions represent the offensive side of the US Army anti-tactical missile or ATM programme. Under this programme Army planners are investigating ways of locating Warsaw Pact missile launchers so that they might be struck before launch or at least before they can be reloaded and prepared for a second strike. Two development programmes figure heavily in the counterfire approach: the joint surveillance and target acquisition radar system (J-STARS) for stand-off target detection and attack direction, and the Army tactical missile system (ATACMS) which is designed to replace the Lance missile as a corps support weapon system. Given the critical importance of the air campaign to both sides, there will be strong incentives during crises to take action. As we have seen on the Warsaw Pact side, both improved long-range conventional capabilities and new operational concepts for exploiting such fires are being deployed and implemented. Without some means of active defence, offensive counterfire solutions promise, at best, to deliver problematic results and, at worst, to stimulate a reciprocal fear of surprise attack.[41]

On their own, offensive solutions (especially ones wedded to ballistic missiles) raise disturbing crisis stability problems. Combined with even modest forms of active defence, however, counterfire against Warsaw Pact missile refire capability would seriously complicate the sustainability of the Pact air operation. As discussed already, brute-force Soviet tactics (such as depending on sheer refire volume to achieve targeting objectives) require not only sufficient launchers but a supporting command and control system to sustain missile operations. A modest ATBM defence such as the dual-mode Patriot would extend the time it takes to meet Pact targeting objectives and thereby offer NATO the chance to employ counterfire effectively to blunt Pact refire capability. The Pact is more vulnerable to refire after the initial missile salvo because of the firing signatures missile launchers offer to NATO target acquisition systems.

From a crisis stability standpoint, natural evolutionary improvements in NATO's force structure (such as new air-delivered munitions) are to be preferred for suppressive fire against Soviet missile launchers over radical increases in ground-launched ballistic missiles.

Integrating Arms Control Policy and Defence Planning

We should expect Soviet political strategists to leverage their considerable asymmetric force advantages toward two objectives: the further denuclearisation of NATO strategy and limiting allied "deep-strike" conventional weapons, especially strike aircraft. The Warsaw Pact's huge remaining arsenal of short-range ballistic missiles will undoubtedly be the centrepiece of any offer. On the surface, this may appear counterproductive in view of the important role conventionally armed ballistic missiles could play in a conventional-only contingency. But Soviet strategists probably see important political and military value in offering to eliminate or substantially reduce missiles with ranges less than 500 km.

Politically, this strategy could deflate the threat of these missiles in much the same way that "double zero" reduced concern in some circles in Western Europe about the short-range missile threat. Managing the Western perception of the threat in this manner could further undermine support for even modest active measures like upgrading Patriot for self-defence purposes. Soviet planners fully recognise that the leveraging pay-off of conventional missiles can be achieved only if they do not have to contend with active defences; even upgrading existing air defences to handle conventionally armed missiles would compel the attacker into saturation attacks that require the expensive addition of extra launchers and create complex missile and aircraft co-ordination problems.

Militarily, Soviet planners would be more than willing to give up conventionally armed ballistic missiles if their reduction or elimination induced further nuclear reductions in NATO. To the extent that arms control can reduce the threat of these systems to the Warsaw Pact ground campaign, the *raison d'être* for Soviet missiles and aircraft is correspondingly diminished.

In general, the Western approach to conventional arms control should be to propose deep cuts in Soviet forces so as to reach a point where NATO and the Warsaw Pact have equal numbers of tanks and artillery in the area of the Atlantic to the Urals. This general propostion is essential in view of the huge Soviet reinforcement potential in the western military districts of the Soviet homeland. Reductions of lesser magnitude, albeit asymmetrical, could be highly disadvantageous for NATO given the requirements of a linear forward defence (force-to-space ratios) and Soviet reinforcement advantages.

West German concerns about a "geographically restricted nuclear risk," or the Soviet asymmetric advantages in short-range nuclear systems (especially missiles), most of which would be used on German territory, is militarily, if not politically, insignificant. Warsaw Pact ballistic missiles are certainly capable of delivering nuclear weapons on German soil, but the Soviets have a strong preference to employ these missiles with conventional warheads. Nonetheless, their range and theoretical capability for massive nuclear attacks make them a potent force for Alliance dissension. We have seen in this chapter that the best way to blunt the conventional military effectiveness of these missiles is through a combination of modest active defences (dual-mode Patriot) and passive measures such as hardening at air bases. This rather simple package of countermeasures plus several other factors could combine to produce an agreement that would alleviate German concerns.

Toward a "Triple Zero" Agreement?

Despite a clear Soviet numerical advantage in short-range ballistic missiles, the evident diminution in the Soviet military's political clout suggests at least the possibility of extending missile elimination downward to cover battlefield as well as intermediate- and shorter-range offensive missiles. Strictly from the standpoint of negotiation, the chief virtue of eliminating all remaining ground-based missiles lies in its simplicity. Rather than attempting to negotiate complex mixed package deals (such as Polish leader Jaruzelski's proposal to trade Warsaw Pact tanks for NATO aircraft) or modernisation bans that freeze in place existing asymmetries (such as East German leader Honecker's proposal that the Pact refrain from modernising its missiles in exchange for NATO abstention)[42], a "triple zero" agreement would simply extend the INF verification regime to a global ban on battlefield missiles of the USA, the Soviet Union, and their respective allies. Such an agreement would eliminate over 2000 launchers and perhaps 7000 missiles on the Eastern side, and roughly 100 launchers and 2000 missiles in the Western arsenal.

When Mikhail Gorbachev signalled Moscow's flexibility to deal with conventional imbalances, he attributed these asymmetries to certain "historical, geographic, and other factors." This book has traced the origin and evolution of these factors and their implications for NATO defence planning. As we have seen, the Soviet military has a strong artillery tradition. Ballistic missiles are just another form of long-range artillery. But perhaps more than any other weapon in the Soviet arsenal, tanks included, ballistic missiles are unabashedly offensive (or counter-offensive) in the role they perform. They create strong hair-trigger incentives for pre-emptive attack in explosive crisis environments.

We should not expect the Soviets to offer an agreement inimical to their security interests. Their stated goal is the elimination of all remaining nuclear weapons in both alliance systems. But there may be a set of incentives that could lead to a mutually advantageous missiles-only deal.

Soviet political leaders now realise the adverse political consequences of their massive SS-20 deployments beginning in the late 1970s. Given NATO's lack of strategic depth on the continent, tactical missiles could become the contemporary analogue to the SS-20. Moreover, Soviet military planners are strongly motivated to remove the West's capacity to couple emerging conventional technologies to the ballistic missile. Certainly, NATO's existing battlefield missile deployments compare unfavourably with the Pact's, but Pentagon planners have discussed as many as 400 ATACMS in the future; and just a short while ago NATO planners looked closely at a concept, as part of the Counterair-90 study, to deploy 600 ground-based ballistic missiles to strike Warsaw Pact airfields in the first minutes of a war.[43] Eliminating these worrisome and potentially unstable deployments may make compelling sense to a current Kremlin leadership desperately in need of respite in high-tech military competition.

There are also sound financial and political reasons why the Soviet leadership might accept a "triple zero" agreement. A combination of modest active and passive measures, as discussed earlier, could seriously blunt Pact missile effectiveness. The only suitable way for the Soviets to counter these measures – through expanding missile launcher force structure in Eastern Europe – is both expensive and politically costly. Indeed, rather than pressuring recalcitrant allies to accept more battlefield missiles on Eastern European soil, the new Soviet leadership might find the alternative of eliminating missiles politically and fiscally appealing.

Notwithstanding NATO's fear of denuclearisation, there are also strong reasons why the West should focus on whether such a deal is possible. Politically, a "triple zero" deal would allay Bonn's nuclear isolation after "double zero." The Western allies are legitimately concerned about any further NATO nuclear reductions. But what best deters the Soviets and plausibly links the US strategic nuclear deterrent to the defence of Western Europe are nuclear capabilities that can primarily strike the Russian homeland from the heart of Europe. Battlefield nuclear missiles possess little of the political coupling value furnished by sea-launched cruise and ballistic missiles or long-range strike aircraft.

Militarily, eliminating battlefield missiles would at once rectify important conventional imbalances favouring the Warsaw Pact and reduce the fear of surprise attack. One NATO worry is that a desperate Soviet Union might be persuaded to use its 3 to 1 advantage in forward-deployed tanks to achieve a lightning grab of NATO territory before the West could muster a sufficient defence. But the first critical shots of any major war in Europe today would come not from tanks but from conventionally armed Soviet missiles. As we have seen, Soviet planners express little hope for achieving success on the ground without first establishing supremacy in the air.

Proponents of ATACMS will undoubtedly argue that a "triple zero" agreement would have NATO forego its most robust deep-attack tank killer. But the loss of NATO's future capability to attack tanks with conventionally armed missiles would be readily offset by eliminating the Soviet missile threat to NATO air bases. A higher survival rate for Western aircraft means more Warsaw Pact tanks at risk. Finally, eliminating the tactical missile threat in Europe suggests that both alliance systems could avoid any significant deployment of anti-tactical ballistic missile systems.

There is certainly danger in venturing into categories of weapons in which the Soviets hold dramatic advantages, especially when negotiating goals are so ill-conceived (as were those that caused the USA in 1981 to seek constraints on Soviet shorter-range missiles). But armed with a better understanding of how these weapons fit within the framework of Soviet strategy, the West should seriously consider how to deal with Soviet battlefield missiles. Compelling political and military reasons suggest that NATO investigate ways of either eliminating battlefield missiles completely or reducing them to levels that would mitigate incentives for pre-emptive use under crisis conditions. Surely, Soviet negotiators will press to fold in other short-range nuclear weapons, but NATO can credibly resist such pressure by focusing on eliminating or controlling the Warsaw Pact's most destabilising offensive advantage. In contrast to the grave numerical advantage the Pact has over NATO in battlefield missiles, there is relative parity in dual-capable aircraft and perhaps even nuclear artillery. A missiles-only approach would not only expose the overwhelmingly offensive character of Soviet military strategy but also offer Moscow the chance to demonstrate its recently expressed intent to practise a genuinely defensive military doctrine.[44] Equally important, drawing attention to Pact battlefield missile advantages would raise the potential political costs for Moscow should the Soviet military begin to test and deploy a legal follow-on to the SS-23 missile or increase the launcher inventory in Eastern Europe.

Barring complete missile elimination, NATO should seek to reduce Pact dual-capable missiles to levels consistent with the goal of easing pre-emptive use and improving NATO's ability to survive the conventional air operation. As the analysis in Chapter 4 and in this chapter shows, there is not much slack in the projected inventory of first-echelon Pact launchers when we consider plausible Soviet strike requirements in support of the air operation. Adding modest levels of active and passive defences stresses this finite launcher inventory even more, liberating critical NATO targets from intensive attack and thereby permitting higher sortie rates for aircraft (as just one example) in the critical early hours of war. To the extent that arms control can lead to reductions in Pact missile launchers, it can directly affect such important decisions as determining the makeup and magnitude of passive measures, the number of upgraded Patriot batteries to deploy, where to deploy them, and how many missiles to buy.

Reducing the Threat of Surprise Attack: Operational Arms Control

There is currently great interest in NATO defence ministries in negotiating truly stabilising operational arms control measures in both the new Conventional Stability Talks (which replace the longstanding and unsuccessful Mutual and Balanced Force Reduction Talks) and continuing CSCE negotiations.[45] Operational arms control entails the negotiation of confidence and security building measures that seek to make military operations more predictable and less prone to misunderstanding.[46] Indeed, any measure that tends to clarify ambiguity during military activities – especially those taking place during periods of heightened tension – could contribute importantly to European stability. Most of the structural and operational arms control measures associated with reducing the threat of surprise attack deal with limits of one sort or another on tanks. As an additional or perhaps alternative proposition, NATO should consider the merits of regulating the operational behaviour of offensive ballistic missiles, which would be used before any Warsaw Pact tanks engaged NATO tanks along the front lines of engagement.

The objective of a CSBM covering battlefield missiles is to uncouple the most destabilising force component from major NATO and Warsaw Pact military exercises. Of concern here is significant out-of-garrison missile activity, especially activity occurring simultaneously with ground-force activity. The threshold between significant and insignificant activity differs markedly for each alliance. The Warsaw Pact requires a high percentage of its first-echelon missile launchers to participate in support of the air operation. NATO has far fewer launchers and, unless there is a dramatic increase in force structure over the next decade, NATO's battlefield missiles will continue to fulfil largely nuclear missions.

Given the dramatic asymmetry between NATO and Pact deployments (there are only 88 Lance launchers in the Central Region while the Pact has around 400 tactical and operational-tactical launchers in East Germany, Czechoslovakia, and Poland), it would seem appropriate to set the threshold at around 50 launchers. Thus, one could propose extending the provision in the Stockholm document on prior notification of certain military activities to include mandatory notification whenever there is any battlefield missile activity of at least 50 missile launchers. Still, one would need to go beyond this simple notificaiton provision to uncouple large-scale out-of-garrison missile activity from major ground-force military exercises. A new provision could prohibit simultaneous out-of-garrison activity involving more than 25,000 troops and 75 battlefield missile launchers.

An alternative approach, which may be amenable to the Soviet Union, is one that includes strict verification procedures to ensure that only training missiles and inert warheads are being employed in connection with any out-of-garrison missile activity. The Soviets and their allies are known to use training missiles and warheads,[47] and the Soviet position with respect to human on-site inspection has changed dramatically as evidenced by INF's strict verification provisions. A useful verification regime might include small inspection teams which would visit garrisons that are declared as part of the notification process. A portal inspection procedure like that envisaged for inspections at missile production facilities under the INF treaty could be established at declared missile garrisons. Inspectors could examine the declared missile units to ensure that only training missiles and inert warheads were being deployed to the field for training. There are a variety of relatively unsophisticated technical devices (simple radiography, for example) that could be employed to reach confident inspection conclusions without becoming excessively intrusive.

In sum, a CSBM regime relating to battlefield missiles represents a military meaningful restraint that could clarify ambiguities during fast-moving periods of tension. The notion of uncoupling might also be wisely applied to other components of the military force structure. Another area worthy of closer evaluation is command and control. The extent to which a military alliance system sets up an elaborate command and control network (as well as other military functions) is a critical barometer of preparations for war. Are there important and observable differences (especially with human inspectors) between routine peacetime activity and actual preparations for war? If a series of CSBMs similar to the ones proposed here were established, a clearer picture of the "normal" pattern of military operations could be formalised. Measures could then be instituted to explain deviations from the norm and to restore an equilibrium before matters get out of hand. Unambiguous and unexplained deviations would help justify prudent military responses. In many respects, a sensible regime of CSBMs could do more to reduce the risk of surprise attack than all but the most asymmetrical of structural arms control agreements, such as equal levels of tanks and artillery from the Atlantic to the Urals.

Notes

1. M. M. Kir'yan, ed., *Military-Technological Progress and the USSR Armed Forces* (Moscow: Voyenizdat, 1982), p. 313.
2. Joseph D. Douglass, Jr., *The Soviet Theater Nuclear Offensive* (Washington, D.C.: USGPO, 1976), *passim*.
3. For an analysis of this and other related issues, see John G. Hines, Phillip A. Petersen, and Notra Trulock III, "Soviet Military Theory from 1945–2000 and the Implications for NATO," *Washington Quarterly*, Fall 1986.
4. Quoted in Hajo Holborn, "The Prussian-German School: Moltke and the Rise of the General Staff," in Peter Paret, ed., *Makers of Modern Strategy* (Princeton: Princeton University Press, 1986), p. 289.
5. Western fascination with the ground war is no doubt partly the product of the extensive analytical basis in the academic literature for making ground (as compared with air) warfare calculations. One of the few exceptions is Joshua M. Epstein, *Measuring Military Power: The Soviet Air Threat to Europe* (Princeton: Princeton University Press, 1984).
6. Paul Kennedy, *The Rise and Fall of the Great Powers: Economic Change and Military Conflict From 1500 to 2000* (New York: Random House, 1987), p. 522.
7. There are certainly other areas (of less importance, in this observer's view) where modest improvements could be made, particularly in the conventional arena. These include NATO's capability to

attack Warsaw Pact follow-on forces; the provision of operational reserves; improvement in NATO's sustainability base; and enhancing NATO's capability to engage Pact forces along the forward line of contact.

8. An excellent treatment of these differing perspectives is found in Leon Sloss, "The Roles of Strategic and Theatre Nuclear Forces in NATO Strategy: Part II," in "Power and Policy: Doctrine, the Alliance and Arms Control," *Adelphi Papers*, No. 205 (London: IISS, 1986), pp. 57–72.

9. Michael Howard, "Reassurance and Deterrence," *Foreign Affairs*, Winter 1982/83.

10. For a useful discussion of theatre nuclear weapons in Europe, see Catherine McArdle Kelleher, "NATO Nuclear Operations," in Ashton B. Carter, John D. Steinbruner, and Charles A. Zracket, eds., *Managing Nuclear Operations* (Washington, D.C.: The Brookings Institution, 1987), pp. 445–469.

11. Of course, this assumes that there has been no pre-delegation authority given to lower-level commanders. For a useful treatment of nuclear use within the theatre, see Bruce D. Berkowitz, *American Security: Dilemmas for a Modern Democracy* (New Haven: Yale University Press, 1986), pp. 128–166.

12. Each rotary cruise missile launcher carries 20 missiles. Thus, 10 to 15 aircraft represent a delivery potential of 200 to 300 cruise missiles.

13. Michael R. Gordon, "Soviet Said to Harden Stance on Missiles," *New York Times*, 14 February 1988, p. 3.

14. Robert Hutchinson, "NATO's Nuclear Stockpile Reductions 'a High Risk'," *Jane's Defence Weekly*, 9 June 1984, p. 903.

15. John J. Fialka, "NATO Planners See Menace in Accuracy of Soviet Short-Range Ballistic Missiles," *Wall Street Journal*, 26 February 1986, p. 29.

16. Paul Bracken, *Command and Control of Nuclear Forces* (New Haven: Yale University Press, 1983), especially pp. 129–178.

17. Such a missile system would be over and above a modernised Lance follow-on. Of course, one of the most important political consequences of the INF treaty is the adverse impact it has had on the prospects of even consummating the Lance follow-on program. The notion of another short-range missile or even an expanded number of follow-on Lance missiles seems highly doubtful under present circumstances.

18. Nuclear artillery storage sites reportedly take around two hours to

evacuate, according to data recently published by the US Senate Appropriations Committee. See John J. Fialka, in Note 15. By contrast, larger rear-area storage sites could take up to a day to evacuate.

19. See, especially, James A. Thomson, "Planning for NATO's Nuclear Deterrent in the 1980s and 1990s," *Survival,* May–June 1983, pp. 98–109.

20. A stockpile of 700 modernised nuclear artillery shells could comprise a mix of non-ER (enhanced radiation) W-79 8-in. rounds and W-82 155-mm rounds. For details on recent stockpile decisions, see Walter Pincus, "Army May Update its Stockpile of Nuclear Artillery in Europe," *Washington Post,* 23 July 1984, p. 14, and Melissa Healy, "NATO Tallies Its Obsolete Nukes," *Defense Week,* 14 January 1985, p. 13.

21. For an excellent examination of this issue, see Condolezza Rice, "Nuclear Weapons and the Warsaw Pact," in *The Nuclear Confrontation in Europe,* Jeffrey D. Boutwell, Paul Doty, and Gregory F. Treverton, eds. (London: Croom Helm, 1985), pp. 185–202.

22. Henry A. Kissinger, *Years of Upheaval* (Boston: Little, Brown and Co., 1982), p. 277.

23. Walter Pincus, "Hill Transcript Lists Nuclear Air Bases," *Washington Post,* 9 July 1986, p. 1.

24. See, for example, Peter Petersen, "NATO's Need for Air Defense," *Air Force Magazine,* August 1986, pp. 74–76 and Warren Strobel, "Think-Tank Report Sees Soviets Able to Humble NATO," *Washington Times,* 5 August 1986, p. 1.

25. Accuracies of 10 m CEP would be required along with munitions designed to penetrate hardened structures or create shock waves of sufficient intensity to collapse the shelter. For a discussion of Soviet commentary on the latter approach, see Kerry L. Hines, "Soviet Short-Range Ballistic Missiles," *International Defense Review,* No. 12, December 1985, pp. 1911–1912. It should also be noted that individual shelters are point targets and, therefore, numerous; they are far more likely to be candidates for precise attack by aircraft-delivered munitions than by ballistic missiles.

26. Typical NATO tactical aircraft require a minimum length of roughly 50 by 3500 ft to recover at an airfield. Preventing recovery therefore requires one or two cuts on a typical 8000-ft runway and parallel taxiway. A Soviet military specialist, while surveying the Western literature, reports a figure of 50 by 3300 ft as the closure criterion. See I. Karenin, "Aviation Weapons for Striking Air-

fields," *Zarubezhnoye Voyernoye Oboyreniye*, No. 12, December 1984, JPRS-UMA-85-031, 7 May 1985, p. 134.

27. In addition to maintenance needs, mission capability depends on the ready availability of fuel, appropriate ordnance, and command, control, communications and intelligence support.

28. Based on interviews with NATO civilian and military officials.

29. Based on interviews in the USA and Europe. It should be noted that modest improvements in passive defence could be obtained without any additional real estate simply by filling in the area between the main runway and taxiway to permit more flexibility for aircraft turnaround. Moreover, Rand analysis suggests that such an approach might increase missile requirements by 50%.

30. Information on R³ activities was obtained from interviews with NATO military and political officials.

31. Hines, *op. cit.* in Note 25, p. 1911.

32. Quoted in Phillip A. Petersen and John R. Clark, "Soviet Air and Antiair Operations," *Air University Review*, March–April 1985, re-printed in *Current News*, Special Edition, No. 1327, 31 July 1985, p. 10.

33. D.J. Alberts, "Deterrence in the 1980s, Part II: The Role of Conventional Air Power," *Adelphi Papers*, No. 193 (London: IISS, 1984), p. 23.

34. Were an agreement possible, which seems doubtful, airfields in France and Spain could perform a useful dispersal function.

35. The notion of extended air defence represents the incorporation of ATBM capabilities into the Alliance's overall air defence posture. On behalf of the NATO Council, the NATO Air Defence Committee took up this formulation in early 1986; it was endorsed by NATO's defence ministers in May 1986. Theatre Defence Architectures will be the product of the Strategic Defence Initiative Organisation's multiple contract awards made in December 1986 to European and US companies to recommend space- and ground-based defences to counter the ballistic missile threat (short- to longer-range) to Europe. For an especially good treatment of the politics of ATBM, see Catherine McArdle Kelleher, "ATBMs and Alliance Politics: The US and Europe," in Donald Hafner and John Roper, eds., *Missile Defenses for Europe: ATBMs and Western Security* (Cambridge, MA: Ballinger Publishing Co., 1988).

36. Obviously, the costs of a modest approach, such as an upgraded, dual-mode Patriot system, are easier to calculate. Multi-tiered,

space-based systems are far more subject to cost (as well as technical) uncertainty. The range of the modest option is the result of assumptions about the size of the missile and radar inventory.

37. *Inside the Pentagon*, Vol. 2, No. 45, 14 November 1986.

38. *Ibid.*

39. Interview with Congressional staff member.

40. The *DMS Market Intelligence Report*, DMS Inc., 1986, reports that the Patriot can handle five targets simultaneously. There is no technical reason barring Patriot's target handling capability for missiles from being improved.

41. A notion suggested long ago in the classic by Thomas C. Schelling, *The Strategy of Conflict* (Cambridge, Massachusetts: Harvard University Press, 1960), pp. 207–230.

42. Such an agreement would be impossible to verify without extremely intrusive verification procedures which permitted each side to inspect old missiles for new guidance components. More important, however, such an agreement would permit the Pact to retain its huge numerical advantage while precluding NATO from even modernising its Lance missiles.

43. One of the hidden consequences of the INF treaty is the "virtual" arms control which has resulted from West Germany's feeling of isolation *vis-à-vis* the Warsaw Pact's great numerical advantage over NATO in short-range missiles. Thus West Germany has backed off the Alliance's decision at Montebello to replace NATO's 88 Lance launchers with an upgraded weapon. The obvious replacement is the ATACMS, which the US Army would like to see as a dual-capable system. But insistence that ATACMS at once accommodate the Lance nuclear follow-on requirement and become a militarily effective means of conventional delivery seems destined to fail in view of West Germany's strong position against any increase in the 88 launcher figure. For ATACMS to become a truly effective conventional means of delivery, significantly more launchers are needed to achieve the required volume of fire within a short time-span. Separating ATACMS from the requirement for a nuclear-armed Lance replacement (and thereby creating at least the theoretical potential for ATACMS' launcher growth) would also give the Alliance some negotiating leverage in any future effort to reduce the Warsaw Pact's dramatic advantage in dual-capable battlefield missiles.

44. One interesting notion promoted by Soviet civilian defence intellectuals is that under the new Soviet military doctrine, Soviet

military authorities may be investigating ways to restructure military thinking and hardware so as to avoid pre-emptive action in a crisis. Andrei Kokoshin, deputy director of the Institute of USA and Canada in Moscow, remarked in a *Defense News* interview (21 March 1988) that the Kremlin's no-first-use pledge in 1982 marked the first step in a doctrinal shift. He claims that the pledge entailed changes in procedures related to the rejection of pre-emptive nuclear strikes. Both Kokoshin in his *Defense News* interview and Minister of Defence Yazov in his meeting with Secretary of Defence Carlucci in Berne, Switzerland, suggest that the USA watch Soviet military exercises closely for signs of their new defensive orientation. But no matter what declaratory statements are made or what number of defencively oriented exercises take place, offensive capability remains largely the product of force structure. Soviet leaders could therefore demonstrate their interest in seriously reducing pre-emptive incentives by accepting an agreement to eliminate or seriously constrain battlefield ballistic missiles.

45. The CSCE negotiations will continue to focus on CSBMs. The Conventional Stability Talks, however, will deal with more than structural arms control. They will seek to produce an equilibrium at lower force levels by eliminating imbalances in force structure. At the same time, the CST forum will seek to eliminate the fear of, and capability for, surprise attack.

46. For more on CSBMs, see James E. Goodby, "Confidence Building Measures and the Stockholm Opportunity," *Arms Control Today,* September 1985, pp. 2–5.

47. Training equipment for INF systems are reported in the INF treaty protocol. See *Arms Control Today,* January/February 1988, pp. 11–16.

Bibliography

Akhromeyev, S., "The Role of the Soviet Union and its Armed Forces in the Achievement of a Sharp Turn in the Second World War and its International Significance," *Voyenno istoricheskiy Zhurnal*, February 1985.

Alberts, D. J., "Deterrence in the 1980s, Part II: The Role of Conventional Air Power," *Adelphi Papers*, No. 193, London, IISS, 1984.

Altmann, Jurgen, Benoit Morel, Theodore Postol, and Thomas Risse-Kappen, *Anti-Tactical Missile Defenses and West European Security*, Frankfurt am Main, Hessische Stiftung Friedens-und Konfliktforschung, 1987.

Andrews, Walter, "Allies' Weapons Said to be Inadequate to Threat of New Soviet Missile Power," *Washington Times*, 1 November 1984.

Arkin, William and Jeffrey T. Sands, "The Soviet Nuclear Stockpile," *Arms Control Today*, June 1984.

Arms Control Today, January/February 1988.

Atkinson, Rick and Fred Hiatt, "The Changing Blue Yonder," *Washington Post*, 7 June 1986.

Azrael, Jeremy, *The Soviet Civilian Leadership and the Military High Command, 1976–1986*, Santa Monica, CA, June 1987.

Baird, Gregory C., "The Soviet Theater Command: An Update," *Naval War College Review*, November/December 1981.

BBC, *USSR International Affairs*, various editions.

Bellamy, Christopher, *Red God of War*, London, Brassey's, 1986.

——"Soviet Artillery and Tactical Rocket Design," *Jane's Defence Review*, No. 8, 1983.

Berkowitz, Bruce D., "An INF Treaty Discredits Arms Control and Promotes Conflict," *Orbis*, Winter 1988.

——*American Security: Dilemmas for a Democracy*, New Haven, Yale University Press, 1986.

Berman, Robert P., *Soviet Air Power in Transition*, Washington, D.C., The Brookings Institution, 1978.
——and John C. Baker, *Soviet Strategic Forces: Requirements and Responses,* Washington, D.C., The Brookings Institution, 1982.
Bluestone, B. L. and J. P. Peak, *Air Superiority and Airfield Attacks: Lessons from History*, DNA-TR-84-161, The BDM Corporation, McLean, VA, 1984.
Blumenstein, Jan, "Frontal Aviation in an Air Operation," *Vojenska mysl'*, August 1975.
Bodansky, Yossef, "Soviets Use Afghanistan to Test 'Liquid Fire'," *Jane's Defence Weekly*, 26 May 1984.
Boyle, Dan, "C³ - The Essential Ingredient to Air Defense," *International Defense Review*, June 1978.
Bracken, Paul, *Command and Control of Nuclear Forces,* New Haven and London, Yale University Press, 1984.
Bronner, Eltran, "U.S. Says Soviet Has A-Arms in E. Europe," *International Herald Tribune*, 2 June 1983.
Brown, Harold, *DoD Annual Report FY 1981*, Washington, D.C., USGPO, 1980.
Builder, Carl H., "The Prospects and Implications of Non-nuclear Means for Strategic Conflict," *Adelphi Papers*, No. 200, London, IISS, 1985.
Central Intelligence Agency, National Foreign Assessment Center, *Estimated Soviet Defense Spending: Trends and Prospects*, Washington, D.C., USGPO, 1978.
Cherednichenko, M. I., "Military Strategy and Military Technology," *Voyennaya mysl'*, April 1973.
Cotter, Donald R., James H. Hansen, and Kirk McConnell, "The Nuclear 'Balance' in Europe: Status, Trends, Implications," *USSI Report 83-1*, Washington, D.C., United States Strategic Institute, 1983.
Defense Intelligence Agency, *The Soviet Conventional Offensive in Europe*, Washington, D.C., 1982.
——*Force Structure Summary - USSR, Eastern Europe, and Mongolia*, DDB-2680-170A-85, November 1985.
DeLauer, Richard D., "Emerging Technologies and Their Impact on the Conventional Deterrent," in Andrew J. Pierre, ed., *The Conventional Defense of Europe: New Technologies and New Strategies* New York, Council on Foreign Relations, 1986.
DMS Market Intelligence Report, DMS Inc., 1986.
Donnelly, Christopher N., "The Soviet Military Under Gorbachev,"

Soviet Studies Research Centre, Royal Military Academy, Sandhurst, December 1986.

Douglass, Joseph, D., Jr., *The Soviet Theater Nuclear Offensive*, Washington, D.C., USGPO, 1976.

——"The Theater Nuclear Threat," *Parameters* No. 4, 1982.

Durch, William and Peter Almquist, "East-West Military Balance," in Barry M. Blechman and Edward N. Luttwak, eds., *International Security Yearbook 1984/85*, Boulder, Westview Press, 1985.

Dzhelaukov, Kh. "The Infliction of Deep Strikes," *Voyennaya mysl'*, February 1966.

Eiseev, A. I., "On Certain Trends in Changes in the Content and Nature of the Initial Period of War," *Voyenno-istoricheskiy zhurnal*, November 1985.

Epstein, Joshua, *Measuring Military Power: The Soviet Air Threat to Europe*, Princeton, Princeton University Press, 1984.

Erickson, John, Lynn Hansen, and William Schneider, *Soviet Ground Forces: An Operational Assessment*, Boulder, Westview Press, 1986.

——"Soviet Military Potential for Surprise Attack: Surprise, Superiority and Time," a paper prepared for the SIPRI workshop on Measures to Reduce the Fear of Surprise Attack in Europe, Stockholm, Sweden, 1–3 December 1983.

Evans, David, "We Still Don't Have the Arms and Tactics for a Major War," *Washington Post*, 3 August 1986.

Fialka, John J., "NATO Planners See Menace in Accuracy of Soviet Short-Range Ballistic Missiles," *Wall Street Journal*, 26 February 1986.

Foreign Broadcast Information Service, various editions.

Galin, P., "Aircraft and Rocket-Carriers of Tactical Nuclear Weapons," in P. T. Astaskenkov, ed., *Atomic Energy in Aviation and Rocket Technology*, Moscow, Voyenizdat, 1959.

Gareyev, M. A., *The Views of M. V. Frunze and Contemporary Military Theory*, Moscow, Voyenizdat, 1985.

Garthoff, Raymond L., *Detente and Confrontation: American-Soviet Relations from Nixon to Reagan*, Washington, D.C., The Brookings Institution, 1985.

Getler, Michael, "New Generation of Soviet Arms Near Deployment," *Washington Post*, 11 October 1983.

Goodby, James E., "Confidence Building Measures and the Stockholm Opportunity," *Arms Control Today*, September 1985.

Gorbachev, M. S., "Political Report of the Central Committee of the CPSU to the XXVII Congress of the Communist Party of the Soviet

Union. Report of the General-Secretary of the CC CPSU Comrade M. S. Gorbachev," Stenographic Report, 1986.

Gordon, Michael R., "Soviet Said to Harden Stance on Missiles," *New York Times*, 14 February 1988.

Gormley, Dennis M., "Understanding Soviet Motivations for Deploying Long-Range Theater Nuclear Forces," *Military Review*, September 1981.

——et al., *Soviet Perceptions of and Responses to U.S. Nuclear Weapon Development and Deployment*, Arlington, V.A., Pacific-Sierra Research Corporation, 1982.

——and Douglas M. Hart, "Soviet Views on Escalation: Implications for Alliance Strategy," *The EAI Papers*, Marina del Rey, CA: European American Institute for Security Research, Summer 1984.

——"A New Dimension to Soviet Theater Strategy." *Orbis*, Fall 1985.

——"The Impact of NATO Doctrinal Choices on the Policies and Strategic Choices of Warsaw Pact States: Part II," in "Power and Policy: Doctrine, the Alliance and Arms Control," *Adelphi Papers 206*, London, IISS, 1986.

Grechko, A. A., *The Armed Forces of the Soviet State*, Moscow, Voyenizdat, 1975.

Gribkov, A. I., "On the Command and Control of Coalition Troop Groupings," *Voyenno-istoricheskiy zhurnal*, March 1984.

Hart, Douglas M. and Dennis M. Gormley, "The Evolution of Soviet Interest in Atomic Artillery," *Journal of the Royal United Services Institute for Defence Studies*, June 1983.

Headquarters, Norwegian Defence Command, *Development of the Soviet Forces in Our Sphere of Interest During the Past 20 Years*, Norwegian Embassy, Washington, D.C., 8 March 1985.

Healy, Melissa, "NATO Tallies Its Obsolete Nukes," *Defense Week*, 14 January 1985.

Hillier, Pat and Nora Slatkin, "U.S. Ground Forces: Design and Cost Alternatives for NATO and Non-NATO Contingencies," Congressional Budget Office, 1980.

Hines, John G., "Soviet Front Operations in Europe-Planning for Encirclement," a paper (No. A-74) published by the Soviet Studies Research Centre, Royal Military Academy Sandhurst, April 1985.

——Phillip A. Petersen, and Notra Trulock III, "Soviet Military Theory from 1945–2000 and the Implications for NATO," *Washington Quarterly*, Fall 1986.

Hines, Kerry L., "Soviet Short-Range Ballistic Missiles," *International Defense Review*, December 1985.

———and John Hines, *Soviet Front Fire Support*, Defense Intelligence Agency, DDB-1130-8-82, September 1982.

Holborn, Hajo, "The Prussian-German School: Moltke and the Rise of the General Staff," in Peter Paret, ed., *Makers of Modern Strategy*, Princeton, Princeton University Press, 1986.

Holloway, David, "Doctrine and Technology in Soviet Armaments Policy," in Derek Leebaert, ed., *Soviet Military Thinking*, London, George Allen and Unwin, 1981.

Howard, Michael, "Reassurance and Deterrence," *Foreign Affairs*, Winter 1982/83.

Hutchinson, Robert, "NATO's Nuclear Stockpile Reductions 'A High Risk'," *Jane's Defence Weekly*, 9 June 1984.

International Defense Review, various editions.

International Institute for Strategic Studies, *The Military Balance*, various editions.

Inside the Pentagon, Vol. 2, No. 45, 14 November 1986.

Isby, David L., *Weapons and Tactics of the Soviet Army*, Jane's, New York, 1981.

Ivanov, S. P., *Initial Period of War*, Moscow, Voyenizdat, 1974.

Karenin, I., "Aviation Weapons for Striking Airfields," *Zarubezhnoye Voyernoye Oboyreniye*, December 1984.

Kazahov, K. P., ed., *Artillery and Missiles*, Moscow, Voyenizdat, 1968.

Kelleher, Catherine McArdle, "ATBMs and Alliance Politics: The U.S. and Europe," in Donald Hafner and John Roper, eds., *Missile Defenses for Europe: ATBMs and Western Security* Cambridge, MA, Ballinger Publishing Co., 1988.

———"NATO Nuclear Operations," in Ashton B. Carter, John D. Steinbruner, and Charles A. Zracket, eds., *Managing Nuclear Operations*, Washington, D.C., The Brookings Institution, 1987.

Keller, Bill, "Soviet Marshal Sees 'Star Wars' Giving U.S. Edge," *New York Times*, 30 October 1987.

Kennedy, Paul, *The Rise and Fall of the Great Powers: Economic Change and Military Conflict From 1500 to 2000*, New York, Random House, 1987.

Kir'yan, M. M., ed. *Military-Technical Progress and the Armed Forces of the USSR*, Moscow, Voyenizdat, 1982.

Kissinger, Henry A., *Years of Upheaval*, Boston, Little, Brown and Co., 1982.

Khrushchev, Nikita, *Khrushchev Remembers: The Last Testament*, ed. and trans. by Strobe Talbott, Boston, Little, Brown, and Company, 1974.

Kolesov, V., "Massing of Artillery under Contemporary Conditions," *Voyennaya mysl'*, November 1972.

Konoplis, P. and A. Mal'shev, "Modern Offensive Battle," *Military Herald*, February 1984.

Koziej, S., "Anticipated Directions for Change in Tactics of Ground Troops,' *Polish Ground Forces Review*, September 1986.

Kozlov, S. N., ed., *The Officer's Handbook (A Soviet View)*, trans. by the DGIS Multilingual Section, Translation Bureau, Secretary of State Department, Ottawa, Canada, Washington, D.C., USGPO, 1977.

Krupnov, V. I. "Dialectics of the Development of Methods and Forms of Armed Conflict," in A. S. Zheltov, ed., *Methodological Problems of Military Theory and Practise*, Moscow, Voyenizdat, 1969.

Kutakhov, P. S., "Experience in Fighting for Strategic Air Supremacy During the Years of World War II and Its Importance in the Contemporary Situation," *Voyenno-istoricheskiy Zhurnal*, December 1984.

——"The Conduct of Independent Air Operations," *Voyenno-istoricheskiy Zhurnal*, June 1972.

Kvitnitsikiy, A. and Yu. Nepodayev,, "The Theory of the Escalation of War," *Voyennaya mysl'*, September 1965.

Lambeth, Benjamin S. and Kevin N. Lewis, *The Strategic Defense Initiative in Soviet Planning and Policy*, Santa Monica, The Rand Corporation, 1988.

Lashchenko, P., "Perfection of Methods of Encirclement and Destruction of Large Enemy Groupings Based on the Experience of the Great Patriotic War," *Voyenno-istoricheskiy Zhurnal*, February 1985.

Lee, W. T., "Trends in Soviet Strategic Ballistic Missile Forces," paper presented at a conference sponsored by the USAF Assistant Chief of Staff for Intelligence, "The Soviet Union: What Lies Ahead? Military-Political Affairs in the 1980s," 25–27 September 1980.

Leites, Nathan, *Soviet Style of War*, New York, Crane Russak, 1982.

Lewis, William J., *The Warsaw Pact: Arms, Doctrine, and Strategy*, Cambridge, MA, Institute for Foreign Policy Analysis, 1982.

Lomov, N. A., "The Influence of Soviet Military Doctrine on the Development of Military Art," *Kommunist voorizhennykh sil*, November 1965.

Mallin, Jay, "Russia at High Level of Battle Readiness," *Washington*

Times, 26 July 1984.

Malyanchikov, S. U., "The Character and Features of Nuclear Rocket War," *Kommunist vooruzhennykh sil*, November 1965.

Markham, James M., "Kohl Would Keep Tactical Missiles," *New York Times*, 7 February 1988.

———"Paris and Bonn Start to Think of a Special Alliance," *New York Times*, 24 June 1987.

Martin, J. J., "How the Soviet Union Came to Gain Escalation Dominance – Trends and Asymmetries in the Theater Nuclear Balance," in Uwe Nerlich, ed., *The Soviet Asset, Military Power in the Competition over Europe*, Cambridge, MA, Ballinger Publishing Co., 1983.

Mauthner, Robert, "NATO Policy is Ripe for Review," *Financial Times*, 19 January 1988.

McCartney, Robert, "Soviet Missile Offer Wins Bonn's Accord," *Washington Post*, 2 June 1987.

McCausland, Jeffrey, "The SS-20: Military and Political Threat?" *The Fletcher Forum*, Winter 1982.

———"Soviet Short-Range Nuclear Forces and Doctrine," *Comparative Strategy*, No. 3, 1985.

McConnell, James M., "The Interacting Evolution of Soviet and American Military Doctrines," Center for Naval Analyses Memorandum No. 80-1313.00, Alexandria, VA, 1980.

———*The Soviet Shift in Emphasis from Nuclear to Conventional*, Alexandria, VA., Center for Naval Analyses, June 1983.

Meyer, Stephen M., "Soviet Theatre Nuclear Forces, Part I: Development of Doctrine and Objectives," *Adelphi Papers*, No. 187, London, IISS, 1983/84.

———"Soviet Theatre Nuclear Forces, Part II: Capabilities and Implications," *Adelphi Papers*, No. 188, London, IISS, 1983/84.

Musial, Aleksander, "The Character and the Importance of Air Operations in Modern Warfare," *Polish Air Defense Review*, No. 2, 1982.

Nepodayev, Yu., "On the 'Nuclear Threshold' in NATO Strategy," *Voyennaya mysl'*, June 1966.

Ol'Shtynsky, L., *Cooperation of the Army and Navy*, Moscow, Voyenizdat, 1983.

Ogarkov, N. V., "On Guard Over Peaceful Labor," *Kommunist*, No. 10, 1981.

———*Always in Readiness to Defend the Fatherland*, Moscow, Voyenizdat, 1982.

———"Military Leader's Thought," *Krasnaya Zvezda*, 2 October 1983.

———*Krasnaya Zvezda*, 9 May 1984.

Ostroumov, N. N., "Employment of Air Forces in Strategic Operations," *Voyennaya mysl'*, September 1975.

Pavlovsky, I., "The Ground Forces," *Voyennaya mysl'*, April 1973.

Penkovsky, Oleg, *The Penkovsky Papers*, New York, Ballatine Books, 1982.

Pentsak, I. N., trans., *The Theory of Flight and Construction of Ballistic Missiles*, Moscow, Voyenizdat, 1974.

Peredel'skiy, G., "Artillery in the Struggle to Attain Fire Superiority," *Voyennaya mysl'*, October 1973.

——"Soviet Artillery Main Assault Force in War," *Voyenno-istoricheskiy Zhurnal*, April 1975.

Petersen, Peter, "NATO's Need for Air Defense," *Air Force Magazine*, August 1986.

Petersen, Phillip A. and John G. Hines, "The Conventional Offensive in Soviet Theater Strategy," *Orbis*, Fall 1983.

——and John R. Clark, "Soviet Air and Antiair Operations," *Air University Review*, March–April 1985.

Pincus, Walter, "Army May Update its Stockpile of Nuclear Artillery in Europe," *Washington Post*, 23 July 1984.

——"Hill Transcript Lists Nuclear Air Bases," *Washington Post*, 9 July 1986.

Pokrovsky, G., "Weapons in a Modern Army," in *Marxism-Leninism on War and the Army*, Moscow, Voyenizdat, 1955.

Record, Jeffrey, *NATO's Theater Nuclear Modernization Program: The Real Issues*, Washington, D.C., and Cambridge, MA, Institute for Foreign Policy Analysis, Inc., 1981.

Rice, Condolezza, "Nuclear Weapons and the Warsaw Pact," in Jeffrey D. Boutwell, Paul Doty, and Gregory F. Treverton, eds., *The Nuclear Confrontation in Europe*, London, Croom Helm, 1985.

Richardson, Robert C., "NATO Nuclear Strategy: A Look Back," *Strategic Review*, Spring 1981.

Samorukov, B., "Combat Operation is Involving Conventional Means of Destruction," *Voyennaya mysl'*, August 1967.

Samorukov, D. and L. Semeyko, "The Increase in Efforts in Nuclear Warfare Operations," *Voyennaya mysl'*, October 1968.

Sandia National Laboratories, *Lab News*, 26 April 1985.

Savkin, V. Ye., *The Basic Principles of Operational Art and Tactics*, Moscow, Voyenizdat, 1972.

Schelling, Thomas C., *The Strategy of Conflict*, Cambridge, MA, Harvard University Press, 1960.

Semenov, N., "Gaining Supremacy in the Air," *Voyennaya mysl'*, April 1968.

Shesterin, F., "The Experience of the Battle for Air Superiority in

World War II and its Significance under Modern Conditions," *Voyennaya mysl'*, February 1969.
Shipler, David K., "Gorbachev Offers to Render Europe Clear of Missiles," *New York Times*, 15 April 1987.
Sidorenko, A. A., *The Offensive (A Soviet View)*, Moscow, 1970, trans. U.S. Air Force, Washington, D.C., USGPO, 1974.
Simon, Jeffrey, "Evaluation and Integration of Non-Soviet Warsaw Pact Forces into the Combined Arms Forces," *Signal*, December 1985.
Simonenko, A., "Artillery of the Reserve of the Supreme High Command," *Krasnaya zveda*, 12 February 1978.
Skirdo, M. P., *The People, The Army, The Commander*, Moscow, Voyenizdat, 1970.
Slocombe, Walter, Book Review, *Survival*, September/October 1984.
Sloss, Leon, "The Roles of Strategic and Theatre Nuclear Forces in NATO Strategy: Part II," in "Power and Policy: Doctrine, the Alliance and Arms Control," *Adelphi Papers*, No. 205, London, IISS, 1986.
Snyder, Jack, "The Gorbachev Revolution: A Waning of Soviet Expansionism?" *International Security*, Winter 1987/88.
Snyder, Jed C., "European Security, East-West Policy, and the INF Debate, *Orbis*, Winter 1984.
Sokolovskiy, V. D. and M. Cherednichenko, "Military Strategy and Its Problems," *Voyennaya msyl'*, October 1968.
Starostin, A., "Tactical Rockets," *Tekhnika i vooruzheniye*, November 1981.
Stern, 20 October 1983.
Strobel, Warren, "Think-Tank Report Sees Soviets Able to Humble NATO," *Washington Times*, 5 August 1986.
Surikov, B. T., *Combat Employment of Ground Forces' Missiles*, Moscow, Voyenizdat, 1979.
Taylor, John W. R., "Fulcrum: A Close Look," *Jane's Defence Weekly*, 2 August 1986.
Thomson, James A., "Planning for NATO's Nuclear Deterrent in the 1980s and 1990s," *Survival*, May-June 1983.
——"Strategic Choices: Their Roles in NATO's Defence Planning and Force Modernization: Part I," in "Power and Policy: Doctrine, The Alliance and Arms Control," *Adelphi Papers* No. 205, London, IISS, 1986.
Tomilin, E., "What to Take from Combat Experience," No. 12, *Report: Military Affairs*, No. 1567, JPRS 77371, 11 February 1981.

Trulock Notra, III, "Weapons of Mass Destruction in Soviet Military Strategy," an unpublished paper presented at the Joint Conference on Soviet Military Strategy in Europe, sponsored by the Boston Foreign Affairs Group and the Royal United Services Institute for Defence Studies, Oxford, England.

——"Soviet Perspectives on Limited Nuclear War," in Fred Hoffman, Albert Wohlstetter, and David Yost, eds., *Swords and Shields: NATO, the USSR, and New Choices for Long-Range Offense and Defense*, Lexington, MA, Lexington Books, 1987.

——*Soviet Military Thought in Transition: Implications for the Long-Term Military Competition*, Pacific-Sierra Research Corporation, 22 May 1987.

——and Dennis M. Gormley, *The Implications of Future Technology on Warfare*, Pacific-Sierra Research Corporation, December 1987.

Turner, Frederick C., *Comments on FM 100-5 from a Soviet Point of View*, U.S. Army War College, Strategic Studies Institute, 15 March 1978.

Tyushkevich, S. A., *The Soviet Armed Forces: The History of Their Development*, Moscow, Voyenizdat, 1978.

U.S. Army, FM 100-2-3, *Soviet Army Troops Organization and Equipment*, Coordinating Draft, August 1982.

U.S. Air Force, trans., *Design of Guided Ballistic Missiles*, Moscow, Voyenizdat, 1969.

U.S. Congress, *Department of Defense Appropriations for FY 85*, Hearings before a Subcommittee of the Committee on Appropriations, House of Representatives, 98th Cong., 2d sess., Washington, D.C., USGPO, 1984.

——*Allocation of Resources in the Soviet Union and China – 1984*, Hearings before the Subcommittee on International Trade, Finance, and Security Economics of the Joint Economic Committee, Washington, D.C., USGPO, 1985.

U.S. Department of Defense, *Report of the Secretary of Defense Caspar W. Weinberger to the Congress on the FY 1987 Budget, FY 1988 Authorization Request, and FY 1987–1991 Defense Programs*, 5 February 1986.

——Secretary of Defense, *The Effectiveness of United States Military Aid to Israel (ISMILAID)*, December 1974.

——*Soviet Military Power 1983*, Washington, D.C., USGPO, 1983.

——*Soviet Military Power 1984*, Washington, D.C., USGPO, 1984.

——*Soviet Military Power 1985*, Washington, D.C., USGPO, 1985.

——*Soviet Military Power 1986*, Washington, D.C., USGPO, 1986.

——*Soviet Military Power 1987*, Washington, D.C., USGPO, 1987.

U.S. Department of State, *Memorandum for the Verification Panel Working Group*, 2 October 1972.

U.S. Government, *Summary of Special Consultative Group, Progress Report to Ministers*, 8 December 1983.

Ustinov, D. F., *We Serve the Motherland and the Cause of Communism*, Moscow, Voyenizdat, 1982.

Voroshilov General Staff Academy, Moscow, various lecture materials.

Yurechko, John J., "Command and Control for Coalitional Warfare: The Soviet Approach," *Signal*, December 1985.

Vorob'ev, I., "Modern Weapons and Tactics," *Krasnaya Zvezda*, 15 September 1984.

Vyrodov, I., "Strategic and Operational Art: On the Leadership of Military Operations of Strategic Troop Groupings in World War II," *Voyenno-istoricheskiy Zhurnal*, April 1979.

Warner, Edward L., *The Military in Contemporary Soviet Politics*, New York, Praeger, 1977.

Weinberger, Caspar W., *Annual Report to Congress, Fiscal Year 1988*.

Wright, Barton, *Soviet Missiles*, Lexington, MA, Lexington Books, 1986.

Yazov, D. T., *On Guard of Socialism and Peace*, Moscow, Voyenizdat, 1987.

Zaitsev, M. M. *Voenny Vestnik*, February 1979.

Zaloga, Steven J., "Soviet Weapons Designations: Part 1" *Jane's Defence Weekly*, 2 May 1987.

INDEX